Praise for *Divided*

"Following in the fine tradition of their [ ] skill-fully blended history and data to profi[ ] *Divided America* is sure to withstand the tests o[ ]al or institutional politics in the United States should read, study, and heed the analysis of Merle and Earl Black."

—*Perspectives on Politics*

"Before any of the 2008 candidates start counting their electoral votes, they should read the latest book by Earl and Merle Black. In their scholarly and ambitious *Divided America,* the Black brothers . . . offer a thoughtful, thorough analysis of the undercurrents that have driven our polarized national politics in recent decades."

—Donna Brazile, *The Washington Post Book World*

"How have the regions of the United States come to be so different in their political behavior, and what does it mean for the future? The Blacks . . . provide a thorough historical and demographic analysis to answer that question. . . . While *Divided America* may get political junkies excited for 2008, it won't help party strategists sleep at night."

—Daniel Heim, *Roll Call*

"*Divided America* is merely brilliant."

—Cragg Hines, *Houston Chronicle*

"A numbers junkie's look at what makes our political map red and blue. . . . The Blacks' simple charts tell complex stories very well. . . . Political junkies can learn a great deal from Merle and Earl Black's expert dissection of the data."

—Karlyn Bowman, *The Weekly Standard*

"An important contribution toward our understanding of the complexities of the contemporary American electorate."

—Claude R. Marx, *The Washington Times*

"Voters should understand the nature of regional differences. Why the regions matter is the subject of a new book, *Divided America.*"

—George Will, *Newsweek*

"Political junkies attempting to understand the current landscape can hardly do better than a perusal of Earl and Merle's latest dissection of the changing American electorate. . . . Unusually detailed and illuminating."

—Keith Monroe, *News & Record* (Greensboro, NC)

"Bedside reading for Karl Rove wannabes preparing for 2008."
—*Kirkus Reviews* (starred)

"For a generation, Earl Black and Merle Black have been enlightening Americans about the politics of the South. It is both a sign of the times and a blessing for all who love politics that they have turned their analytical genius and clarity of thought to regional politics in the whole country. This book would have been important even without the electoral earthquake of 2006. Now it is more important than ever in providing a road map for 2008 and beyond. You can't understand the future of American politics without understanding the importance of the new regionalism. To understand how it works and why it matters, you need to read *Divided America*."
—E. J. Dionne, Jr., syndicated columnist and author of
Why Americans Hate Politics

"Forget the Middle East. The real struggle for the future will take place in the Middle West. As Earl and Merle Black show in this lucid and informative account, the smartest way to think about American politics is the old-fashioned way—by region. *Divided America* explains why we will have close elections in this country as far as the eye can see. This is a complete picture of where we stand politically, with important historical context."
—Jonathan Alter, senior editor, *Newsweek,* and author of *The Defining Moment: FDR's Hundred Days and the Triumph of Hope*

"*Divided America* is a sophisticated study of how Americans vote—and why the country has become almost impossible to govern. It is a book of frustrating answers rather than the usual clueless questions. A valuable book."
—Richard Reeves, author of *President Reagan* and *President Kennedy*

ALSO BY EARL BLACK AND MERLE BLACK

The Rise of Southern Republicans

The Vital South: How Presidents Are Elected

Politics and Society in the South

THE FEROCIOUS POWER STRUGGLE IN AMERICAN POLITICS

DIVIDED AMERICA

EARL BLACK and MERLE BLACK

Simon & Schuster Paperbacks

New York   London   Toronto   Sydney

SIMON & SCHUSTER PAPERBACKS
A Division of Simon & Schuster, Inc.
1230 Avenue of the Americas
New York, NY 10020

First Simon & Schuster trade paperback edition March 2008

SIMON & SCHUSTER PAPERBACKS and colophon are registered trademarks
of Simon & Schuster, Inc.

For information regarding special discounts for bulk purchases,
please contact Simon & Schuster Special Sales at 1-800-456-6798
or business@simonandschuster.com.

Book design by Ellen R. Sasahara

Manufactured in the United States of America

1   3   5   7   9   10   8   6   4   2

The Library of Congress has cataloged the hardcover edition as follows:

Black, Earl, 1942–
Divided America / Earl Black, Merle Black.
p.   cm.
Includes bibliographical references and index.
Contents: Competitive America—America's political regions—The Republican
strongholds—The Democratic strongholds—The divided Midwest—The presidential
power struggle—The power struggle in the House of Representatives—The power
struggle in the Senate—The American power struggle.
1. Political parties—United States.   2. Party affiliation—United States.   3. Divided
government—United States.   4. Political culture—United States—Regional
disparities.   5. United States—Politics and government—2001–
I. Black, Merle.   II. Title.

JK2261.B614   2007
324.273—dc22   2006051187

ISBN-13: 978-0-7432-6206-4
ISBN-10:   0-7432-6206-9
ISBN-13: 978-0-7432-6207-1 (pbk)
ISBN-10:   0-7432-6207-7 (pbk)

For our families
Sena, Shameem, and Andy
Debra, Claire, and Julia

CONTENTS

PREFACE

W HY DO THE DEMOCRATIC AND REPUBLICAN
PARTIES always seem on the verge of winning—or
losing—the White House and Congress? *Divided
America* is the first book in the twenty-first century to emphasize
the importance of *regions* in understanding the evenly fought and
intensely ideological battles to win control of American government. Most books on American politics focus almost exclusively on
national trends and patterns. Our approach is different. Important
geographical divisions, we believe, are at the heart of the very close
national battles between Democrats and Republicans. American
politics becomes much more interesting—and easier to understand—when the party battles are examined region by region.

The United States spans a continent. We divide this immense
country into five regions: the Northeast, South, Midwest, Moun-
tains/Plains, and Pacific Coast. For each region we identify and integrate social and partisan trends during the past half century into the
story of how American politics has become so intensely competitive. We show the emergence of a substantial Democratic advantage
in the Northeast, the continuation of a Democratic edge in the Pacific Coast, the convergence of partisan strength in the Midwest, and
Republican realignments in the Mountains/Plains and the South.

Divided America analyzes *long-term regional patterns* of partisan
conflict in American politics. We develop the story of America's competitive two-party politics from the 1950s through the early 2000s. By

using surveys and election results over a half century to trace major trends and shifts in the partisan preferences of important social groups, we help readers understand why the United States continues to be such a closely divided nation in the twenty-first century.

The regional trends described in the book are borne out by the Democrats' impressive House and Senate victories in 2006. Understanding each party's regional strengths and weaknesses as they have developed over the past half century is the essential starting point for assessing close national outcomes.

Regional analyses are especially valuable because the United States has no genuinely *national* elections. Instead, elections for the presidency and Congress are won by aggregating state-level outcomes (in presidential and Senate elections) or district-level winners (for the House of Representatives). Democratic strength is greatest in the Northeast and the Pacific Coast, whereas the South and the Mountains/Plains give the Republicans areas of strong support. The Midwest is the crucial swing region.

America's close national battles are the product—the net result, so to speak—of offsetting partisan and ideological preferences among the different groups of voters who predominate in the various regions. Because neither Democrats nor Republicans can win national majorities simply by sweeping their regional strongholds, America's two parties are locked in a power struggle in which victory or defeat is possible in *every* round of elections for *every* national institution.

The 2006 elections confirm the methods and conclusions of the book by showing how partisan control of the House of Representatives and the Senate can shift dramatically in each election cycle. Because of the Republicans' slim majorities in both houses of Congress, Democrats needed net gains of only 6 seats in the Senate and 15 seats in the House of Representatives to secure control. All the short-term forces in 2006—especially President George W. Bush's unpopularity and voter dissatisfaction with the Iraq war—heavily favored Democratic candidates. Indeed, Democrats picked up House seats in every region and gained in contests for the Senate everywhere except in the Pacific Coast. However, the leads won by the Democrats in 2006 are not insuperable, and Republicans will vigorously attempt to reclaim both houses of Congress in the next round of elections.

Even more to the point, the 2006 congressional elections clearly demonstrate the importance of the partisan regional strongholds identified in *Divided America*. The rival parties continue to hold majorities of Senate and House seats in their regional strongholds. Democrats emerged with *larger majorities* of the Northeastern and Pacific Coast delegations to the House of Representatives. Democrats also expanded their majority of the Northeastern Senate delegation and kept their already large Pacific Coast Senate majority. Republicans ended up with *smaller majorities* of the Southern and Mountains/Plains delegations to both houses of Congress. Republican losses in the Mountains/Plains, in particular, will prompt even more aggressive Democratic campaigns in that region. The Midwest, the swing region, moved in a pro-Democratic direction in both House and Senate contests. Democratic gains in the Midwest added to the party's prior majority of the region's Senate delegation and demolished the previously large Republican surplus among the region's House delegation.

The enlarged Democratic majority in the Northeast was the most significant regional development in American politics in 2006. The Northeast solidified its position as the most Democratic region in the United States. Democratic majorities in the Northeastern House and Senate delegations appear to be finally catching up with the powerful underlying Democratic advantage in the Northeastern electorate, a trend that has been under way for decades. In 2006, the emergence of a stronger Democratic Northeast in the Senate and House of Representatives trumped—for the immediate future, at least—the rise of a Republican South.

The relentless power struggle analyzed in *Divided America* will intensify as the nation approaches the 2008 elections. Democrats will seek to consolidate their gains and expand their majorities in the Senate and House of Representatives, but Republicans will enter the election cycle needing only a small number of seat changes to reclaim control of both institutions. And in the battle for the presidency, the greatest prize in American politics, candidates and strategists of both parties will seek to hold their regional strongholds while attempting to win Midwestern battleground states and to pick up states in their rival party's strongholds. Understanding regional patterns of partisan strength and weakness, the subject of this book, highlights the different strategies of the Democratic and Republican parties for winning the White House, Senate, and House of Representatives in 2008.

In *Divided America* we give special emphasis to racial and ethnic groups as the principal building blocks of partisan coalitions. Understanding modern American politics requires tracing patterns of partisanship for whites, African Americans, and the New Minorities of Latinos, Asians, and other ethnic groups. Because whites still cast large majorities of all votes in American elections, particular attention is also paid to the partisan and ideological preferences of Protestants, Catholics, and non-Christians.

We tell the story of modern American politics in a straightforward manner. After establishing national trends in the opening chapter, we then argue that America's old sectional division between the North and the South has given way to a new division based on five regions. Chapters 3–5 analyze the changing regional electorates in the two Republican strongholds, the two Democratic strongholds, and the Midwest. Within each region significant transformations have occurred in the size and partisanship of key groups.

Having portrayed five distinctive regional landscapes among voters, we then relate the regions to national outcomes. Chapters 6–8 reveal the new regional structure of elections for president, the

House of Representatives, and the Senate. In each institution, the close national party battle results from Democratic strength in the Northeast and Pacific Coast, Republican dominance in the Mountains/Plains and South, and the Midwest as a crucial swing region.

In the last chapter we return to the level of the entire nation and show the changing racial/ethnic, religious, and ideological composition of the rival parties over the past half century. America has two political parties whose centers of gravity rest in different geographic regions. The dominant social groups in the competing parties differ profoundly by race and ethnicity, religion, and ideological preferences.

Through our assessment of regional and national trends, we seek to provide a realistic understanding of the strengths and weaknesses of the Republican and Democratic parties across the entire country. Tremendous changes in the racial, ethnic, and religious composition of the American electorate, as well as substantial shifts in partisanship among important social groups, have culminated in a tight national party battle. The United States has no majority party in the electorate; instead, Republicans and Democrats constitute sizable minorities of the nation's voters.

America's new regional divisions do not ordinarily result in landslide national victories, much less stable governing majorities. Neither Democrats nor Republicans, neither conservatives nor liberals, represent governing majorities in the United States. Because the dominant constellations of social forces vary considerably from region to region, governing America successfully may be even more challenging in the future than in the past.

In this book we have used two sources of surveys to describe and analyze the American electorate. We have made use of American National Election Studies (ANES) from 1952 to 2004 conducted by the

Center for Political Studies of the Institute for Social Research at the University of Michigan. We have also made use of exit polls conducted by CBS News and *The New York Times* from 1976 to 1988, exit polls conducted by the Voter News Service from 1992 to 2002, and the National Election Pool (NEP) exit polls conducted by Edison Media Research and Mitofsky International in 2004. All of these surveys were obtained through the Inter-University Consortium for Political and Social Research. We are grateful to the consortium for the use of these data collections; neither the collector of the original data nor the consortium bears any responsibility for the analysis or interpretations presented here.

1

COMPETITIVE AMERICA

THE BIGGEST STORY OF MODERN AMERICAN POLITICS—a story with no end in sight—is the ferocious power struggle between conservative Republicans and liberal Democrats over each elected institution of the national government. Because the two major parties are now evenly balanced in the national electorate, control of the presidency, the Senate, and the House of Representatives can shift with each round of elections. And because Republicans and Democrats disagree so fundamentally over the direction of countless public policies, changes in partisan control can seriously affect millions of people in the United States and even larger numbers elsewhere in the world.

America's tight national battle results from opposing political developments in five different regions. Each party has developed two regional strongholds: the Northeast and the Pacific Coast for the Democrats versus the South and the Mountains/Plains for the Republicans. The Midwest is the nation's swing region. In this opening chapter, however, our focus will be on the entire nation. Once national trends have been established, the rest of the book will show how Republicans and Democrats have worked themselves into distinctive tight corners. Regional strengths are offset by regional weaknesses. Democratic and Republican leaders can ordinarily aspire—at best—to narrow national victories.

Permanently competitive *and* ideologically charged politics is a new reality for America. Governing the United States requires agreement among "separated institutions *sharing* powers."[1] America's unstable power politics generates relentlessly bitter conflicts over a huge range of domestic and foreign policies and motivates activists in both parties to compete fiercely all the time. The 9/11/01 terrorist attacks on New York and Washington restored national security issues to the forefront of American politics. In response, President George W. Bush's decision to confront terrorism in Afghanistan and Iraq divided the nation along prowar and antiwar lines and further intensified the national party battle. Close national elections between ideologically distinct parties give American politics its harsh tones and its extraordinarily high stakes, thus magnifying the difficulties of governing the world's only superpower.

By comparison with the national landslides underlying Franklin D. Roosevelt's New Deal or Lyndon Johnson's Great Society, in 2000 Bush barely won the electoral vote and lost the popular vote. His victory in 2004 was solid but not overwhelming. He won reelection by an electoral vote margin of 53 percent to 47 percent and a popular vote majority of 51 percent to 48 percent. Had the Republicans lost either Ohio or Florida, their most challenging contests in large states, John Kerry would have been elected president. Republicans maintained their majority in the House of Representatives by the identical close margin of 53 percent to 47 percent. They did improve their majority in the Senate, emerging after the election with a lead of fifty-five to forty-five seats. Even in the Senate, however, Republicans lacked the sixty votes needed to break any determined Democratic filibuster.

Conservative Republicans and liberal Democrats—as politicians, financial contributors, activists, and voters—are more than ever the driving forces in American politics. Ideological purity has been achieved most dramatically in Congress, where strong partisans prevail as both leaders and followers. Far more than they ever did in the past, senators and representatives in both parties vote with their leaders most of the time. Some of the most die-hard participants in American politics are the members of Congress who daily settle scores and recount the latest partisan outrages on network news, cable news, and C-SPAN.

Ideological purity is trickier to achieve in presidential politics. Here the fundamental challenge for each party is building winning coalitions that begin with a party's ideological base but also reach into the "center" of the electorate to achieve national majorities. Finding ways to disguise, finesse, or modify ideological positions that repel as well as attract centrist voters has thus become a basic task of campaign strategy. Republicans Ronald Reagan and George W. Bush and Democrat Bill Clinton all found creative ways to retain their most ideological partisans while attracting support that transcended their bases.

The tremendous personal, partisan, and ideological differences that polarize Democratic and Republican politicians are paralleled among the voters that make up the rival parties. The liberal wing of the Democratic Party—white liberals plus minorities—is a substantial majority among voters who claim to be Democrats, just as the Republicans' conservative wing—white conservatives plus minorities—makes up a large majority among voters who identify as Republicans. In 1976 only 37 percent of America's Democrats belonged to its liberal wing. In 2004 white liberals plus minorities comprised 63 percent of all Democrats. The size of the Republicans' conservative wing grew from 52 percent in 1976 to 66 percent in the 2004 election.[2] Ideologically, as political scientists Alan I. Abramowitz and Kyle L. Saunders have shown, America's two major parties are more polarized than ever before.[3]

Yet while liberals and conservatives are sizable majorities within their parties, their influence on American politics represents a tremendous leveraging of their actual size among all voters. In the 2004 presidential election, 15 percent of the voters were liberal Democrats, and 24 percent were conservative Republicans. Members of the two polar groups comprise about two-fifths of the entire electorate.[4] Finding sufficient allies outside their respective bases to forge majorities is the perennial task of conservative Republican and liberal Democratic politicians.

Increased ideological clarity within the Republican and Democratic parties has made the American party battle more divisive than in the past. For decades Democrats had an influential conservative wing that moderated the policies pursued by national party leaders. Though located primarily in the South, conservative Democrats were also present in much of rural and small-town America. Along with moderate Democrats, conservative Democrats influenced policy and constrained the liberal wing of the party. As late as 1976, the Democratic Party included almost as many white conservatives (19 percent) as white liberals (22 percent). By 2004 conservative Democrats were almost extinct: white liberals outnumbered white conservatives 27 percent to 6 percent among all Democrats.

Republicans traditionally had a moderate wing, as well as a few liberals, that restrained its conservatives. Within the Republican Party, white moderates declined from 42 percent in 1976 to 34 percent in 2004. The white liberal wing of the Republican Party, only 8 percent of all Republicans in 1976, was down to 4 percent in 2004. Ideological splits *within* the parties have largely been transformed into sharpened ideological divisions *between* the parties. Leaders of both parties still have to formulate policies that will satisfy their moderates, but Democratic leaders do not worry about the opinions and interests of conservatives, just as Republican leaders pay no attention to liberal viewpoints.

America's confrontational politics, reported and interpreted by an extraordinarily diverse array of news media, talk radio, bloggers, and Internet advocacy forums on a nonstop basis, places extraordinary demands on politicians who aspire to the presidency or leadership roles in Congress. When each new wave in the political ocean is sincerely believed to make all the difference between winning or losing power, bitter fights can and do occur over practically everything. Robust conflict is obviously inherent in a democracy, but incessant personal attacks mean that especially thick skins are necessary for America's leading politicians. President Bush and Senator Kerry must have wondered from time to time if winning the White House was worth the personal abuse that each of them received during the 2004 presidential campaign.

THE NEW WASHINGTON BATTLEGROUND

A hallmark of the modern American power struggle is the revival of the Republicans as a governing party. Republicans once dominated American politics. Emerging from the Civil War as the victorious champions of Union and emancipation, for seven decades Republicans usually controlled the White House and both houses of Congress. GOP domination collapsed with the Great Depression. Under Roosevelt's charismatic and optimistic leadership, Democrats became the country's new majority party. In the New Deal era, Democrats won five straight presidential elections, a feat never again approached by either party. Indeed, Democrats held the White House and both branches of Congress in nine of the ten elections from 1932 through 1950.

It is now considerably more difficult for either party to control the White House, the Senate, and the House of Representatives at the same time. Between 1952 and 2004, national elections resulted in divided partisan control—that is, one party controlled two institutions, and the other party controlled the third—in 63 percent of the elections.[5] Democrats last achieved unified control of the national government for more than a single Congress during Jimmy

Carter's presidency in the late 1970s. Until their back-to-back victories in 2002 and 2004, Republicans had to look back to the 1920s to find a similar accomplishment.

Republicans' recovery from the Great Depression took generations. A good way to appreciate the GOP's utter devastation is to identify the points at which the Republican Party next won consecutive victories in specific national institutions. The initial Republican revival came in presidential elections, with General Dwight D. Eisenhower's victories in 1952 and 1956. The hero of World War II, untainted by the Republicans' domestic failures and unrivaled in the area of national security, reestablished the Republican Party in presidential politics. Republicans have won nine of the fourteen presidential elections from 1952 through 2004.

Presidential recovery did not extend to Congress. The GOP's first sustained majorities in the Senate arrived three decades after its presidential breakthrough. Consecutive majorities in 1980, 1982, and 1984, aided enormously by Reagan's decisive victories, reestablished the Republicans as a frequent governing party in the Senate. Between 1980 and 2004, Republicans were more successful than Democrats (eight to five victories) in controlling the Senate. Every senator is now well aware that partisan control of the chamber can change in the next election.

The House of Representatives proved far more resistant to Republican recovery. Democrats held the House in all but two of thirty-two congressional elections from 1930 through 1992. All Democrats and most Republicans believed that Democrats were an unchallengeable, permanent majority party. In 1994 Republicans achieved a breakthrough victory in the House. They did so by overcoming some Democratic incumbents and capturing many open seats. Many of their gains came in districts previously won by Republican presidential candidates. Republicans' success in the House of Representatives was no fluke. From 1994 through 2004, the Republicans won six consecutive national majorities. However, Republican House majorities have been slim and fragile in comparison with preceding Democratic majorities.

Republican gains in 1994 transformed the national political landscape far beyond the House of Representatives. Democrats' defeat in the House greatly magnified the stakes of the partisan power struggles already being waged over the White House and the Senate. It has been a long, long time since most American politicians really believed that partisan control of every single national institution could shift in every election cycle.

AMERICA'S COMPETITIVE
MINORITY PARTIES

America's power struggle is waged in a political system that does not have a majority party. Close national elections rest upon the nearly equal size of the two minority parties. Drawing upon a half century of public opinion polling, figure 1.1 tracks the American party battle in the national electorate. Excluding independents, it charts the percentage of American voters who classified themselves as Republicans or Democrats in presidential elections from 1952 through 2004.[6]

The Democratic Party's national advantage persisted long after the Great Depression and the Second World War. Although no longer attracting a majority of voters, midway through the twentieth century Democrats remained the dominant minority party. From 1952 through 1980, on average, 45 percent of all presidential voters were Democrats, while only 29 percent were Republicans. This substantial Democratic lead in the national electorate underlay virtually continuous Democratic control of the Senate and the House of Representatives, though obviously it did not produce similar success for the party's presidential candidates.

Reagan's presidency reshaped the national party battle. Beginning with his reelection in 1984, the wide gap between Democrats

Figure 1.1
The American Party Battle

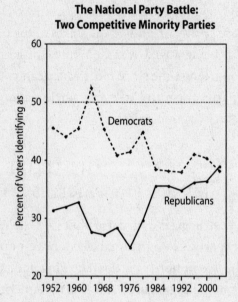

The National Party Battle:
Two Competitive Minority Parties

and Republicans narrowed to a smaller Democratic lead and, by 2004, to a partisan tie. During the presidential elections from 1984 through 2004, on average, Democrats fell to 39 percent, and Republicans rose to 36 percent of American voters. In the 2004 exit poll, 39 percent (rounding up) of voters were Republicans, and 38 percent were Democrats. A huge Democratic advantage in the electorate has thus narrowed to a partisan dead heat in the opening decade of the twenty-first century.

Three Patterns of Partisanship

To understand the dynamics of modern American politics, the crucial first step is to analyze voters by their race or ethnicity. In the United States, the three main building blocks of Republican and Democratic coalitions are whites, African Americans, and New Minorities (Latinos plus other minorities). For any group, the key political resources are its size and unity. How big is the group? How unified is it politically? The answers to these basic questions reveal the big picture of party politics in America.

We begin with size (see figure 1.2). In presidential elections, what proportion of voters are whites, African Americans, and New Minorities? White voters have historically dominated the electorate. As late as 1952, whites made up 96 percent of voters in the United States. Since the 1950s, new groups have entered the electorate and reduced the relative size of white voters.[7] Black Americans, ruthlessly excluded from the Southern electorate, began to participate in large numbers in the 1960s because of the civil rights movement and federal voting-rights legislation. African Americans now cast about one-ninth of the presidential vote. Latinos, America's largest minority group in the general population, increasingly began to vote in the 1980s. In 2004, however, Latinos continued to make up a smaller percentage of actual voters than did African Americans.

Much attention has been focused on the growing diversity of the electorate. Although whites are a smaller share of voters than fifty years ago, it is also crucial to emphasize that whites remain the largest group of voters in the United States. According to the 2004 exit poll, 78 percent of American voters were whites, 11 percent were African Americans, and 8 percent were Latinos. Other minorities, mainly Asian Americans, account for the remaining 3 percent of voters. Because partisanship differs profoundly by race and ethnicity, it is essential to analyze each group separately. Whites are much more closely divided between Republicans and Democrats than are the New Minorities or African Americans.

White Americans

White Americans have a plurality—rather than a majority—party. We use the term *partisan realignment* to indicate the emergence of a new plurality or majority advantage among a particular group of voters. Among white voters, party-identification trends over the past

Figure 1.2
American Size and Partisan Unity

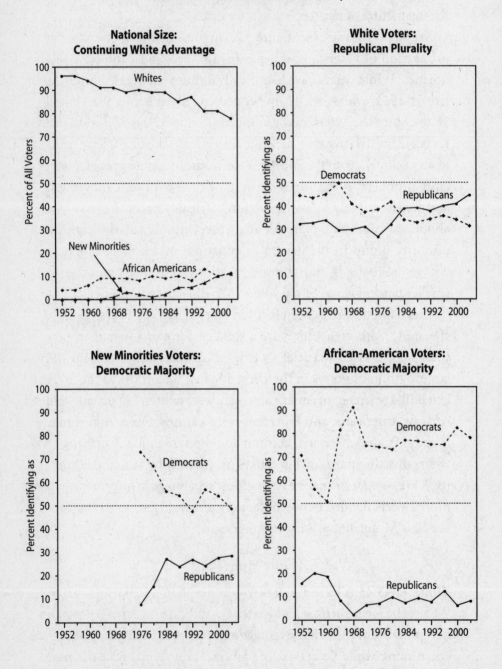

fifty years clearly show a realignment—stopping short of a majority—favoring the Republicans (see "White Voters" in figure 1.2). The old Democratic advantage among white voters, established during the New Deal, ended during the Reagan years. An average Democratic lead of 12 points between 1952 and 1980 (43 percent to 31 percent) gave way to a 6-point Republican edge during the elections from 1984 through 2004 (40 percent to 34 percent). President George W. Bush's first term widened his party's advantage among white Americans. In the 2004 presidential election, 45 percent of white voters were Republicans, while only 31 percent were Democrats. This crucial partisan shift in America's immense white electorate has made the Republican Party once again genuinely competitive.

The New Minorities

America's New Minorities have a majority party (see "New Minorities Voters" in figure 1.2). However, the Democratic advantage among Latinos and Asian Americans is considerably less than that prevailing among African-American voters. In 2004, according to the aggregated state exit polls, 52 percent of Latino voters were Democrats, and 29 percent identified themselves as Republicans.[8] Democrats outnumbered Republicans 40 percent to 28 percent among Asian Americans. Among the entire group of New Minority voters in the 2004 election, Democrats led Republicans by 49 percent to 28 percent.

African Americans

Black Americans have an unmistakable majority party.[9] From the early 1950s through 2004, huge majorities of African Americans have called themselves Democrats, while only tiny minorities have reported a Republican identification. After peaking in 1968 at the end of Johnson's Great Society administration, blacks' identification with the Democratic Party stabilized at exceptionally high levels. Democratic identification among African-American voters averaged 78 percent during the elections from 1984 through 2004, 44 points higher than the average Democratic identification among white voters. In 2004, 78 percent of African-American voters were Democrats, and only 8 percent were Republicans. In no other racial or ethnic group did one political party maintain such overwhelming majority support.

THE WHITE REALIGNMENT

America's transformed party battle, its shift from a substantial Democratic edge to a fight between parties of roughly equal size, is thus primarily the product of the long-term realignment of white voters dating from the Reagan presidency. Because of the size of the white electorate, and because white voters are the main source of increased Republican competitiveness, the dynamics of the white realignment need to be examined.

The Importance of Ideology

How did the Republicans engineer their white realignment? In modern American politics, ideology plays a central role in separating the parties. Conceding white liberals to the Democrats, Republican leaders have pursued two basic goals in their efforts to shift the partisan balance among white voters: *realign the conservatives and neutralize the moderates.*[10] Efforts to achieve these strategic objectives were targeted especially at the Southern white electorate, where both conservatives and moderates had long been Democrats, but they were pursued in the rest of the nation as well. The long-term results have been the development of large Republican majorities among white conservatives, the disappearance of sizable Democratic leads among white moderates, and the consolidation of Democratic strength among white liberals.[11]

Accordingly, the most realistic way to understand the divisions among white voters is to classify them according to their ideology—

as liberals, moderates, and conservatives—and then to examine the changing partisanship of these ideological groups. Using the national election exit polls conducted by news organizations, figure 1.3 shows that the relative sizes of the three ideological groups remained fairly similar from 1976 through 2004. On average, nearly half of white voters classified themselves as moderates, about one-third thought of themselves as conservatives, and fewer than one-fifth identified themselves as liberals.

Realigning White Conservatives

As late as 1976, conservative white voters were far from sold on the Republican Party (see "Conservatives: Republican Realignment" in figure 1.3). Only two-fifths of conservative whites thought of themselves as Republicans, one-third of them were independents, and one-fourth were still Democrats. White conservatives, those individuals most likely in principle to identify as Republicans, became the main targets of GOP realignment efforts. Some conservatives were longtime voters who had been raised as Democrats or who thought of themselves as independents. Other targets were conservatives who had seldom or never voted. Republican efforts toward these individuals sought to get them registered and voting.

Reagan's presidency was indeed a watershed era for many white Americans. He was elected in 1980 on a platform that promised to strengthen the military, cut taxes, reduce domestic government spending, and honor traditional moral, religious, and cultural values. "Ronald Reagan's legacy as a party builder has gotten short shrift," former Republican Speaker of the House Newt Gingrich observed shortly after the former president's death in 2004. "One of President Reagan's great strengths was his commitment to big ideas and his willingness to remain cheerful no matter what the difficulties were," Gingrich emphasized. "It made him likable and approachable and easy to support. Despite being the son of an alcoholic father, entering the job market in the Great Depression, and watching his ca-

Figure 1.3
White Voters: Ideology and Party

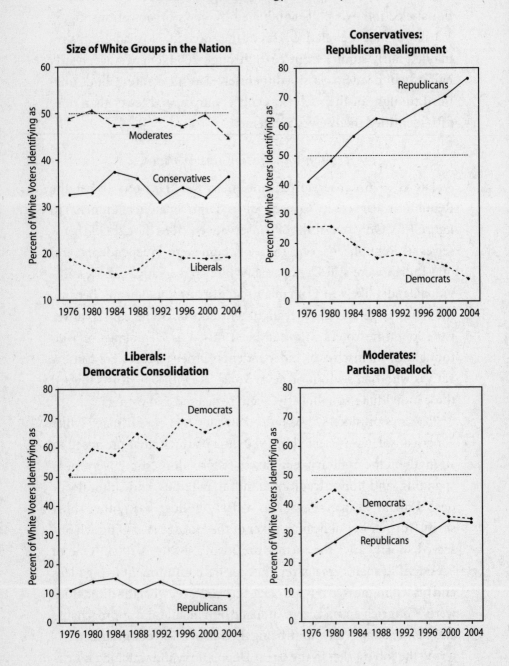

reer in movies fade out, Reagan remained a steadfast optimist. That disposition was a tremendous, politically potent change from the angry pessimism of traditional conservatism." [12]

Reagan's optimism and performance in office legitimated Republicanism as the party of choice for most American conservatives. [13] When his presidency began, fewer than half of conservative white voters (48 percent) in the United States were Republicans. Only in the West, where Reagan's brand of conservative Republicanism had originated, did majorities of white conservative voters already think of themselves as Republicans. Abandoning the me-too approach of earlier Republican presidents, the Californian advocated conservative policies on a wide range of issues. Across the nation, Reagan attracted large numbers of white conservatives into the Republican Party. By 1988, at the end of his presidency, 63 percent of conservative white voters were Republicans, 23 percent were independents, and only 15 percent still thought of themselves as Democrats.

Even more important for the American party battle, the conservative gains that Reagan stimulated have endured. In 2004, 76 percent of white conservative voters were Republicans, while a mere 8 percent were still Democrats. Realigning conservatives created reliable bases of support in many areas of the country where the Republican Party had previously been an uncompetitive minority. The increased conservative presence—especially in the South and the West—reshaped the national Republican Party.

White Liberals Become More Democratic

Reagan's philosophy and governing style directly challenged several of the most important assumptions that had dominated American politics since the New Deal. He called for reductions in the rate of increase of federal programs and for lowering income tax rates. Instead of accommodating to the Cold War, Reagan believed that Russian Communism was an evil economic and political system that delivered neither freedom nor a high standard of living to its subjects.

Angered and alarmed by Reagan's rejection of their fundamental beliefs, values, and interests, liberal whites responded by aligning more strongly with the Democratic Party. In 1976, 51 percent of liberal white voters were Democrats, 38 percent were independents, and 11 percent were Republicans. By 1988, 65 percent of white liberals were Democrats, a percentage that rose to 68 percent in 2004 (see "Liberals: Democratic Consolidation" in figure 1.3). As more liberal whites became Democrats, and as minority voters—African Americans, Latinos, Asian Americans, and others—became more prominent within the party, the liberal wing of the national Democratic Party was greatly strengthened at the expense of its conservative wing.

Neutralizing the White Moderates

Simply realigning white conservatives was not sufficient to make the Republicans truly competitive with the Democrats. Nationally, Republican leaders confronted a size problem. Their potentially most loyal supporters made up only about one-third of America's white voters. If the Republicans continued to lose moderate whites by large margins, and if they lost liberal whites and racial/ethnic minorities by even wider margins, even the most solid bloc of white conservatives could not possibly overcome Democrats' strength in the rest of the electorate.

Hence enlarging the Republican Party in the national electorate also depended upon the success of a second strategic imperative: neutralizing the customary Democratic advantage among moderates, the nation's largest group of white voters. In 1976 Democrats led Republicans 40 percent to 23 percent among these voters. Moderate whites, as figure 1.3 shows, displayed a sizable Democratic advantage until 1984, when Reagan's decisive reelection victory helped neutralize the long-standing Democratic advantage. In the 2000 and 2004 elections, the Democratic advantage dropped to a single point, 35 percent to 34 percent. No longer did America's white moderate voters provide a reliable surplus of votes for Democratic candidates.

Moderation, unlike conservatism or liberalism, is not a fighting faith. White moderates do not ordinarily have polarized views of the parties and candidates. In general they are liberal on some issues, conservative on others, and without clear tendencies on many other issues. Because their policy preferences are so diverse, it is difficult for either a distinctly *liberal* Democratic Party or a distinctly *conservative* Republican Party to attract majority identification from white moderates. Neither Bill Clinton's "New Democrat" policies nor George W. Bush's "compassionate conservatism" brought majorities of moderates into their respective parties. Clear and unmistakable performance failure by one of the parties—as happened to the Republicans during the Great Depression—may be necessary before majorities of white moderates identify with a particular party. One party would have to be perceived as culturally unacceptable, politically useless, or some of both.

Thus heightened ideological divisions between Republican and Democratic voters increasingly shape the partisan policy battles among American politicians. Power struggles between conservative Republican and liberal Democratic elected politicians in the White House, the Senate, and the House of Representatives are based upon the rapidly changing ideological composition of voters who make up the Democratic and Republican parties and nominate their respective parties' candidates.

Neither of the ideological orientations commonly associated with party elites attracts anything close to majority support among all white voters. In 2004 self-identified moderates (45 percent) far outnumbered conservatives (34 percent) and liberals (21 percent). Liberal Democrats cannot win by appealing primarily to liberals, nor can conservative Republicans prevail by exclusively targeting conservatives. Presidential candidates therefore must unify their core ideological bases but also attract millions of moderate voters.

Republican gains and Democratic losses among the nation's huge group of white moderate voters have powerfully reshaped the party balance. These ideological trends have, of course, affected the relative strength of the liberal and conservative wings within each of the parties. As Democratic primary voters have become more liberal and less conservative, liberal candidates have thrived. At the same time, as Republican primary voters have become more conservative and less moderate, conservatives have more often been winners.

This partisan sorting out of white voters according to their ideology has profoundly affected the two national parties. The net effect of these trends has been to strengthen the association in the white electorate between voters' ideologies and their partisan identifications. Each party has become more ideologically homogeneous and more distinct from the other. The Republican Party has become more conservative; the Democratic Party has become more liberal.[14]

White Men and White Women

Republican efforts to attract white support have succeeded far more with men than women. In the 1950s, Democrats led Republicans in both groups, and white men were even more Democratic and less Republican than white women. Since the early 1980s, the Democratic advantage has collapsed dramatically among white men and more subtly among white women.

White men, the driving force in the Republican surge, have clearly realigned their partisanship. Beginning in the Reagan-Mondale contest of 1984, and persisting in every subsequent presidential election, more white men have labeled themselves Republicans than Democrats. In 2004 Republicans led Democrats among white men by 20 points, 47 percent to 27 percent. White women, by contrast, displayed a different pattern of partisan change. Democratic strength has eroded, but a sustained Republican advantage has not emerged. In 2004, however, a substantial Republican lead appeared, 43 percent to 35 percent, among white women.

The greater Republican strength among white men than white women rests upon the different ideological composition of the groups. There are more conservatives and fewer liberals among white men than among white women. In the 2004 exit poll moderates were similar in number among men and women (44 percent and 45 percent, respectively). The important gender differences concerned the relative numbers of conservatives and liberals. Conservatives swamped liberals 40 percent to 16 percent among white men. While there were also more conservatives (33 percent) than liberals (22 percent) among white women, the ratio of conservatives to liberals was far less pronounced.

Ideology, Religion, Gender, and Party

White American voters continue to divide their partisanship along religious lines, although modern cleavages differ from those of the past in several respects. Nationally, most white voters are Christians (94 percent in the 1950s, 82 percent in 2004). Because whites made up virtually all of the electorate in 1952, white Christians were more than nine-tenths of all American voters. By 2004 white Christians had become a much smaller majority (63 percent) of American voters due to the smaller percentages of whites among all voters *and* to smaller percentages of Christians among all white voters.

Enormous changes have occurred in the size of the nation's major religious groups.[15] In the 1950s Protestants made up 70 percent of the nation's white voters, followed distantly by Catholics (24 percent) and even more distantly by whites who were not Christians (6 percent). By 2004 the religious affiliations of white voters were considerably more diverse. The relative size of white Protestants declined to 55 percent of the white electorate. Catholics increased slightly, to 27 percent of white voters. The non-Christian whites—

Figure 1.4
White Voters: Religion and Party

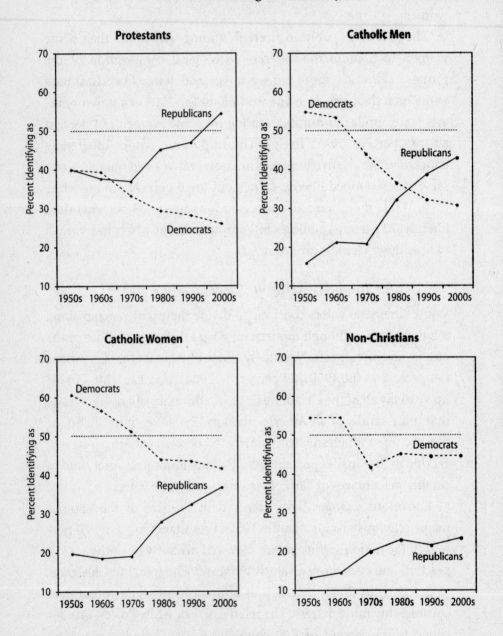

Jews, adherents of religions other than Christianity and Judaism, and those with no religious affiliation—tripled in size, to 18 percent of all white voters.

To track the changing political dynamics of America's religious traditions, we divide white voters into four groups: Protestants, Catholic men, Catholic women, and non-Christians. Figure 1.4 shows the partisanship of these groups by decades from the 1950s through the early 2000s. America's white Protestants have seldom behaved as a cohesive partisan bloc. From the 1950s through the 1970s, they were evenly split in partisanship. Commencing in the 1980s, however, white Protestants moved decisively toward the Republican Party. Republican ascendancy among white Protestants represents a tremendous departure from the old national pattern.

Ideology is the central explanation of the white Protestants' political transformation. White Protestants have the highest ratio of conservatives to liberals of any voting group in the nation. In 2004, for example, 45 percent were conservatives, and 13 percent were liberals. Reagan's presidency was the obvious turning point for white Protestants. His emphasis on conservative themes concerning national security, taxation, cultural, racial, and religious issues resonated with many of the values, beliefs, and experiences of Protestant whites throughout the nation. By the 2002 and 2004 elections, for the first time in the history of the United States, majorities of white Protestants—men *and* women—were Republicans.

The changing partisanship of white Catholic voters has been equally important in reducing Democratic strength and enhancing Republican competitiveness. Political scientist William B. Prendergast has summed up this major development as "The Passing of the Democratic Monolith."[16] Historically many Catholics viewed the Republican Party as the political instrument of Protestants. As such, they had little interest in the Republicans. In the 1950s and 1960s, most white Catholics were Democrats, and through the 1970s, barely one-fifth of them were Republicans. Not until the Reagan years did white Catholics display a sharp upward movement toward the Republicans. According to Prendergast, "In the 1980s a notable realignment of Catholic voters took place. The proportion of Catholics of Democratic affiliation and voting habits shrank; the ranks of Catholic Republicans and Independents increased; and the activist cadres in the Republican Party were diversified by an infusion of Catholics in party and public office."[17] By the first decade of the twenty-first century, there were slightly more Republicans than Democrats among white Catholic voters—an astonishing shift within the nation's second largest religious group.

Gender impacts partisan trends for white Catholics (see figure 1.4). A Republican realignment has occurred among white Catholic men. During the past half century, this group shifted from a Democratic majority to a Republican plurality. The Democratic advantage narrowed markedly during Reagan's presidency, and by the 1990s, a clear Republican lead had emerged. These gains have continued in the twenty-first century. In 2004, 46 percent of white male Catholic voters were Republicans, while only 27 percent remained Democrats.

White Catholic women, on the other hand, display a pattern of *partisan dealignment.* This is a process of partisan change in which a party's traditional majority or plurality advantage collapses without a rival party emerging with a new majority or plurality lead. Among white Catholic women, huge Democratic leads of the 1950s and 1960s have narrowed to much smaller Democratic advantages. Based on the average of the 2002 and 2004 elections, Democrats still held a small lead. In the 2004 presidential election, however, the Democratic lead fell to two points, 40 percent to 38 percent.

Catholic women have been harder to realign than Catholic men because of their different ideological perspectives. In 2004, 53 percent of Catholic women were moderates, only 27 percent were conservatives, and 19 percent were liberals. While 50 percent of all Catholic men were moderates, 36 percent were conservatives, and

14 percent were liberals. Realigning white Catholic women would require the GOP to attract far more moderates. Yet even without a Republican realignment among white Catholic women, the old pro-Democratic patterns in partisanship have been transformed.

Non-Christian white voters have always been far more Democratic than Republican (see figure 1.4). Their substantial impact on national politics derives from their reliable Democratic unity combined with their growing size. Three groups comprise the non-Christian whites. Jews, 3 percent of the white electorate in 2004, are by far the nation's most Democratic and most liberal group of white voters. Among Jewish voters, there were four times as many Democrats as Republicans (63 percent to 15 percent) and almost four times as many liberals as conservatives (45 percent to 12 percent). No other group of white voters provides such strong partisan and ideological support for the Democratic Party.

Smaller Democratic advantages characterize the other two groups of non-Christian whites. White voters who belong to a religion other than Christianity or Judaism were 5 percent of the white electorate in 2004. They also identify far more as Democrats than as Republicans (42 percent to 25 percent). The Democratic advantage is rooted in the more than two-to-one liberal-to-conservative makeup of the group, as well as a Democratic advantage among moderates.

Voters who reported no religious affiliation accounted for one-tenth of the white electorate in 2004.[18] Democrats outnumbered Republicans among these voters by nearly 2 to 1, 43 percent to 23 percent. While moderates are a plurality (44 percent) of the group, liberals overwhelm conservatives, 40 percent to 16 percent. All in all, the stability of Democratic support among non-Christian whites over recent decades stands in distinct contrast to all other white religious groups.

Taken together, the net impact of these changes in the white electorate has been quite substantial. The Republican Party has become far more conservative and the Democratic Party far more liberal than in the past. The conservative wing of the national Democratic Party has virtually disappeared, as has the liberal wing of the Republican Party. A more liberal Democratic Party and a much more conservative Republican Party are unlikely to attract majority support from the many voters who do not think of themselves as either liberals or conservatives.

NATIONAL PARTY BASES IN 2004

The 2004 elections are a convenient benchmark for understanding the group composition of the national Democratic and Republican parties. Using the exit polls, we have divided voters into eight groups: African Americans, New Minorities, and six categories of whites. The white groups are evangelical Protestants, nonevangelical Protestant women, nonevangelical Protestant men, Catholic women, Catholic men, and non-Christians.

Realistic bases for each party can be created by adding ideology to partisanship. In the ideologically charged climate of modern American politics, liberal independents and conservative independents generally join their respective partisans in providing emphatic support for the party closest to their ideological orientation. Thus the "Democratic base" consists of Democrats plus liberal independents. Likewise, Republicans plus conservative independents constitute the "Republican base." Adding conservative independents to Republicans and liberal independents to Democrats produced in 2004 a national tie—44 percent to 43 percent in favor of the Republicans—in the size of the two party bases. Neither party attracted a majority of voters even when partisans are supplemented by the appropriate category of independents.

Table 1.1 ranks the eight groups from most Democratic to least Democratic based on the difference between the Democratic and Republican party bases. The final column reports the size of each

Table 1.1
Democratic and Republican National Party Bases in 2004 (%)*

Political Group	Democratic Base	Republican Base	DB–RB	Group Size
African Americans	82	11	+71	11
Non-Christians	58	26	+32	14
New Minorities	55	34	+21	11
Catholic women	44	42	+2	11
Nonevangelical Protestant women	41	45	–4	11
Nonevangelical Protestant men	33	52	–19	10
Catholic men	32	52	–20	10
Evangelical Protestants	21	71	–50	22
All	43	44	–1	100

* Democratic base = Democrats + liberal independents;
Republican base = Republicans + conservative independents;
Group Size = percent of all voters; New Minorities = Latinos +
other minorities. Aside from African Americans and New Minorities,
all other groups are categories of white voters. Percentages are rounded
to the nearest whole number.
Source: 2004 exit polls.

group in the 2004 national electorate. Hence the table summarizes the American power struggle according to the partisan unity and size of important groups of voters. It allows us to understand how race and ethnicity, religion, and gender greatly impact modern American politics.

The strongest Democratic groups are African Americans, non-Christian whites, and New Minorities. No other group matched African Americans in the magnitude of partisan advantage. Among black voters there was a 71-point gap in party bases. Non-Christian whites gave the Democrats their second largest advantage, while the New Minorities were the final group with a substantial Democratic advantage. Together, these three pro-Democratic groups cast 36 percent of the national vote in 2004.

For the Republicans three groups also produced large party bases. First and foremost were white evangelical Protestants, the only group with an overwhelming—71 percent to 21 percent—Republican advantage. The white men and women who classify themselves as evangelical Protestants represented 22 percent of all American voters in 2004.[19] Two other groups of white men—Catholics and nonevangelical Protestants—each gave the Republicans 20-point leads. These pro-Republican groups accounted for 42 percent of the national vote.

Located in the middle of the national electorate were two groups of white women: Catholics and nonevangelical Protestants. As of 2004, the Democratic and Republican party bases gave neither party any advantage. These groups are especially important in determining winners and losers in national elections because they represent slightly over one-fifth of all voters.

Neither party can create national majorities simply by mobilizing its key groups and turning them out. The high stakes of each presidential election encourage each party to find ways to motivate its strongest partisans while also appealing to enough moderate independents—13 percent of the voters in 2004—to win elections. Part of the difficulty for each party is that the politicians and issues identified with the most lopsidedly partisan groups—white evangelical Protestants and white conservatives for the Republicans, and African Americans and white liberals for the Democrats—mobilize opponents as well as supporters. The very striking differences in how these groups contribute to the Democratic and Republican party bases reflect remarkable changes in the social composition of the two parties in the past half century.

THE TRANSFORMATION
OF THE NATIONAL PARTIES

While great changes have occurred in the relative size of key groups in the American electorate, even more dramatic changes have taken place *within* each of the major parties. The modern American power struggle is waged between groups of partisans who are more starkly different in terms of race and ethnicity, religion, and gender than they were in the early 1950s. Common political ground is thus harder to find and maintain as the two major parties become more distinct in their group composition.

The greatest transformations concern the Democratic Party. Figure 1.5 compares the two parties according to the relative size of three important categories of voters: white Protestants, white Catholics, and the combination of all minorities plus non-Christian whites. In the 1950s, white Protestants were a large majority of all

Figure 1.5
Transformation of the National Parties

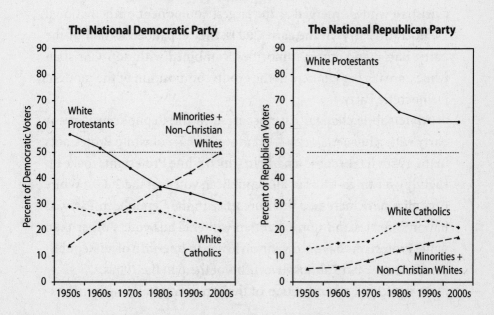

Democrats in the United States. They were, in short, the dominant social group within the nation's largest party. White Catholics were the second biggest group of Democrats, and minorities plus non-Christian whites were a distant third. Over time the size of these three groups of Democrats has shifted remarkably.

White Protestants have steadily declined as a percentage of Democratic voters. By the 1970s, white Protestants were no longer a majority of all Democrats, and by the 1990s, they were in second place behind minorities and non-Christian whites. As of the early 2000s, white Protestants were a diminishing presence within a smaller Democratic Party. White Catholics have also declined in relative size within the Democratic Party. Of the three groups, they have become the smallest force among all Democratic voters.

Within the Democratic Party, the rising social groups are racial/ethnic minorities and non-Christian whites. By the 1970s, these combined groups slightly outnumbered white Catholics, and a decade later they were more or less tied with white Protestants. The 1990s were a breakthrough decade in the history of the Democratic Party. For the first time, racial/ethnic minorities and non-Christian whites emerged as the largest component of the national Democratic Party. In the early 2000s, they expanded to half of the party. Racial and ethnic minorities, combined with non-Christian whites, are the big winners in the group composition of the modern Democratic Party.

More subtle changes have occurred in the Republican Party. A party with a huge majority—over four-fifths—of white Protestants in the 1950s has become a party in which white Protestants make up slightly over three-fifths of all Republican voters in the 2000s. White Catholics have increased their presence in the Republican Party, as have minorities and non-Christian whites. Thus voters other than white Protestants have grown from less than one-fifth of all Republicans in the 1950s to almost two-fifths of them in the 2000s.

In the 1950s, as a reflection of their majority standing in the national electorate, white Protestants dominated both the Democratic and Republican parties. A Democratic Party in which white Protestants were a large majority faced a Republican Party in which white Protestants were a much larger majority. Fifty years later, fewer and fewer white Protestants were comfortable with the Democratic Party. Because white Protestants remain the single largest group in the American electorate, the steady decline of white Protestants as a proportion of all Democrats marks a significant transformation in American party politics.

Historically, white Catholics had a much larger presence in the Democratic Party than in the Republican Party. As old divisions between white Protestants and white Catholics have faded, white Catholics have become somewhat less prominent within the Democratic Party and somewhat more prominent within the Republican Party. As of the early 2000s, they accounted for about one-fifth of both Democrats and Republicans. In the 1950s, they were 29 percent of Democrats but only 13 percent of Republicans.

The most obvious difference between the Democratic and Republican parties is the relative prominence of racial/ethnic minorities plus non-Christian whites. Never before in American history has this combination of groups accounted for half of a major party. In modern American politics, a Republican Party dominated by white Protestants faces a Democratic Party in which minorities plus non-Christian whites far outnumber white Protestants. The American power struggle thus rests on two parties whose group composition is increasingly distinct.

FROM THE NATION TO SECTIONS AND REGIONS

This book is organized to help readers understand how and why the United States has arrived at its current form of close and intensely ideological partisan conflict. Having begun our book with the national perspective, in the following chapters we shall identify and integrate different partisan trends in the sections and regions of the nation into the story of how American politics has become so intensely competitive and so ideologically driven.

To understand the momentous transformation of the national party battle, we shall first analyze different trends in the South and the North, historically the two great sections of the United States. The South, defined as the eleven states of the former Confederacy, still remains highly distinctive in aspects of its political behavior. The North—the rest of America—is too large and too complex to be useful as an analytic category except in comparison with the South.

The battles characteristic of modern American politics result from very different patterns of partisan and ideological development in the major regions of the country. We engage in regional political analysis in order to better understand the real politics of this continental nation. Assessing trends in the various regions generates an improved awareness of the competing forces that shape the American power struggle over the presidency, the Senate, and the House of Representatives. Accordingly, we shall separate the North into the Northeast, the Midwest, the Mountains/Plains, and the Pacific Coast regions.

In the United States, the closely competitive national battles to control the White House and Congress derive from Republican strength in the Mountains/Plains and the South, Democratic strength in the Northeast and the Pacific Coast, and closely divided support for the two major parties in the Midwest. Although the relentlessly competitive nature of American national politics is visible for all to see and ponder, the regional patterns underlying this new state of affairs are not well understood. This book tells the story of these remarkable developments.

2

AMERICA'S POLITICAL REGIONS

To GRASP THE WHOLE, WE NEED TO UNDERSTAND THE PARTS. The United States is a federal system in which national political power is built up from local, state, regional, and sectional bases of support. Understanding American politics requires examining party battles in the nation's principal geographic areas. In recent American history, the close struggles for national power reflect increased Republican strength in the South and a diminished Democratic advantage in the North. Paying attention to the main trends in the South—and contrasting these patterns with those in the rest of the nation—is an essential starting point for comprehending modern American politics. In this book, the South is defined as the eleven former Confederate states: Alabama, Arkansas, Florida, Georgia, Louisiana, Mississippi, North Carolina, South Carolina, Tennessee, Texas, and Virginia. The North consists of the thirty-nine other states plus the District of Columbia.

Without the Republicans' Southern victories in 2004, Democrats would have regained the presidency and both houses of Congress. John Kerry won 65 percent of the Northern electoral votes but still fell short of the 70 percent he needed when President George W.

Bush won all of the South's electoral votes. Northern Democrats outnumbered Northern Republicans in the Senate, but massive Republican strength in the South's delegation gave the GOP formal control of that institution. In the House of Representatives, a small Democratic lead in the North was overwhelmed by a huge Republican surplus from the South. In each national battle, very large Republican surpluses of electoral votes and congressional seats in the South trumped much smaller Democratic surpluses in the rest of the nation.

The division between the North and the South has long been the prime example of geographically based conflict in the United States. After discussing the most salient changes in the South and in the North, we shall then examine four distinct Northern regions—the Northeast, the Midwest, the Mountains/Plains, and the Pacific Coast—that vary in the types of people who reside in them and in the relative strengths of the rival parties.

BATTLEFIELD SECTIONALISM

The Civil War and Reconstruction bequeathed a political system in which the two major parties long pursued fundamentally different sectional strategies to achieve national victories. Death and destruction in the Civil War, followed by unsuccessful Northern efforts to change the behavior and attitudes of defeated Southern whites during Reconstruction, forged durable partisan loyalties in all Confederate states and in many Union ones. Battlefield Sectionalism, a concept that emphasizes the rigid connection between the geography of the Civil War and subsequent Republican and Democratic strongholds, molded the American party system for generations. The Republican Party became the designated political instrument of the triumphant North, while the defeated South emerged as the most reliable stronghold of the Democratic Party.[1]

From the Civil War through the first half of the twentieth century, the Republican Party was strictly a Northern enterprise. Abraham Lincoln and other Republican leaders in the 1850s had understood that the North's immense size was the key to national success. Provided that Republicans could win around two-thirds of the electoral votes, Senate seats, and House seats contained in the Northern states, Republicans could literally write off the South. And in fact they did. In the 1860 presidential election, Lincoln's party was not even on the ballot in any of the Southern states.

A sufficiently unified North could always prevail because the North was roughly three times larger than the South. The Lincoln Strategy of 1860—attack the South in order to unite the North—proved to be eminently practical for seventy years. Republicans presented themselves as the party of the North but never dominated "their" section to the same extent that Democrats achieved in the smaller South.

America's classic sectional cleavage collapsed first in the North when voters held the Republicans responsible for the Great Depression of the 1930s. Democrats became the new majority party of the North during Franklin D. Roosevelt's New Deal. The former New York governor expanded the Northern Democratic Party, especially in the largest cities. Lincoln's exclusively sectional strategy now ensured national Republican defeats. Eventually the GOP recovered from its New Deal lows and again became competitive in many Northern states. Nonetheless, at the midpoint of the twentieth century, Republicans remained a minority party in the North. Democrats may no longer have commanded the loyalties of a majority of Northern voters, but there were still more Northern Democrats than Northern Republicans.

For generations after the Civil War, Southern political leaders invested all of their political capital in the Democratic Party and leveraged their influence in that party on behalf of the practices and institutions of southern racism. Black men who began to vote in the Southern states supported the Republicans as the party of emancipation and Reconstruction. By preventing former slaves and their descendants from voting, Southern whites generated massive majorities of electoral votes and congressional seats for the national Democratic Party. Until the 1930s, Democrats were a minority party in the United States, and the Southerners constituted, according to historian David M. Potter, "a majority wing in a minority party." Southerners especially used their influence in the Senate to filibuster—or threaten to—any legislation that challenged the institutions and practices of Southern racism. When Northern Democrats swept into Congress during the early New Deal, the Southerners immediately shrank to "a minority wing in a majority party." Yet their reduced size did not end their influence within the Democratic Party. Roosevelt needed Southern support to pass his New Deal agenda. By refusing to advocate civil rights legislation and by allowing Southerners to amend bills in ways that maximized benefits to their white constituents, Roosevelt retained the support of most Southern senators and representatives.[2]

Something for nothing is the greatest formula for political success the world has ever known. Roosevelt sent more federal dollars into the Southern states than any previous president but did not tax the incomes of the vast majority of Southerners. Nearly all Southerners, whites as well as blacks, earned so little that their incomes were not subject to federal income taxes. According to historian Jordan A. Schwarz, one Texas congressional district, for example, "was so poor that in 1935 it was estimated that less than two-thirds of 1 percent had ever filed an income tax return." Roosevelt thus gave Southern whites what they wanted—money, jobs, and racial segregation—at no direct cost to themselves, while protecting them from what they did not want: civil rights laws and income taxes. Yet the New Deal did provide benefits to impoverished Southerners, both whites and blacks, and thus indirectly began to reduce the dependence of blacks upon white Southerners.[3]

Northern Democratic strength peaked in the early years of the

New Deal. By 1938 Republicans began to regain some of their traditional seats in Congress. Northern Democrats therefore still needed huge Southern surpluses of electoral votes and seats in Congress to ensure continued Democratic control of the national government. As late as the 1950 elections, all of the South's senators and almost all of its House members were Democrats. As long as the South remained overwhelmingly Democratic, the Democratic Party could hold the White House and both houses of Congress without ever needing to win majorities in the North.

Through the end of World War II, the Solid Democratic South continued to be the great "given" of American political life. To many white Southerners, the Republicans were still the party of Lincoln's war and Hoover's depression. Bitterness and resentment toward the victorious Yankees and Republicans lasted well into the second half of the twentieth century.

In the South, Battlefield Sectionalism ended at different times. Republicans first began to divide the Southern presidential vote in 1952. Beginning with the 1964 presidential election, and continuing in every subsequent presidential contest, more Southern whites have voted Republican than Democratic. The white switch in partisanship—more Republicans than Democrats—occurred twenty years later. Starting in 1984, and continuing in every subsequent presidential election year, more whites have identified themselves as Republicans than Democrats. In 1994 Southern Battlefield Sectionalism finally ended for the Senate and the House of Representatives when Republicans gained—and kept—majorities of the South's delegations to both institutions.[4]

SOUTHERN CHANGE
VERSUS NORTHERN STABILITY

The Republican advance among Southern whites is the most spectacular example of partisan realignment in modern American history. Figure 2.1 reveals enormous partisan shifts in the South versus fairly modest partisan change in the rest of the nation during the second half of the twentieth century. The upper figures contrast the scope of partisan change among white voters alone, while the bottom figures chart the results for all voters. Massive changes in partisanship have occurred among Southern white voters as well as much smaller shifts among Northern whites. In both sections, the initial turning point in whites' party identification occurred in 1984—the midpoint of Ronald Reagan's presidency. Because of Democratic strength among the growing numbers of minority voters, Democrats still held a lead in the North, and the Republican advantage among all Southern voters was much smaller than among white voters.[5]

As the 1950s began, the traditional institutions and practices of white supremacy remained firmly in place across the South. In 1952 blacks made up 25 percent of the Southern population but only 5 percent of voters—and that estimate may be on the high side. Blatant obstacles to blacks' voting, low turnout rates among whites, and the absence of real two-party competition made the South the most undemocratic area of the United States. When asked whether they thought of themselves as "a Democrat, a Republican, an independent, or something else," 78 percent of Southern white voters gave the politically correct answer. Only 11 percent broke the cultural line and identified themselves as Republicans. Another 11 percent thought of themselves as independents. Nowhere else in America were white voters so completely attached to the Democratic Party.[6]

Political and social events in the 1960s rocked the foundations of the Southern Democratic Party. Black protests against Southern segregation and shifts in Northern white public opinion favorable to federal intervention eventually forced presidential and congressional action. Democratic president Lyndon B. Johnson of Texas led a bipartisan coalition of Northern Democrats and Northern Republicans that finally overcame Southern Democrats' resistance to pass-

Figure 2.1
Trends in South vs. North

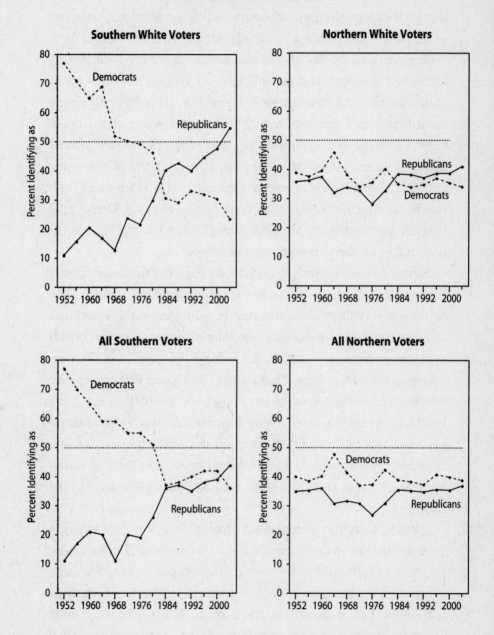

ing the Civil Rights Act of 1964 and the Voting Rights Act of 1965. These laws prohibited many of the most flagrantly racist practices that had made public life in the South so different from that of the rest of the nation and greatly stimulated voting by African Americans.[7]

Johnson's Great Society, unlike Roosevelt's New Deal, boldly combined economic and racial liberalism. During Johnson's presidency, the national Democratic Party emerged as a distinctly liberal institution. The Great Society, with its War on Poverty, expansion of federal government responsibilities and programs, higher income taxes, and commitment to ending segregation in the public sector and enforcing the right to vote, sought to transform American politics in ways never before attempted by the national Democratic Party. Many Southern whites interpreted these developments as direct attacks on their interests and traditions.[8]

Johnson's decisive shift to the left broke the ties that bound many conservative Southern whites to the Democratic Party. From 1968 to the early 1980s, only about half of Southern white voters still called themselves Democrats. Many white Southerners now considered themselves independents. Yet beyond some hard-core conservatives, white voters did not rush to the Republican Party in massive numbers. Few white Southerners viewed the Republican Party as a legitimate and useful social institution. Because nearly all of the new black voters were Democrats, their numbers offset the party's losses of departing whites. Thus the Southern Democratic Party, reconfigured as a biracial coalition, continued to flourish—at least in the short run.[9]

The 1984 election was the great turning point for white voters in both the South and the North. Reagan's realignment of white voters, the most important shift in white partisanship since the New Deal, occurred in the North as well as in the South. The Southern transformation was much more dramatic than the Northern realignment, but the same process was at work in both sections (see the top half of figure 2.1). Since 1984 Republicans have consistently outnumbered

Democrats among white voters in every presidential election. By 2004 Republicans had grown to a majority—55 percent—of Southern white voters, while only 24 percent of Southern whites remained Democrats. Smaller and more subtle partisan shifts occurred among Northern white voters: Republicans outnumbered Democrats 41 percent to 34 percent, according to the 2004 exit poll.[10]

While white voters in both sections have shifted to the Republicans, increasing racial and ethnic diversification has brought new Democratic supporters into both electorates. Virtually all-white electorates, the reality everywhere in America in the 1950s, have vanished. Racial and ethnic minority groups now account for 30 percent of Southern voters and 20 percent of Northern voters. Democrats have been the primary beneficiaries of increased participation by African Americans, Latinos, and other ethnic groups. Among all voters, Democrats have retained a small advantage in the North and did so in the South until 2004.

A DIVIDED NORTH

Although the North provides a useful standard of comparison with the South, it is too large and too diverse to justify sustained analytical interest. The North encompasses regions that have experienced quite different patterns of partisan conflict. Accordingly, we have divided the North into four regions: the Northeast, the Midwest, the Mountains/Plains, and the Pacific Coast.[11] A good way to appreciate Northern diversity is by comparing trends in Democratic and Republican identification among white voters alone and then among all voters.[12]

In this book the Northeast is defined as New England (Connecticut, Maine, Massachusetts, New Hampshire, Rhode Island, and Vermont), the Middle Atlantic (Delaware, Maryland, New Jersey, New York, and Pennsylvania), and the District of Columbia. Illinois, Indiana, Iowa, Kentucky, Michigan, Minnesota, Missouri, Ohio, West

Figure 2.2
Patterns Among White Voters

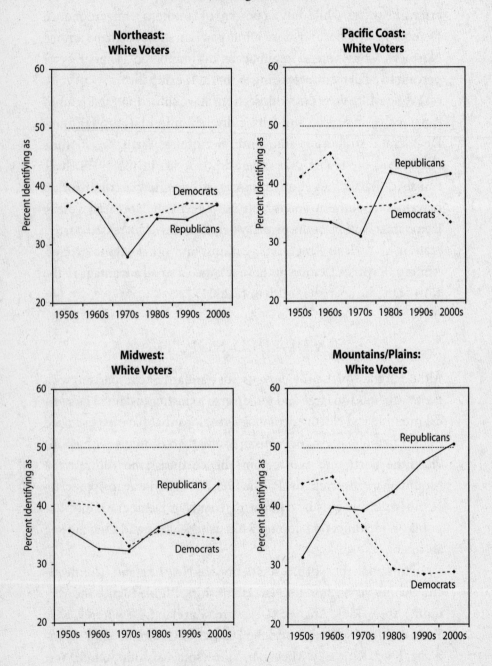

Virginia, and Wisconsin constitute the Midwest. The Mountains/ Plains states are Arizona, Colorado, Idaho, Kansas, Montana, Nebraska, Nevada, New Mexico, North Dakota, Oklahoma, South Dakota, Utah, and Wyoming. The Pacific Coast is composed of Alaska, California, Hawaii, Oregon, and Washington.

To what extent did the modest Republican realignment among white voters in the North occur in each of the Northern regions? Figure 2.2 provides the answers. The earliest, largest, and most enduring pro-Republican shift among whites came in the Mountains/ Plains. Democrats had easily dominated the region in the 1950s, but Republicans surged upward in the 1960s and established a small lead in the 1970s. Whites in the Mountains/Plains responded positively to Reagan's presidency. A huge Republican plurality emerged in the 1980s, and this lead continued to widen during the 1990s and the early 2000s. By the first decade of the twenty-first century, a majority of white voters in the Mountains/Plains were Republicans. No other Northern region experienced such a powerful Republican realignment among its white voters.

Although white voters in the neighboring Pacific Coast states also moved away from the Democrats and toward the Republicans, the timing and magnitude of these partisan shifts differed from those in the Mountains/Plains. Democrats held large leads over Republicans in the 1950s and 1960s, but both parties lost ground during the 1970s. The presidency of a California Republican stimulated Pacific Coast whites to realign in the 1980s. Yet while Republicans have outnumbered Democrats in subsequent decades, GOP growth among Pacific Coast white voters has not accelerated as it did in the Mountains/Plains.

Midwestern whites show another pattern of Republican realignment. Democrats held leads in the 1950s and 1960s, and both parties attracted similar levels of white support in the 1970s and 1980s. A small Republican lead appeared among Midwestern white voters in the 1990s and then expanded in the early 2000s. Thus three of the four Northern regions have displayed pro-Republican shifts in white partisanship in recent decades.

Northeastern whites provide the conspicuous exception to the central trend in Northern white partisanship. During the 1950s, the Northeast was the sole region in which white Republicans outnumbered white Democrats. In the early twenty-first century, it was the only region where white voters evenly divided their partisanship. Republican losses commenced when moderate Northeastern Republicans lost control of the presidential wing of the Republican Party, an institution they had dominated for generations. The new centers of gravity for presidential Republicanism shifted to the West and the South, bringing more conservatives into the party leadership and displacing the more moderate Northeastern Republicans. Many Northeastern whites began to desert the Republican Party during the 1960s.[13] Others left during the 1970s. In subsequent decades, Republicans usually lagged behind Democrats among Northeastern white voters before drawing even, on average, in the 2002 and 2004 elections.

Since the 1960s, the major source of new Democratic strength in the national electorate has been increased participation by racial and ethnic minorities. African Americans began to enter Northern big-city electorates in sizable numbers after World War II and accelerated in participation during the 1960s and subsequent decades. Latino voters have been more recent arrivals, as have Asian Americans and other ethnic minorities. Because of very small numbers of these specific groups in some of the regions, we have combined them as nonwhite minorities. In every region, voters in these groups have greatly increased in size during the past fifty years. The prime beneficiary, of course, has been the Democratic Party.

Figure 2.3 tracks the partisan identification of all voters in the Northern regions. The Northeast has experienced the strongest Democratic realignment in the nation during the past fifty years. A tiny Republican lead in the 1950s has been transformed into a sub-

Figure 2.3
Patterns Among All Voters

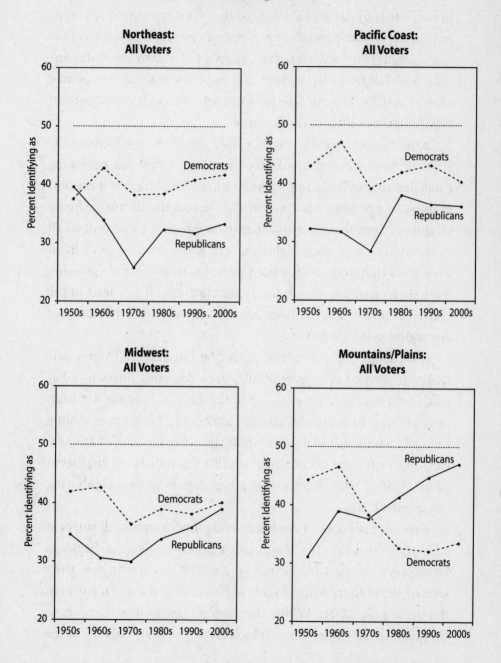

stantial Democratic advantage. From the 1960s onward, Democrats have maintained an impressive plurality advantage over the Republicans. The rival parties have battled to a draw among white voters, but Democrats have greatly benefited from increasing minority participation. Whenever Democrats can split the white vote while winning landslide minority support, the result is sustained Democratic success and Republican failure—precisely the central tendency of Northeastern politics in recent years.

In the Midwest and the Pacific Coast, more cohesive Democratic strength among rising numbers of minority voters has overcome small Republican leads among white voters. The Midwest is the best example of a persistent but narrowing Democratic advantage in the electorate. Even though minorities make up only 13 percent of all Midwestern voters, their high Democratic cohesion—especially in the region's large cities—has been sufficient to overcome a growing Republican lead among whites. Democrats hold a tiny lead in the entire electorate. The Midwest has the closest partisan balance of any region in the United States.

The Pacific Coast shows an enduring but smaller Democratic lead over the past fifty years. Whites are a declining portion of Pacific Coast voters, and their shift to the Republicans has not been large enough to overcome strong Democratic preferences among minority voters, especially the rapidly growing number of Latinos. Racial and ethnic minorities in the Pacific Coast make up 28 percent of the Pacific Coast electorate—far higher than in the neighboring Mountains/Plains.

The only instance of Republican realignment among all voters in a Northern region is the Mountains/Plains. Republicans displaced Democrats among white voters in the 1980s—Reagan was their kind of Republican. Minorities made up only 1 of every 6 voters in the region in 2004. While the region's minorities were pro-Democratic, they were too small to reverse the party balance in the entire electorate. A Republican majority among whites became a Republican plurality among all voters.

THE NEW AMERICAN REGIONS

Because of the large number of white voters, their values and preferences heavily shape the regional variations among all voters. A compelling way to visualize the importance of regions as distinctive settings for partisan conflict in modern America is by examining a series of figures—all based on the 2004 elections—that plot ideology and partisanship for white voters and for all voters. In the following figures, the regions are arrayed on a partisan continuum from left to right. The Northeast occupies the most Democratic position on the left, while the South anchors the most Republican position on the right. Adjacent to the Northeast is the Pacific Coast; next to the South is the Mountains/Plains. In the middle is the Midwest, symbolizing its location in the center of American political life.

From Ronald Reagan to George W. Bush, Republicans have sought to compete nationally by emphasizing conservative ideology to realign white voters. The strengths and weaknesses of such an assertive ideological approach to expanding a minority party can be appreciated by focusing first on the relative size of white conservatives, white liberals, and white moderates from one region to another. How do the regional white electorates differ in terms of their ideological settings? The answers appear in the upper left-hand chart of figure 2.4.

Tremendous regional variation exists in the size of the white ideological groups. Self-identified moderates dominate the white electorates of the Northeast, the Pacific Coast, and the Midwest. In these three regions, there are far more moderates than conservatives, their closest competitors. Everywhere, liberals are the smallest ideological category of white voters. However, in the Northeast and the Pacific

Figure 2.4
Regional Settings: Party and Ideology

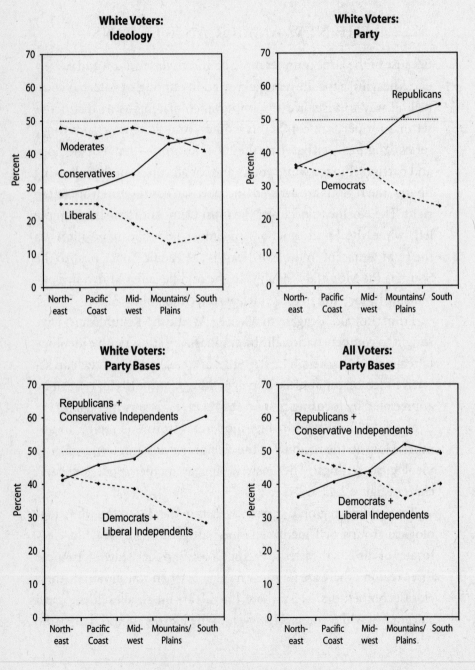

Coast, liberals are almost as common as conservatives. In the Midwest, the gap between conservatives and liberals is much wider than in the Northeast and the Pacific Coast.

Very different ideological configurations characterize white voters in the other two regions. Conservatives are about as numerous as moderates in the Mountains/Plains, and they actually outnumber moderates in the South. The huge conservative domination over liberals in the South and the Mountains/Plains contrasts greatly with the much smaller conservative edge over liberals in the Northeast and the Pacific Coast.

Republican growth in the United States has depended upon attracting white conservatives, and the upper-right chart shows a pattern of Republican identification that closely tracks regional variations in the percentage of white conservative voters. Among white voters alone, the parties are tied in the Northeast, show rather small Republican leads in the Pacific Coast and the Midwest, and then swell to substantial Republican advantages in the Mountains/Plains and the South. White voters in the Pacific Coast and the Midwest closely mirror the Republican lead among whites in the national electorate, while the Northeast and the Republican strongholds show large departures from the national pattern. Among white voters in 2004, the Democratic Party possessed not a single regional stronghold.

To produce realistic bases for each party, ideology can be added to partisanship. Thus the Republican base consists of self-identified Republicans plus the conservative independents. In a similar way, self-identified Democrats plus the liberal independents constitute the Democratic base. The 2004 party bases show a slightly larger Democratic base among white voters only in the Northeast. In every other region, the white Republican base exceeded the white Democratic base. As the lower left-hand chart in figure 2.4 shows, the Republican white base grows larger in every region as we move away from the Northeast, culminating in a 32-point advantage among Southern white voters.

Offsetting white Republicanism, of course, is pronounced Democratic strength among minority voters. The lower-right chart in figure 2.4 plots the regional bottom lines in 2004: the Democratic and Republican party bases among all voters. It reveals acutely different regional bases of party strength in the United States.

The largest Democratic advantage is located in the Northeast. Republicans are now distinct underdogs in the Northeast, where they trail slightly among white voters and lose 4 to 1 among minorities. The Democratic base now includes nearly half of all Northeastern voters. Joining the Northeast as a Democratic stronghold is the Pacific Coast. This region contains the nation's largest percentage of racial and ethnic minorities, as well as the biggest percentage of non-Christian whites. Democratic strength among these groups easily overcomes the Republican edge among white Christians.

Among all voters, the Mountains/Plains and the South stand out as Republican strongholds. Although the greater Republican advantage among white voters occurs in the South, a larger Republican lead among all voters appears in the Mountains/Plains because racial and ethnic minorities make up a smaller portion of its voters than in the South. In both regions, the Republican base exceeds or approaches half of all voters.

In the Midwest, the 2004 party bases were virtually equal, with the Republicans holding the slimmest of advantages—a partisan balance that paralleled Bush's very narrow victory over Kerry in the region. Democratic strength among minority voters residing in the large cities of the Midwest turns the region into an unusually close partisan battleground. The virtual parity of the Republican and Democratic Parties in the Midwest most resembles the closeness of the national party battle—a conclusion shared by the strategists of both political parties.

Considered in sequence, the four charts in figure 2.4 summarize the grand regional story of modern American politics. Regional patterns involving ideology and party are the best initial guides for understanding American elections. Emphatically, these regional patterns are not fixed in stone. Partisan preferences of white and minority voters may—or may not—be the same in the future, and the relative sizes of whites and minorities will surely change. Indeed, party strategists will surely try to solidify their advantages in favorable regional strongholds while trying to make inroads into rival regional strongholds.

THE USEFULNESS OF REGIONAL COMPARISONS

The utility of regional analysis to show different preferences of white voters in the United States is illustrated by their responses to major war, tax, and cultural issues in the 2004 election exit polls (see figure 2.5). When asked in November 2004, "Do you think the Iraq War has improved the long-term security of the United States?" white voters split into two large groups. By 51 percent to 49 percent, a slight majority believed that the Iraq War had advanced the nation's security. When their preferences are arrayed across the nation's regions, large differences appeared among white voters (see the upper-left figure). Greatest opposition to the war was present in the Northeast, followed by the Pacific Coast and the Midwest. Large majorities of white voters in the two Republican strongholds, however, believed that the war had improved the nation's long-term security interests. The sharpest regional differences among white voters separated the Northeast from the Mountains/Plains and the South.

Bush had campaigned in 2000 on a platform of lowering income tax rates and had persuaded Congress to cut rates in his first term. Voters were asked in 2004 whether they believed the Bush tax cuts were good for the economy, bad for the economy, or made no difference on the economy. Nationally a plurality of whites (47 percent) evaluated the tax cuts as good, while 30 percent believed the effects were bad. Regional variations were pronounced among white

Figure 2.5
Regional Differences on Key Issues

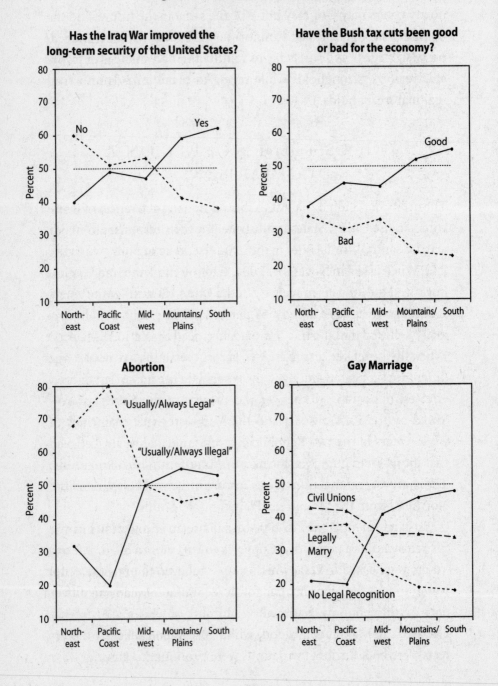

Has the Iraq War improved the long-term security of the United States?

Have the Bush tax cuts been good or bad for the economy?

Abortion

Gay Marriage

voters. In every region, more whites viewed the tax cuts positively than negatively, but the size of the differences, as the upper-right figure shows, fluctuated across the regions. Among white voters, the differences ranged from only a 3-point edge in the Northeast, to small double-digit leads in the Pacific Coast and the Midwest, to a 28-point advantage in the Mountains/Plains and a 32-point lead in the South. In the Republican Party's two regional strongholds, majorities of white voters thought the tax cuts had been good for the economy.

Two cultural issues, the legality of abortion and the legal status of gay and lesbian couples, also divided white American voters in 2004. When voters were asked whether they preferred abortions to always or usually be legal, or if they preferred them to always or usually be illegal, proabortion whites outnumbered antiabortion whites, 56 percent to 44 percent. When the preferences are charted across the regions, the political impact of the abortion issue differs dramatically among white voters. Support for the legality of most abortions greatly outweighed opposition among Northeastern and Pacific Coast whites. More than two-thirds of Northeastern whites and four-fifths of Pacific Coast whites favored the legality of most abortions. Outside the Democratic Party regional strongholds, however, white preferences about abortion were not overwhelmingly liberal. Midwestern white voters were evenly split over the legality of most abortions. In the Mountains/Plains and the South, small majorities of white voters believed that most abortions should always or usually be illegal.

Controversies about the legal status of gay and lesbian couples also showed large regional differences among white voters. The exit poll question asked voters to choose among three preferences for the legal treatment of gay and lesbian couples: no legal recognition, civil unions, and marriage. None of the three options attracted a majority among the nation's white voters: 38 percent favored civil unions, 36 percent opposed any legal recognition of gay and lesbian couples, and 27 percent favored legal marriage. The preference orders of white voters in the entire nation, however, did not appear in any of the five regions (see the bottom-right figure).

In the two Democratic regional strongholds, pluralities of white voters preferred civil unions, followed closely by those who supported gay and lesbian marriages. Only about one-fifth of white voters in the Northeast and the Pacific Coast opposed any legal recognition of gay and lesbian couples. Opposition to legal recognition of these relationships was the plurality position of white voters in the Midwest and the Mountains/Plains and came close to a majority of white voters in the South. In these three regions, civil unions fell to second place, and support for gay marriage dropped to small minorities of white voters.

These visual comparisons highlight the regional structure of political conflict among whites in the United States in the opening decade of the twenty-first century. Cultural liberalism was strongest in the Northeast and the Pacific Coast; cultural conservatism characterized white voters in the South and the Mountains/Plains. On both abortion and gay marriage, white voters in the Midwest were closer to those in the Republican strongholds than in the Democratic strongholds. The Iraq War polarized white voters in the Northeast against those in the South and the Mountains/Plains, but whites in the Pacific Coast and Midwest were closer to those in the Northeast than those in the Republican strongholds. Differences between the Northeast and the Republican strongholds about the effects of the Bush tax cuts also stood out.

To further demonstrate the advantage of regional analysis, we shall conclude this chapter by comparing variations in the sizes of Protestants and Catholics, the two largest groups of white voters in the nation. In 2004 white Protestants made up 42 percent of all voters in the United States. For generations white Protestants were divided in their partisanship by the realities of Battlefield Sectionalism. From the Civil War to the Great Depression, far more Northern white Protestants were Republicans than Democrats. Southern white Protestants were overwhelmingly Democrats. Although the New Deal attracted many Northern white Protestants into the Democratic Party, two-thirds of white Protestants in the Northeast were Republicans in the 1950s. In the other Northern regions, however, the partisan allegiances of white Protestants were divided more evenly, and Republicans held only small leads. Southern white Protestants in the 1950s were, of course, still overwhelmingly attached to the Democratic Party and alienated from the Republicans.

Fifty years later, the regional partisan preferences of white Protestants were very different. White Protestants have been the main driving force in the resurgence of the Republican Party. The upper-left chart of figure 2.6 shows huge regional variations in the size of Protestants among white voters. While Protestants were a majority of the nation's white voters in 2004, their presence in the regions ranged from barely more than one-third of white voters in the Northeast to more than two-thirds of them in the Mountains/Plains and the South.

In addition to the numerical dominance of white Protestants in the Republican strongholds, there are significant qualitative differences in the nature of Protestant religious beliefs.[14] Half of white Protestant voters in the United States considered themselves evangelical or "born-again" Christians. White evangelicals are the most culturally conservative voters of any large group active in American politics. According to the 2004 exit poll, 72 percent of the nation's white evangelical Protestants thought that abortions should be usually or always illegal, 65 percent believed that no legal recognition should be given to gay and lesbian couples, 77 percent approved of the U.S. decision to go to war with Iraq, and 81 percent approved of the way George W. Bush was handling his job as president. Seventy-nine percent voted for his reelection.[15]

Evangelical Protestants are not randomly distributed across the

Figure 2.6
Regions and Religion

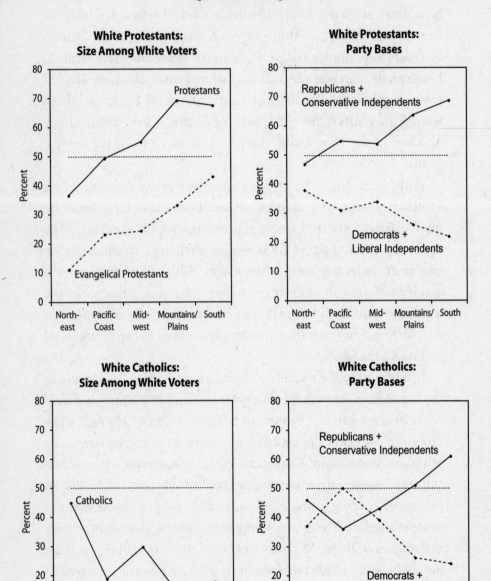

White Protestants:
Size Among White Voters

White Protestants:
Party Bases

White Catholics:
Size Among White Voters

White Catholics:
Party Bases

regions. Variations in the size of evangelicals speak volumes about the differences in the cultural conservatism of white Protestants. In the 2004 election, evangelicals made up 64 percent of Southern white Protestant voters and 48 percent of white Protestant voters in the Mountains/Plains region. Over two-fifths of all white voters in the South—led by President George W. Bush—were evangelical Protestants, as were nearly one-third of white voters in the Mountains/Plains. By contrast, only 30 percent of white Protestants in the Northeast were evangelicals, and they constituted merely 11 percent of Northeastern white voters.

Conservatives—at 45 percent—were the largest ideological group among America's white Protestant voters. Moderates trailed closely (42 percent), but only 14 percent were liberals. The relative numbers of moderates and conservatives signal important differences in the tone or spirit of white Protestantism in different parts of the nation. Moderates outnumbered or equaled conservatives among Protestants in the Northeast, the Pacific Coast, and the Midwest. In the two Republican strongholds, however, conservatives exceeded moderates among Protestants. Combined with their greater numbers of evangelical Protestants, the South and the Mountains/Plains display much greater potential for the success of conservative Republicanism than do other regions of the nation.

Republicans outnumbered Democrats among white Protestants in every region. The smallest Republican advantage appeared in the Northeast, which decades earlier had generated the largest Republican lead among white Protestants. Republicans had large plurality leads in the Pacific Coast and the Midwest and a majority lead in the Mountains/Plains. In the South, their weakest region fifty years earlier, Republicans now enjoyed a sizable majority advantage among white Protestants.

When conservative and liberal independents are added to their respective parties, the Republican bases among white Protestants moved into landslide territory in the Republican geographical strongholds and into majority status in the Pacific Coast and the Midwest (see "White Protestants: Party Bases" in figure 2.6). So weak was the Republican appeal in the Northeast, however, that even the addition of conservative independents failed to move the Republican base into a majority among white Protestants. Northeastern white Protestants, once the backbone of the national Republican Party, were much less attracted to the new Republican Party than their counterparts in the other four regions.

White Catholics have also become more Republican and less Democratic during the past fifty years.[16] Historically Catholics differed greatly from Protestants in their party ties. Often the victims of discrimination by and hostility from Protestants, politically active Catholics generally sided with the Democratic Party. In the 1950s, adherence to the Democratic Party and rejection of the Republicans united white Catholics. Everywhere, majorities of white Catholic voters were Democrats, while the percentages of Catholics identifying as Republicans ranged only from 10 percent to 20 percent across the regions.

Over the past half century, American Catholic voters have realigned their partisanship. In the 2004 election, Republicans outnumbered Democrats 42 percent to 32 percent, a GOP advantage that would have been inconceivable to their parents and grandparents. The erosion of Democratic strength and the rise of Republican identification among white Catholics have been major factors in generating more competitive partisan politics in the United States.

In 2004 Catholics were 27 percent of white voters and 21 percent of all voters in the United States. The partisan impact of white Catholic voters varied with their size and their partisanship in the regions (see the bottom two charts in figure 2.6). The lower left-hand chart identifies two large regional concentrations of white Catholics. The Northeast was the only region where Catholics (45 percent) outnumbered Protestants (37 percent) among white voters. Catholics also constituted a sizable minority (30 percent) of white voters in the Midwest. In the South and the two Western regions, however, Catholics accounted for less than one-fifth of white voters. Moreover, in contrast to the tremendous regional variation in the number of evangelical Protestants, evangelical Catholics were practically nonexistent in every region.

As a group, white Catholics differed ideologically from white Protestants: 53 percent were moderates, 31 percent were conservatives, and 17 percent were liberals. Moderates were the largest group of white Catholics in every region. In both Republican strongholds, however, conservatives rose well above their levels in the other three regions. Striking regional differences appeared in the party battle among white Catholics. In the South and the Mountains/Plains, white Catholic voters displayed strong Republican tendencies. By contrast, the direction and size of partisan differences were much more competitive in the Democratic strongholds and the Midwest. When the appropriate ideological groups are combined with the partisans, Republicans and conservative independents led Democrats and liberal independents among Catholic whites in every region except the Pacific Coast (see "White Catholics: Party Bases" in figure 2.6).

The Republican advantage among white Christians extended to white Protestant men in all five regions, white Protestant women in all five regions, white Catholic men in all five regions, and white Catholic women in the South and the Mountains/Plains. In 2004 the Democrats had a larger party base only among white Catholic women in the Pacific Coast, the Northeast, and the Midwest. All in all, to a much greater extent than ever before, the Republican Party as of 2004 united white Protestants and white Catholics.

Regional comparisons thus help to clarify the nature and closeness of the national partisan battles. Reversing its earlier position in American politics, the Northeast has emerged during the past forty years as the nation's most Democratic region. The Republican Party has lost strength among white Protestants and gained among white Catholics in the Northeast. Neither group generates majority support for the Republican Party. With the two white Christian groups weakly pro-Republican, the Democratic Party has benefited from majority support from the growing numbers of non-Christian whites and racial minorities, especially in the large cities.

Democratic attachments have also been strengthened in the Pacific Coast region. White Protestants are the only group of significant size still giving majority support to the Republican Party in that region. White Catholics have continued to favor the Democrats. The two groups most rapidly increasing in size in the Pacific Coast are non-Christian whites (30 percent of white voters, the largest concentration anywhere in the nation) and racial and ethnic minorities (26 percent of all voters, a share that will surely increase in the future). The dominant tendencies of non-Christian whites and the racial/ethnic minorities strongly favor Democrats over Republicans. As a result of these trends, the Pacific Coast has also emerged as a Democratic stronghold in elections for national office.

In the center of American politics are the states of the Midwest. Close presidential elections rest upon very close partisan divisions in the Midwestern electorate. Comparative analysis highlights why the Midwest—thus far—has not become a stronghold for either party. White Protestants are the only group showing majority support for the Republicans, and GOP leads among this group are smaller than in the Republican strongholds. White Catholics are divided in their partisanship, and while they showed a slight Republican advantage in the 2004 election, it was also much smaller than in the regions where Republicans have realigned white Catholic voters. Non-Christian whites and racial/ethnic minorities are the bulwarks of the Democratic Party, as in every region, but both groups are smaller in the Midwest's electorate than in the Democratic strongholds. The result is—at present—a partisan standoff between two competitive minority parties.

The greatest transformations of white partisan attachments have occurred in the South and the Mountains/Plains. Fifty years ago, Southern white Protestants and white Catholics wanted nothing to do with the Republican Party. Today landslide majorities of white Protestants and white Catholics underlie Republican strength in the South. In the Mountains/Plains, Republicans began with a lead among white Protestants and later realigned white Catholics. Only in the South and the Mountains/Plains have majorities of the two largest white religious groups realigned their partisan preferences to create a new political party. As a consequence of these developments, the Republican Party is stronger in the Mountains/Plains and the South than anywhere else in the nation.

We now turn to more detailed analyses of the party battles in the Republican regional strongholds. Partisan shifts in these regions have mightily reshaped the national party battle. For the first time since the 1920s, Republicans are sufficiently strong across the entire nation to compete realistically with Democrats for control of both houses of Congress and the presidency. There is no better way to understand the modern American power struggle than by beginning with the Mountains/Plains and the South, where the most pro-Republican changes have occurred and where Republicans now outnumber Democrats in the electorate.

3

THE REPUBLICAN STRONGHOLDS

REPUBLICAN STRENGTH IN THE UNITED STATES is greatest in the South and the Mountains/Plains. These regions commonly generate strong Republican surpluses of electoral votes and House and Senate delegations, surpluses that are the geographic foundations of national Republican competitiveness. The turning point in the revival of the Republican Party was Ronald Reagan's presidential victory in 1980. His presidency reinforced existing Republican strength in the Mountains/Plains and invigorated the Republican Party in the South.

The Reagan realignment of white conservatives and dealignment of white moderates took root primarily in the two regions where white Protestants were sufficiently numerous and influential to set the political agenda. Reagan's success in presidential politics prepared the ground for the Republicans' 1994 victories in the House and the Senate, victories that came in the aftermath of President Bill Clinton's failed attempt to legislate a national system of health care. Later, the South and the Mountains/Plains responded to the 9/11/01 terrorist attacks on the United States by supporting the leadership of President George W. Bush.

These two regions differ enormously in population size. Three of every ten Americans live in the South, making it by far the largest region in the United States. The Mountains/Plains, containing only one-tenth of the national population, is the smallest region.[1] In institutions where population size is crucial to political power—seats in the House of Representatives and votes in the electoral college—the Republican realignment in the South has contributed more to competitive national elections than have changes in the Mountains/Plains states. For the Senate, though, what counts is not population but simply the number of states (thirteen in the Mountains/Plains, eleven in the South). Republican strength in the Senate hinges upon surpluses of Republican senators from both regions, which together account for almost half of the one hundred Senate seats.

During the past half century, both regions have experienced Republican realignments. Democratic leads during the 1950s and 1960s gave way to more balanced partisan divisions and eventually to electorates where Republicans now outnumber Democrats. Based on their advantage among voters, Republicans seeking national office would be expected to win far more elections than Democrats in these regions. Yet because the new Republican advantage typically amounts to a plurality of voters, Democratic candidates, given enough favorable short-term conditions, can still realistically compete and sometimes win in particular states.

In the Republican strongholds, the main Republican advantage is based upon the large size and increasing Republican identification of white Protestants. White Protestants have long dominated the electorates of the Mountains/Plains and the South, and they continue to be the largest group of voters in both regions. In 2004 Protestants accounted for nearly 7 of every 10 white voters in the Republican strongholds. By contrast, they were only about half of all white voters in the Pacific Coast and the Midwest and less than two-fifths of white voters in the Northeast. So numerous were white

Protestants in the Republican strongholds that they made up a majority of all Mountains/Plains voters and nearly half of all Southern voters. Nowhere else in the United States did white Protestants enjoy such enormous advantages in size.

A second factor—the prominence of evangelical or born-again Protestants—highlights the unique character of white religious culture in the Republican strongholds. White evangelical Protestants have been crucial to the party's success in the South and Mountains/Plains. As GOP strategist Warren Tompkins told reporters Dan Balz and Ronald Brownstein, "Until the religious conservative movement broke its behavioral Democratic patterns and started voting in large part in Republican primaries and for Republican candidates, we weren't winning elections in the South."[2]

In 2004 evangelicals made up 59 percent of white Protestants in the Republican strongholds. Two of every five white voters in these regions were evangelical Protestants, by far the largest concentration of religious conservatives in the United States. In the Republican strongholds, Republicans trumped Democrats among evangelical white Protestants by 65 percent to 19 percent. The GOP also enjoyed a large lead, 54 percent to 24 percent, among nonevangelical white Protestants. Such sizable Republican strength among evangelical *and* nonevangelical white Protestants has not appeared outside the Republican strongholds.

White Protestants who have attended college have driven Republican growth. These voters reached critical mass during Reagan's presidency. Their views define conventional notions of success and set the tone for white partisanship in the Republican regions. From their ranks have increasingly come the regions' new political, business, and professional elites, decision makers, and wielders of influence.

Reagan's conservative message—reduce the size and responsibilities of the federal government, cut tax rates, rebuild the military, get tougher with the Soviet Union, oppose affirmative action and abortion—played very well among college-educated white Protestants.[3] More than any previous Republican president, Reagan expressed many of their deepest values and beliefs. For the most part, Reagan told them exactly what they wanted to hear, and he received 78 percent of their vote in 1984. George W. Bush later matched Reagan's popularity with this group. In 2004 huge majorities liked Bush's national security and economic policies, his religious conservatism, and his conduct in office. Bush won 76 percent of the vote cast by college-educated white Protestants in the Republican strongholds.

Republicanism has become the party of respectability and influence for college-educated white Protestants in the South and the Mountains/Plains. Given the choice between an increasingly liberal Democratic Party and an increasingly conservative Republican Party, they preferred Republicans over Democrats 61 percent to 19 percent in 2004. The ideological profile of college-educated white Protestants is one of many conservatives, fewer moderates, and very few liberals. When asked in the 2004 exit poll, "On most political matters, do you consider yourself to be liberal, moderate, or conservative?" 54 percent of white college-educated Protestant voters in the Republican strongholds labeled themselves conservative, 36 percent moderate, and only 10 percent liberal.

From Barry Goldwater to George W. Bush, Republicans have sought to attract conservative whites and to reduce Democratic leads among moderate whites. Depending upon how persuadable different segments of the electorate appear to be, the party has even sought to open leads among moderate white Protestants. In their geographical strongholds, the Republicans have succeeded among college-educated white Protestants. In 2004 Republicans swamped Democrats 82 percent to 3 percent among the large group of conservatives and also led 44 percent to 30 percent among moderates. Democrats won a majority only from the small group of liberals.

Most white Protestants in these regions characterize themselves as deeply religious. More than seven of every ten college-educated white Protestants agreed that religion had a "great deal" or "quite a bit" of importance in their lives.⁴ Baptists are the largest group, followed by Methodists and other denominations. Evangelical churches without clear denominational ties draw huge numbers of worshipers. Although there are exceptions, these churches generally preach conservative social agendas on issues such as abortion and same-sex marriage.

An old Protestant prayer goes, "Ask God for help in your work, but don't ask Him to do it for you." College-educated white Protestants believe strongly in the importance of individual responsibility for the financial well-being of themselves and their families. When asked if it was the responsibility of the individual or the government to provide a job and a good standard of living, 68 percent chose individual responsibility, while only 16 percent opted for governmental responsibility.⁵ The family, they believe, is the primary unit of economic and social advancement. Many aspire to upward mobility. Their political views are probably influenced more by where they want to end up in life than by where they started out. They want to make money, keep most of it, and then spend, invest, or give it away as they see fit. Members of this group respond enthusiastically when Republican politicians—such as Reagan and Bush—tell them that it is their money, not the government's money, and promise to cut their income tax rates.

Consistent with their robust individualism, college-educated white Protestants in principle prefer limited government. In the 2000 exit poll, more than seven-tenths of these voters in the Republican strongholds preferred less government to more government. According to the 1992–2000 American National Election Studies (ANES hereafter) polls, 58 percent of this group wanted fewer governmental services even if it meant reductions in some programs, while only one-fifth wanted more services.

While the interests, values, priorities, and concerns of college-educated white Protestants have set the tone for the nationwide Republican advance, the party's appeal in the South and the Mountains/Plains has gone far beyond this social group. White Protestants who have not gone to college have also rejected the Democrats and joined the Republicans. In addition, the old Protestant-Catholic rivalry, a source of tremendous bitterness and conflict in the not-too-distant past, has mainly faded. White Catholics, led by those who have attended college, have shifted to the party of white Protestants. Republican strength in both regions now rests on majorities among white Protestants, supplemented by a majority of white Catholics in the South and a plurality of white Catholics in the Mountains/Plains.

REPUBLICAN EMERGENCE
IN THE MOUNTAINS/PLAINS

Republican realignment occurred first in the Mountains/Plains states. It was a shift predicted by Kevin P. Phillips in his influential 1969 book, *The Emerging Republican Majority*. The "Plains and Mountain States," he asserted, "constitute the conservative geographical heartland of the emerging Republican majority."[6] In the 1950s and 1960s, Democrats led Republicans in the region's entire electorate, but the parties drew very close during the 1970s. Republicans opened a wide advantage during Reagan's presidency, an edge that has increased in subsequent decades. In the 2004 election, Republicans led Democrats 46 percent to 32 percent among all Mountains/Plains voters. Moreover, when conservative independents are added to Republicans and liberal independents are combined with Democrats to form the party bases, the Republican advantage in the region's electorate increased to 16 points, 52 percent to 36 percent.

Several factors have converged to shift partisan power to the Republicans.[7] Individual responsibility for the well-being of oneself and one's family is very important. Western suspicion of the

Northeast—now increasingly Democratic—has deep roots in American history. The type of aggressive economic and Cold War conservatism championed by Goldwater, an Arizona senator, won considerable support, although his root-and-branch rejection of the New Deal did not play well in a region where federal aid for large construction, transportation, and water projects remains crucial. Goldwater carried only his home state in 1964. Reagan's career was based in California, but his optimism, praise of individual liberty, and suspicion of the federal government resonated with many citizens in the Rocky Mountains and the Great Plains.

Figure 3.1 presents two perspectives concerning the setting for party battles in the Mountains/Plains over the past fifty years. The left-hand chart shows the changing racial and ethnic composition of the region's voters, while the right-hand chart traces the changing size of white Protestants, white Catholics, and the combination of non-Christian whites and racial/ethnic minorities in the electorate.

Figure 3.1
Settings: Mountains/Plains

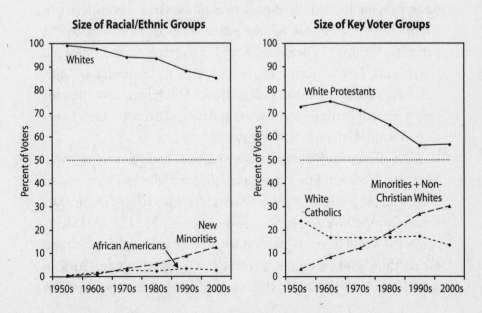

Whites made up 99 percent of the region's voters in the 1950s, and they have continued to dominate the electorate. In 2004 whites accounted for 84 percent of all Mountains/Plains voters. Democrats originally held a plurality advantage among white voters. Forty-four percent of whites were Democrats in the 1950s, while fewer than one-third were Republicans. As late as 1974, Democrats still out-numbered Republicans. Beginning with Jimmy Carter's campaign in 1976, however, more white voters in the region have identified as Republicans than Democrats. The GOP took a much larger lead during Reagan's presidency, and this advantage has widened over time. In 2004, 50 percent of Mountains/Plains whites were Republicans and only 28 percent were Democrats. The Republicans' lead in the total regional electorate is based on their strength among the huge white majority. The Democratic "size" problem among white voters is that less than three-tenths of them now consider themselves Democrats.

To the extent that the region's electorate has diversified, most of the change has come from increasing numbers of Latinos and other ethnic groups. They made up 13 percent of voters in the 2004 elections, ranging from minute presences in the Great Plains states to sizable minorities in the Southwestern states of New Mexico (32 percent), Arizona (12 percent), Nevada (10 percent), and Colorado (8 percent). Few African Americans live in the Mountains/Plains states. According to the exit polls, African Americans accounted for only 3 percent of the region's voters and ranged from less than 1 percent in South Dakota to 7 percent in Nevada.

All in all, ethnic and racial minority groups have grown from only 1 percent of Mountains/Plains voters in the 1950s to 15 percent in 2004. Their increased weight in the electorate has helped Democrats remain competitive despite their losses among whites. In 2004 Democrats led Republicans 47 percent to 29 percent among Latinos and other ethnic groups, and 66 percent to 17 percent among African Americans. Non-Christian whites provide the other important new source of Democratic support. In 2004 they made up 18 percent of white voters and 15 percent of all voters. Non-Christian whites favored Democrats to Republicans by 41 percent to 25 percent.

The Mountains/Plains is the only region in the United States where white Protestants remain a majority of all voters. Fifty years ago, nearly all of the region's white voters were Christians, and most of the Christians were Protestants. In the 2004 election, white Protestants still accounted for 59 percent of all voters. Because of their large number and cohesion, white Protestants have largely shaped the region's partisan balance. In 2004 evangelicals constituted nearly half (48 percent) of white Protestants in the Mountains/Plains, and Republicans outnumbered Democrats by 64 percent to 22 percent. Republicans also enjoyed more than a two-to-one lead over Democrats, 53 percent to 25 percent, among the region's nonevangelical white Protestants.

Republicans did not begin their ascent among Mountains/Plains white Protestants at ground zero. In the 1950s, nearly two-fifths of white Protestants were already Republicans, slightly more than the group's Democrats. Protestants began to abandon the Democratic Party during Carter's presidency, and the Republican advantage has steadily increased. During the 1990s and 2000s, the Republican-Democratic gap widened enormously when bigger majorities of white Protestants became Republican. In 2004 Republicans swamped Democrats among the white Protestants, 58 percent to 23 percent.

Republican growth in the Mountains/Plains has been led by college-educated white Protestants. These voters already favored the GOP in the 1950s: 53 percent were Republicans, and only 32 percent were Democrats. Their initial political influence was limited, however, because they made up only 14 percent of the region's voters. Since the 1950s the region's college-educated white Protestant voters have increased in number while continuing to prefer the Republican Party. In 2004 college-educated white Protestants were 44 percent of all Mountains/Plains voters. Republicans led Democrats by 61 percent to 21 percent among this influential group.

Conservative ideology has played a crucial role in the Republicanism of the region's college-educated white Protestants. In 2004 half of these Protestants were conservatives, and Republicans overwhelmed Democrats by 83 percent to 4 percent among these conservative voters. Another two-fifths thought of themselves as moderates. Republicans also led among this group, 45 percent to 33 percent. The Republican Party has thus consolidated the conservatives and realigned the moderates among the largest and most influential group of white voters in the region. Conservative Republicans concede the small group of college-educated liberal Protestants to the Democrats because they do not need the votes of liberal whites to win elections. Indeed, Republicans welcome the growing influence of white liberals in the Mountains/Plains Democratic Parties because this trend highlights the ideological differences between the two parties.

Until the 1980s, most white Protestants in the Mountains/Plains had not attended college, and their partisan loyalties were divided. In response to Reagan's presidency, however, these voters also shifted to the GOP. In 2004 noncollege white Protestants favored Republicans over Democrats by 51 percent to 34 percent. The realignment of less educated Protestants solidified Republican strength among white Protestants generally: Republicans outnumbered Democrats at every income level, and women were nearly as Republican as men. The Protestant reformation in the Mountains/Plains appeared to be complete.

Republicans' gains in the Mountains/Plains have not been limited to white Protestants. Many white Catholics have also shifted to the Republican Party. In the 1950s and 1960s, they were overwhelmingly Democratic. Few Catholics in the Mountains/Plains wanted to be associated with the Republicans, the party historically dominated by white Protestants. However, Democratic identification among white Catholics plummeted during the 1970s, and in the following decade Republican identification increased sharply. In the 1990s, white Catholics became slightly more Republican than Democratic. College-educated Catholics, now a large majority of white Catholic voters, led the realignment in the region. White Catholics who have not attended college still seesaw between the parties, but this group gets smaller with each passing year.

Democratic strength in the Mountains/Plains is based on the small group of liberal Christian whites, a shrinking number of moderate Christian whites, plus large majorities of non-Christian whites and racial/ethnic minorities. In some states, more recent demographic trends—chiefly the rising Latino populations—are reshaping electorates in ways that could help Democrats return to power.

In the benchmark 2004 election, the Republican Party base (Republicans plus conservative independents) far exceeded the Democratic Party base (Democrats plus liberal independents) among Protestant white men, Protestant white women, Catholic white men, and Catholic white women. In short, white Christians—both women and men—gave the Republican Party very broad support in the Mountains/Plains. The Democrats drew their large advantages from minority women, non-Christian white women, minority men, and non-Christian white men.

The Republicans' advantage in the 2004 presidential vote began at the fundamental level of race and ethnicity. Although John Kerry carried the small African-American vote handily, he achieved only a modest majority among the New Minorities. Whites in the Mountains/Plains gave Bush a 2-to-1 victory. The broad scope of the president's landslide white majority is evident when voters are analyzed according to religion, income, and education. Bush defeated Kerry by more than 4 to 1 among evangelical Christians, and he won over three-fifths of the vote among nonevangelical Christian men and women. Majority white support for Kerry was limited to non-Christians. High-, medium-, and low-income whites all gave Bush large majorities, as did every educational category (high school, college, and graduate and professional).

THE TRANSFORMATION OF THE MOUNTAINS/PLAINS PARTIES

In the Mountains/Plains, the two parties have experienced important but slightly different transformations during the past fifty years. The Democrats have become smaller in relative size and somewhat different in their social composition. The Republicans have grown in size but have remained rather similar in social composition. Figure 3.2 tracks the changing social composition of the parties (Democrats on the left and Republicans on the right). In the 1950s, the Mountains/Plains parties were quite similar in their group composition. Almost all self-identified Republicans *and* Democrats were white Christians. Moreover, white Protestants held majorities in both parties, though a considerably larger majority in the Republican Party.

Racial and ethnic minorities and non-Christian whites have entered the political system primarily as Democrats. Simultaneously, Reagan drew many white Christians, Protestants and Catholics, into the Republican Party. Because of the entry of minorities and non-Christian whites and the departure of white Christians, the composition of the Democratic Party has been dramatically transformed. In the first decade of the twenty-first century, white Christians were only a slight majority over non-Christian whites and racial/ethnic minorities. White Protestants remain the largest group among Mountains/Plains Democrats, but they are now a minority.

As the Republican Party has revived in the Mountains/Plains, its composition has also changed but in a less striking fashion. The Republican Party continues to be dominated by white Protestants and supplemented by white Catholics. White evangelical Protestants

Figure 3.2
Transformation of the Mountains/Plains Parties

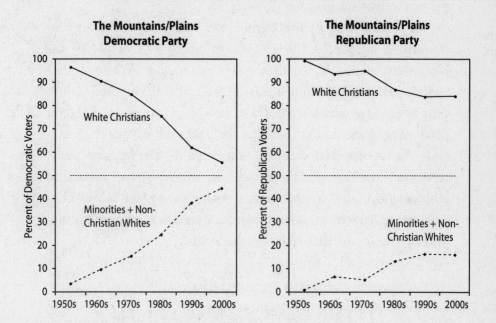

made up 39 percent of the Mountains/Plains Republican Party in the 2004 election. White Christians still constitute well over four-fifths of all Republicans. Compared to the era from 1950 through 1970, minorities and non-Christian whites have become a slightly larger minority in the Republican Party.

Today the two regional parties no longer resemble each other. White Protestants have become a smaller majority in the Republican Party and have dropped to a plurality of Democrats. White Christians continue to make up a huge majority of the region's Republicans but have declined to a small majority of Mountains/Plains Democrats.

Changes in the Mountains/Plains electorate have sharpened the ideological differences between the rival parties. In the 2004 election, the conservative wing of the Republican Party—white conservatives plus minorities who identify as Republicans—made up 69 percent of the region's Republican voters. Only 30 percent of Mountains/Plains Republicans were white moderates, and merely 1 percent were white liberals.

The liberal wing of the Democratic Party, white liberals plus minorities, accounted for 46 percent of all Democrats in the Mountains/Plains, the smallest share in any region. White moderates (42 percent) were almost as large as the liberal wing, and 12 percent of the Democrats were still white conservatives—the highest percentage in the nation. Thus far the liberalization of the Democratic Party—apparent in every other region—has failed to penetrate the Mountains/Plains parties. The smaller size of racial and ethnic minorities, combined with a smaller percentage of white liberals, has given white moderates and conservatives a larger portion of the Democratic Party than the liberal wing.

THE UNRAVELING
OF THE DEMOCRATIC SOUTH

At the midpoint of the twentieth century, white Democrats completely dominated Southern politics. Virtually every elected official—from top to bottom—was a Democrat. In 1950 all 22 of the South's senators and 103 of its 105 representatives were Democrats. All elected statewide officials, almost all state legislators, and thousands of locally elected officials were Democrats. The one-party monopoly of officeholders rested upon a huge preponderance of Democratic voters. Nearly 80 percent of Southern voters were Democrats, while only one in nine was a Republican. The South's incredibly weak and inefficient Republican Party attracted the scorn of political scientist V. O. Key Jr. "It scarcely deserves the name of party," Key concluded in *Southern Politics in State and Nation*. "It wavers somewhat between an esoteric cult on the order of a lodge and a conspiracy for plunder in accord with the accepted customs of our politics."[8]

By the beginning of the twenty-first century, the Southern party

Figure 3.3
Settings: South

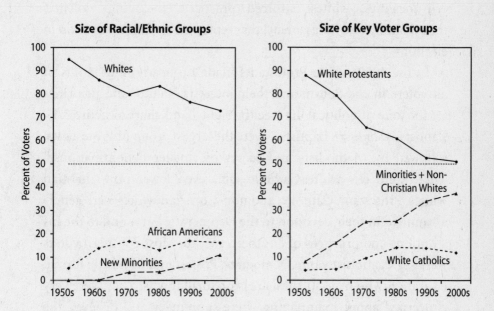

Size of Racial/Ethnic Groups   **Size of Key Voter Groups**

Left chart (Size of Racial/Ethnic Groups): Whites; African Americans; New Minorities. Percent of Voters, 1950s–2000s.

Right chart (Size of Key Voter Groups): White Protestants; Minorities + Non-Christian Whites; White Catholics. Percent of Voters, 1950s–2000s.

system was very different. In the 2002 and 2004 elections, for the first time in modern history, more voters in the South called themselves Republicans than Democrats. When conservative and liberal independents are added to these partisans, the Republican base exceeded the Democratic base by 9 percentage points, 49 to 40, in 2004. Republicans now hold the upper hand in Southern elections for national offices. No other region of the United States has experienced such a drastic reversal in its party battle.[9]

To understand this transformation, it is helpful to view the region's voters first in terms of their race and religion (see figure 3.3). The left-hand figure shows the changing racial composition of the Southern electorate. The 1950s was the final decade of virtually total white domination. Whites were three-fourths of the Southern population but 95 percent of all voters. Black men had been violently excluded from the electorate during the late nineteenth century, and few black women had been allowed to register and vote after the Nineteenth Amendment was ratified in 1920. Each Southern state had restrictive voter registration laws, and in many Southern localities, whites enforced practices (including violence, intimidation, and harassment) that repressed black participation in elections.[10]

In the 1950s white Protestants made up nearly nine-tenths of all voters in the South, and their interests, values, and priorities set the tone of political life (see the right-hand chart in figure 3.3). Baptists—*Southern* Baptists—were the largest group of Protestants, followed by Methodists and scores of smaller denominations.[11] There were few white Catholics and even fewer non-Christian whites. Protestant, Catholic, and non-Christian whites were generally united in their devotion to the Democratic Party and to the institutions and practices of Southern racism. Most Southern voters were segregationist white Democrats, Protestants with little formal education who lived in rural areas or small towns. They were very concerned about maintaining white supremacy and believed the Democratic Party represented the interests of "common folks" like themselves.[12]

As in the rest of the nation, the most important change in the Southern electorate in the first half of the twentieth century had been the entry of women, almost all of whom were whites. By the 1950s, white women were nearly as numerous as white men in the Southern electorate. This change had not disturbed the region's party balance because Southern white women were almost as emphatically Democratic as Southern white men.[13]

Growing protests against segregation in the early 1960s by the civil rights movement eventually led to federal intervention under the presidential leadership of Texas Democrat Lyndon B. Johnson. Enforcement of the Civil Rights Act of 1964 and the Voting Rights Act of 1965 ended many of the most blatant practices of state-sponsored racism that had separated the South from the rest of America.[14] By 1968 majorities of eligible black adults were registered to vote in every Southern state. African Americans increased to 14 percent of the region's voters in the 1960s. Four decades later, according to the 2004 exit poll, African Americans made up 19 percent of Southern voters. Almost all of the new black voters were Democrats, and extraordinary majorities of black voters have remained Democrats for more than four decades.

Black voters brought into the electorate quite different views about the importance and responsibilities of government from those held by most Southern whites. A basic indicator of liberal or conservative preferences is the proportion of voters who favor "more government" or "less government." By this standard, African Americans are the largest group of liberal, progovernment voters in the South. In the 2000 exit poll, by a margin of 3 to 1, Southern blacks favored "more government" over "less government." According to the 2004 exit poll, 72 percent believed that "government should do more to solve problems" while only 28 percent agreed that "government is doing too many things." During the elections from 1992 through 2000 according to the ANES surveys, three times as many African-American voters in the South preferred more government services (57 percent) to fewer services (19 percent).

Southern whites took opposing positions on each of these questions. Two-thirds of whites wanted less government, 60 percent believed the government was already doing too many things, and 47 percent preferred fewer governmental services (only one-fourth wanted more services). In the 2004 exit poll, only 11 percent of Southern blacks thought President Bush's tax cuts were good for the economy, in contrast to 55 percent of Southern whites.

Because of their personal and/or their ancestors' experiences on the receiving end of state and locally sponsored racism directed at them *as a group,* many African Americans remain skeptical about the extent to which they have been or will be judged solely on the merits of their individual efforts.[15] During the period from 1992 to 2000, nearly half of African Americans in the South (48 percent) believed that government should be primarily responsible for providing individuals with a job and a good standard of living. Only 29 percent believed individuals themselves had this responsibility, a perspective that put many African-Americans at odds with the individualistic values of three-fifths of white Southerners.[16]

Specific racial controversies also have continued to separate most blacks from most whites in the South, as they also have done in much of the rest of the nation. More than three-fourths of African Americans in the South believe the federal government should be responsible for public school desegregation, a point of view rejected by two-thirds of Southern whites. More than three-fifths of black Southerners believe that slavery and generations of discrimination have created unusual difficulties for African Americans, a view rejected by a majority (51 percent) of Southern whites. More than seven of every ten Southern black voters believe they have not received what they have deserved in recent years, while more than three-fifths of Southern whites think blacks have received what they (as a group) have deserved.[17]

Because of their fundamentally different views about the proper role of government and the resolution of specific racial controversies, it is hard to imagine majorities of Southern whites and blacks coexisting in the same political party.[18] Beginning in the 1950s, and accelerating after federal intervention in the 1960s, white and black Southerners have generally moved in opposite partisan directions. The interests and priorities of white Democrats and African Americans are not identical, of course, but blacks have far more points of agreement with white Democrats than they do with white Republicans.[19]

"Republicans remain unacceptable to black voters because of their continued opposition to racially liberal policies and the identification of their party with Southern symbols, like the Confederate flag, that reek of racism to many African-American Southerners," political scientist David Lublin has argued. "Even for blacks attracted to the Republicans because of their positions on nonracial issues, the continued partisan divide over racial issues renders the Republicans largely unacceptable." [20] Many African Americans are convinced that Republicans are actively hostile or indifferent to their most pressing concerns and needs. These realities have produced rates of African-American identification with the modern Democratic Party reminiscent of the resolute loyalty that white Southerners once displayed for the old Democratic Party. In the 2004 election, to take the most recent example, 80 percent of African Americans in the South were Democrats, while only 7 percent were Republicans. By contrast, 55 percent of Southern white voters were Republicans, and only 24 percent still thought of themselves as Democrats.

Other ethnic groups also contribute to a more diverse Southern electorate. African Americans remain the largest minority group of voters in the South except in Texas and Florida, where Latinos now cast more votes. Latinos are far less homogeneous in their histories, current situations, and political outlooks. In 2004 Democrats led Republicans by only 4 points, 41 percent to 37 percent, among the New Minorities of Latinos and other ethnic groups. African Americans and the New Minorities now make up about three-tenths of the Southern electorate, six times the size of African Americans in the 1950s.

While the racial and ethnic diversification of the modern electorate is a significant break with the past, the enduring political power of whites is one of the main continuities in Southern politics. Their negative responses to the increasing racial, economic, and cultural liberalism of the national Democratic Party in subsequent decades, as well as their more positive responses to the conservatism of Reagan and George W. Bush, have produced a viable Republican Party for the first time in the history of the South.

Federal intervention in the 1960s encouraged the development of an institution important for the practice of democracy that had long been absent in the South: the growth of a rival political party to challenge the Democratic monopoly. Many conservative Southern whites objected to President Johnson's liberalism on civil rights, economics, social policy, and cultural issues, as well as his handling of the Vietnam War. The negative reaction among Southern white voters appeared earliest and most clearly in presidential elections. An estimated 55 percent of Southern whites voted for Goldwater in 1964. From that point on, in every presidential election, the Republican presidential candidate has received more votes from Southern whites than has the Democratic candidate.[21]

The Republican advantage in presidential elections in the South is based on many factors. Since 1964 Southern white voters have generally viewed Republican presidential candidates as more likely than Democratic presidential candidates to limit their income taxes, promote their economic interests, preserve their economic gains, defend their cultural values, limit racial change, and advance the nation's interests in international affairs than their Democratic opponents.[22]

By championing Goldwater in 1964 and opposing federal intervention, Southern Republicans threw away any chance of attracting black support just as the minority group was beginning to vote in large numbers. Republicans therefore needed huge, landslide majorities of white votes to prevail in the new biracial electorate—at a time when they commanded the loyalties of only about one-fifth of Southern white voters. Democrats, by contrast, no longer needed to win majorities from Southern whites. If they could win 90 percent or more of an increasingly large African-American vote, they needed only a sufficiently large minority of the Southern white vote to prevail.[23]

During the 1970s, the Democratic biracial coalition continued to produce many victories. The main symbolic success of Democratic biracial politics was the election of Democrat Jimmy Carter, a former governor of the Deep South state of Georgia, as president in

1976. Carter lost the Southern white vote to a Michigan Republican, Gerald Ford, by 47 percent to 53 percent, but he won the region because he carried 82 percent of the African-American vote and a sufficiently large share of the white vote. The 1976 election, with Carter victorious in ten of the eleven Southern states, was the high point of the new "Democratic" South in presidential elections. Democrats continued to hold huge majorities of the region's delegations in the U.S. Senate and House of Representatives.

Yet even in 1976, there were signs of potential problems for the success of the Democratic Southern strategy. A prominent Baptist who openly practiced his faith, Carter was nonetheless rejected by his fellow white Protestants, 58 percent to 42 percent. Carter lost decisively among business, professional, and white-collar whites, and he trailed Ford even among blue-collar whites. As Southern white voters became more prosperous, more employed in commerce and industry, and more exposed to higher education, Republican presidential candidates would run even more strongly than Ford did in 1976.

THE EMERGENCE OF
SOUTHERN REPUBLICANS

Ending legally required segregation eventually reduced racial unrest in the South and accelerated many other positive changes. The spread of higher education, the shift from an economy based on agriculture to one based on services and industry, and the growth of large cities and suburbs helped to modernize the South.[24] Better job opportunities motivated many whites and blacks to leave the region's small towns and rural areas and move to metropolitan areas. In addition, the South began to attract many migrants from the rest of the United States (and other countries) who now found it a more desirable place in which to live, work, and retire.

Prospects for a two-party South improved after Johnson's Great

Society identified the national Democratic Party with racial, economic, and cultural liberalism, but white reaction against federal intervention, though intense, was not sufficiently widespread to immediately create a competitive Republican Party. There were still far more Democrats than Republicans among white voters. For most whites, becoming a Republican was neither sound practical politics nor socially respectable behavior. Southern Republicans needed national, state, and local leaders who could effectively market the party as a practical alternative for conservative and moderate whites. The minority party also had to increase the size of its reliable supporters: voters who identified as Republicans and activists who were willing to support the party's candidates with their time and money.

Thus the realignment of white *partisanship* in the South came much later than the white switch in presidential voting. Another two decades—roughly a generation in politics—were required for such a critical mass of Republicans to emerge in the South after federal intervention in the 1960s had destabilized the Democratic Party. The white realignment of partisanship—the first time more Southern whites actually called themselves Republicans than Democrats—took place twenty years later during Reagan's presidency. Finally, another two decades passed before Republicans attained majority status among Southern white voters in 2002 and 2004.[25]

The Southerners most likely to shift to the Republicans were white Protestants, the region's most conservative group.[26] Protestant whites in the South switched to the Republicans much later than those elsewhere in the United States because they first had to shed their inherited Democratic loyalties. Even more important, they had to become convinced that the party they had been taught from childhood to hate and despise might now better represent their interests, values, and priorities in national politics. Until the 1980s, political power in the South rested largely upon the votes of relatively uneducated white Protestants, and far more of them had been raised as Democrats than as Republicans.

Many trends worked in the Republicans' favor. By the 1980s, according to the exit polls, majorities of Southern voters had gone to college (even if they had not graduated) and now lived in metropolitan areas. College-educated white Protestants became the most important source of political power in the South. They now made up a majority of Southern white voters and were the largest group in the total electorate. By virtue of their wealth, status, and power, they exerted political, social, and economic influence well beyond their numbers. From this group, especially among those who lived in large cities, suburbs and exurbs, came the new models of success, the new embodiments of upward mobility, whose affluent lifestyles continue to be on display in every issue of *Southern Living* magazine. College-educated white Protestants were the heart of the region's new urbanized middle and upper classes, the social group most strongly attracted to the Republican Party.

Beginning in the 1950s with Dwight Eisenhower, many of the members of this group had voted for Republican presidential candidates. They became even more disenchanted with the national Democrats in the 1960s. President Johnson's Great Society agenda of racial and economic liberalism alienated many of them, but they were not yet sold on the Republican Party. The Nixon presidency's disgraceful end in 1974 destroyed an early opportunity for partisan realignment, but Carter's ineffective performance in office reinforced their many doubts about national Democratic leaders. In 1980 many college-educated white Protestants were still looking for a party and a politician willing to champion their interests and values.

At this opportune moment, the Republicans nominated Reagan for the White House. On matters of race, religion, philosophy of government, taxes, national defense, and culture, he gave voice to many of their most cherished conservative values and aspirations as well as their most practical and material interests. Reagan put an optimistic and reassuring face on messages that Goldwater had delivered in 1964 and Nixon had employed in 1968 and 1972. Warming immediately to the messenger and his message, they responded with even greater enthusiasm to his performance in the White House.

Reagan's presidency resonated with their beliefs and values, and many responded by becoming Republicans. A slight Democratic lead in the 1970s among college-educated white Protestants turned into a sizable Republican lead during the Reagan years. Republican identification among the group increased to a majority during the 1990s and then expanded to landslide proportions in the early twenty-first century. In 2004, 61 percent of Southern college-educated white Protestants were Republicans, while only 18 percent were still Democrats. By virtue of its size, unity, prestige, and financial resources, this new group of voters finally gave the Republican Party legitimacy and respectability among white Southerners generally.

The main beliefs, values, and interests of college-educated white Protestant Southerners strongly dispose them toward the Republican Party. They are very religious. Nearly three-fourths of them say religion is very important or quite a bit important in their lives. Almost three-fifths are evangelical Christians. More than half attend church on a weekly basis. At the same time, many are powerfully motivated by visions of upward economic and social mobility for themselves and their children. A very large majority (67 percent) accept personal responsibility for their own (and their families') economic well-being; only 17 percent of them believe this should primarily be a responsibility of government. By more than 2 to 1, they preferred private health insurance to government-provided health insurance in the period from 1992 through 2000. A large majority wants less government and believes the government is already trying to deal with too many problems. Over the elections from 1992 through 2000, those wanting fewer government services outnumbered those wanting more government services by 3 to 1.[27]

College-educated white Protestants have accepted the desegregation of the public sector brought about by federal intervention in the 1960s, but majorities of them generally take conservative positions on many racial issues that still divide whites and African Americans. Nearly three-fifths believe there has been too much emphasis on equality in recent years. By a 6-to-1 margin, they reject the proposal that governmental programs should be designed specifically for African Americans. Most do not believe the federal government should be responsible for public-school desegregation. Although split over the question of how much slavery and past generations of racial discrimination have affected African Americans, nearly half of these whites rejected the idea that such past treatment still affected current behavior. More than three-fifths of the Southern college-educated white Protestants disagreed with the statement "Over the past few years, blacks have gotten less than they deserve." Only 23 percent believed that "blacks have gotten less than they deserve." On most of these questions, their attitudes are similar to those of other white Protestants and white Catholics in the South and elsewhere in the nation.[28]

Huge Republican gains have occurred among both conservative *and* moderate college-educated white Protestants. In the 2004 election, a large majority—55 percent—identified as conservatives. These educated conservatives have thoroughly realigned: 81 percent were Republicans, and only 3 percent were still Democrats. Bush won 96 percent of their vote. Republicans also outnumbered Democrats 43 percent to 28 percent among moderate college-educated white Protestants. Sixty-three percent of them voted for the Republican presidential candidate. Merely 11 percent of the college-educated Protestant whites in the South thought of themselves as liberals. Only among this small group did Democrats outnumber Republicans and Kerry defeat Bush.

Republican success among college-educated white Protestants is important because of their numbers (35 percent of all Southern voters) and their role as opinion leaders for other groups of white voters. As their influence has extended downward through the social structure (especially through conservative Protestant churches) and moved beyond the large cities, suburbs, and exurbs, Protestants of less education and those living in small towns and rural areas have also moved to the Republicans. White Protestants who had not attended college shifted to the Republicans in the 1990s and increased their attachment to the GOP during Bush's first term. In 2004 Republicans outnumbered Democrats among noncollege white Protestants by 62 percent to 23 percent.

White Protestants made up 48 percent of all Southern voters in 2004, and among them Republicans led Democrats by 59 percent to 21 percent. Sixty-four percent of Southern white Protestants were evangelicals—highest by far of any region in the nation—and Republicans led Democrats in this group by 65 percent to 18 percent. The smaller group of nonevangelical white Protestants also preferred Republicans to Democrats, by 55 percent to 23 percent.

Conservative white Protestants favored Republicans over Democrats by 80 percent to 6 percent, as did moderates by a smaller margin, 42 percent to 32 percent. Democrats claimed a majority only among the 10 percent of Southern white Protestants who were liberals. Indeed, Republicans outnumbered Democrats in virtually every demographic subgroup. Republicans led Democrats among men *and* women and on every income level. White Protestants in the South had historically invested all of their national political capital in a single party—the Democrats—and now again appeared to be concentrating most of their national political resources in the Republican Party.

The GOP's appeal in the South has gone well beyond white Protestants. In 2004 Republicans led Democrats 54 percent to 27 percent among white Catholics, who accounted for 12 percent of all

Southern voters. Republicans outnumbered Democrats among both white Catholic men and women. The Republicans led among both conservative and moderate white Catholics. Thus in the South the two largest groups of white Christians have come together in the same political party. Republicans have also attracted support from the small numbers of non-Christian whites who think of themselves as conservatives, and have even made some inroads among similarly identified racial minorities.

In the 1980s, the explosion of college-educated voters and the shift of voters into metropolitan areas intersected in the South to magnify the political influence of college-educated white Christians who live in cities, suburbs, and exurbs. Old Protestant-Catholic divisions are now often irrelevant. Most members of the Southern Christian white middle class are Protestants, but sizable numbers are Catholics. Urbanized white middle-class Christians (mainly Protestants but also supplemented by Catholics) generate huge leads for Republican candidates.

The power and influence of this new social group were most clearly visible in those suburbs and exurbs where whites constituted large majorities of the voters. Eventually the new suburbs (and later exurbs) became areas where middle-class college-educated white Christians brought old values and new interests into fresh settings that they could dominate. They became the most important social, economic, and political influences in suburban and exurban political life. In the early 2000s, Republicans opened up a lead over Democrats in the old Democratic rural and small-town strongholds. At times the impact of this new social group was less visible in cities, especially if the cities had large minority populations that voted heavily Democratic. In these areas, the role of the new white Christian middle class was to hold down Democratic victory margins rather than to carry the large cities.

In the 2004 elections, the Republican Party base included huge majorities of Protestant white men, Protestant white women, and

Catholic white men, and a lesser majority among Catholic white women. As in the Mountains/Plains, Republican strength in the South was consistently strong among female as well as male white Christians. The Democratic Party base held sizable majorities among minority women, non-Christian white women, and minority men and a plurality lead among non-Christian white men.

According to the 2004 exit poll, Kerry defeated Bush by almost 9 to 1 among black voters but narrowly lost to Bush among the New Minorities (mainly Latinos in the South). Southern whites favored Bush over Kerry by 70 percent to 29 percent. Among white Southerners, Bush lost by more than 20 points among non-Christians, but otherwise he achieved landslide white majorities. Bush defeated Kerry by about 4 to 1 among both evangelical Christians and nonevangelical Christian men and by nearly 2 to 1 among nonevangelical Christian women. White Southerners of every income and educational level gave Bush landslide support of at least 60 percent (usually much higher).

THE TRANSFORMATION OF THE
SOUTHERN PARTIES

The most important change in the Southern Republican Party is its size in the electorate. A once hopelessly uncompetitive minority party has become the South's new plurality party. Much less has changed in the characteristics of Southerners who think of themselves as Republicans. As a small party, most of its followers were white Protestants. As a large party, most of its followers are still white Protestants. Indeed, white evangelical Protestants made up 44 percent of the Southern Republican Party in the 2004 election. With the addition of white Catholics, the Southern Republican Party is thoroughly dominated by white Christians. The largest group of Christian whites in the Republican Party consists of those who have gone to college. Racial and ethnic minorities, as well as non-Christian whites, still account for very few Southern Republicans.

By contrast, the Southern Democratic Party has experienced tremendous changes in its relative size and social composition. Fifty years ago, the Democratic Party, dominated by white Protestants, was overwhelmingly the majority party of the South. In general, college-educated white Protestants provided leadership and white Protestants with little formal education constituted the party's grassroots base.

Because white Democrats did not allow most blacks to vote, and because few Latinos voted in the South in the 1950s, there was practically no minority presence within the traditional Democratic Party. Racial and ethnic minorities have increased over time to nearly half of the modern Southern Democratic Party. Perhaps the most vivid indication of the transformed Southern Democratic Party is the fact that racial and ethnic minorities now outnumber not just white Protestants but white Christians. Groups once deliberately barred from the Southern Democratic Party are now its most numerous and reliable supporters.

In recent decades, white and black voters in the South have moved in opposite partisan directions. Blacks and whites in large numbers have never been in the same political party in the South, and their differences in philosophy, economic situation, and attitude toward government—in addition to all of their differences on specifically racial issues which are still on the table—make it difficult to overcome the past and the present.[29]

Figure 3.4 charts the transformation of the Democratic and Republican parties in the South. When voters are reduced to two categories—white Christians versus minorities and non-Christian whites—the results again show the emergence of remarkable differences between the two parties from the 1950s to the early 2000s. The Southern Democratic Party, historically a party of white Christians with relatively few minorities and non-Christian whites, has be-

Figure 3.4
Transformation of the Southern Parties

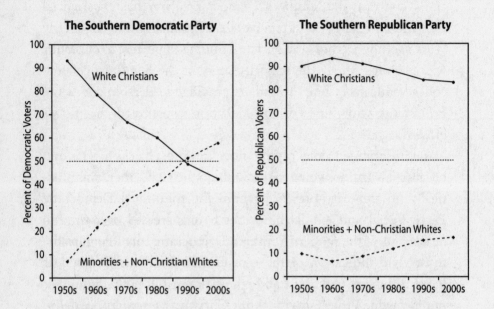

The Southern Democratic Party

The Southern Republican Party

come a party in which white Christians are now in the minority. The South's Republican Party, by comparison, has expanded enormously without experiencing much change in the relative number of white Christians. In their fundamental group composition, the two Southern parties are more dissimilar than ever before.

The ideological composition of the two Southern parties is very different. African Americans, Latinos, other ethnic groups, and white liberals now make up a large majority of Southern Democrats. The liberal wing of the party outnumbers the moderate wing, and white conservatives are about as scarce among Southern Democrats as racial minorities were fifty years ago. Just as the Democrats have become more liberal, the Southern Republicans have become more conservative. They attracted the Goldwater voters from the 1960s, and their move forward came when they began to organize the evangelical Christian churches in the 1980s. They are certainly more conservative than the Republican Party of the 1950s.

Thus the South and the Mountains/Plains have become the two Republican strongholds in modern American politics. When the regional party bases for all voters are considered, the Republicans as of 2004 had a 16-point advantage in the Mountains/Plains (52 percent to 36) and a 9-point advantage in the South (49 percent to 40). With their two regional strongholds, the Republicans were a highly competitive minority party. Uniting the South with the Mountains/Plains has given the Republican Party its firmest basis for national competitiveness since Northern Battlefield Sectionalism vanished in the Great Depression of the 1930s.

While the Mountains/Plains and the South have been highly receptive to the conservative message of the modern Republican Party, the Republicans' regional strongholds are too small to produce national victories by themselves. Moreover, the Republicans' strong dependence on evangelical white Protestants as the principal group attracted to such a conservative message has rebranded the national Republican Party in ways that have severely weakened the GOP in other important regions. Republican success in the South and the Mountains/Plains has helped to develop and consolidate two equally impressive Democratic strongholds in response to the Republican challenge.

4

THE DEMOCRATIC STRONGHOLDS

POLITICAL JUDGMENTS ALWAYS INVOLVE COM-PARISONS. The politicians, issues, and symbols promi-nently associated with America's two national parties affect voters quite differently from region to region. Just as an ag-gressively liberal Democratic Party repulses and angers many voters in the South and the Mountains/Plains, so too an assertively conser-vative Republican Party—particularly one in which evangelical Christians play prominent roles—alienates and alarms many voters in the Northeast and the Pacific Coast. What seems obviously wise and reasonable to liberals, especially secular liberals, appears foolish and unreasonable to conservatives, especially religious conserva-tives, and vice versa. Ronald Reagan and George W. Bush's conserva-tive challenges to liberal Democratic policies have given Democratic strategists many opportunities to attack Republicans in the North-east and the Pacific Coast. Democrats have become more highly ac-tivated and energized in the two regions of the United States where liberal traditions formed in the New Deal and reinforced by the Great Society retain widespread elite and grassroots support and where evangelicals are less numerous.

Democratic strength in modern America is foremost in the Northeast and the Pacific Coast. Both regions now produce impressive Democratic majorities of electoral votes and delegations to the Senate and the House of Representatives. Those regional surpluses are the geographic keys to Democratic competitiveness in the nation. America's Democratic strongholds differ in their size and political leverage. In 2000 the Northeast contained one-fifth of the nation's population, ranking it slightly behind the Midwest but well behind the South. One out of six Americans lived in the Pacific Coast states, making that region larger than the Mountains/Plains but smaller than the other regions.[1]

The political weight of the Northeast has been slowly but steadily declining because of anemic population growth, whereas the Pacific Coast has emerged in recent decades as a high-growth region. In 1950 the Northeastern states sent 127 members (29 percent) to the House of Representatives. After the 2000 reapportionment of House seats, the Northeast had shrunk to 92 representatives—21 percent of all members. While the Northeast was losing more than one-quarter of its congressional representation, the Pacific Coast expanded from 33 to 70 seats—16 percent of the House. For the 2002–2010 elections, the combined Northeast and Pacific Coast delegations account for 37 percent of the House of Representatives and 37 percent of the electoral college. The Democratic strongholds are weaker in the Senate. There the eleven states of the Northeast plus the five states of the Pacific Coast produce only thirty-two of the one hundred senators.

In both regions, the Democratic advantage in presidential and congressional politics is firmly grounded in the electorate. Democratic strength is based upon the increasing size of two pro-Democratic groups, racial/ethnic minorities and non-Christian whites, combined with the decreasing size of white Protestants, the most pro-Republican group in the nation. In the 2004 election, racial/ethnic minorities and non-Christian whites together cast one-half of the Pacific Coast's vote and two-fifths of the Northeastern vote. The combined pro-Democratic groups easily outnumbered white Protestants in both the Pacific Coast (40 percent) and the Northeast (29 percent). White Catholics differed in their size and partisanship. Comprising nearly one-third of all Northeastern voters in 2004, white Catholics were evenly divided between the two parties. Pacific Coast Catholics were more Democratic than Republican, but they represented about one-sixth of the electorate.

Because of the diverse racial, religious, and nationality groups that comprise its highly urbanized population, the Northeast has long been the most pluralistic part of the United States.[2] New York City, the nation's leading metropolis, is the preeminent symbol of Northeastern multiculturalism. The region's Democrats have had generations of experience in constructing and maintaining coalitions based on highly diverse social groups. More recently, similar changes—especially involving the massive growth of the Los Angeles metropolitan area—have also transformed the Pacific Coast electorate.

Organized labor in the Northeast and the Pacific Coast is a substantial Democratic institutional advantage. There are far more union members in the Democratic strongholds than in the Republican strongholds. American labor unions have declined in size during recent decades, but they still exert considerable political leverage in the Northeast, the Pacific Coast, and the Midwest. According to the 2004 exit poll, 18 percent of Northeastern voters and 17 percent of Pacific Coast voters were union members. In the Democratic strongholds, union members gave Democrats a large lead over Republicans, 52 percent to 28 percent. Democrats even slightly outnumbered Republicans among nonunion voters, 37 percent to 35 percent. In the Republican strongholds, by contrast, only 7 percent of voters belonged to a union. While Democrats also claimed a majority among the small number of union members in the Republican strongholds, a very different pattern of partisanship appeared in the South and the Mountains/Plains among the huge numbers of nonunion voters: Republicans outnumbered Democrats 46 percent to 33 percent.

Finally, Democrats in the Northeast and the Pacific Coast benefit considerably from the relative strength of white liberals and the weakness of white conservatives. Compared to the Republican strongholds, there are more white moderates, more white liberals, and fewer white conservatives in the Democratic strongholds. White conservatives by and large operate against the grain of public and media opinion in the Northeast and the Pacific Coast.

Metropolitan voters, those residing in big cities, suburbs, and exurbs, have long dominated the electorates of the Democratic strongholds. Urbanization was so far advanced by the 1950s that 75 percent of the Northeastern vote and 70 percent of the Pacific Coast vote came from large cities and suburbs. During the past fifty years, the metropolitan vote has passed 85 percent in the Northeast and reached nearly 90 percent in the Pacific Coast. More votes now come from suburbs than large cities. In many of the regions' biggest cities, the Republican Party does not exist as a practical alternative for voters in national elections. Democratic candidates for statewide office, who can build huge leads in the largest cities, are difficult for Republican opponents to overcome. Democrats have also become very competitive in many suburbs. Only in rural areas and small towns, which provide smaller shares of the vote each decade, has a Republican advantage persisted, and even that has ended in the Northeast.

THE DEMOCRATIC NORTHEAST

The Northeast is the only region in the United States where Democrats have displaced Republicans as the preferred party in the electorate during the past fifty years. This region is the starting point for a nationally competitive Democratic Party. Northeastern Republicans lost ground during the New Deal but revived after the Second

World War and held a slight lead during the early 1950s (see figure 2.3). However, Democrats moved ahead of Republicans in the late 1950s and solidified their advantage during the turbulent 1960s. Since then Democrats have always outnumbered Republicans in the entire Northeastern electorate.

Democratic candidates who can unite their large party base and attract modest support from independents are therefore strongly favored throughout the Northeast. Republican politicians face steeply uphill battles because their base of reliable support is so small. Successful Republican candidates need to unite their base but also run exceptionally well among moderate independents and even some Democrats.

Figure 4.1 shows the long-term transformation of the Northeastern electorate. The figure on the left charts the changing racial and ethnic composition of voters in the Northeast. Whites made up 95 percent of the entire electorate in the 1950s and declined to 78 per-

Figure 4.1
Settings: Northeast

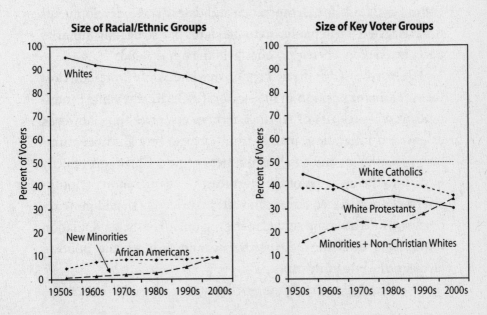

cent in the 2004 election. However, unlike whites elsewhere in the United States, Northeastern whites *as a group* display little partisan cohesion. They were evenly divided in 2004. Thirty-seven percent of Northeastern whites were Democrats, and 36 percent identified as Republicans, a very unusual pattern of partisanship. In every other region, including the Pacific Coast, Republicans outnumbered Democrats among white voters.

Democratic ascendancy in the Northeast owes much to the growing size of racial and ethnic minorities in the electorate. Always strongly pro-Democratic, racial and ethnic minorities have begun to vote in larger numbers. In 2004 African Americans were 12 percent of Northeastern voters, while the New Minorities of Latinos and others accounted for an additional 10 percent of the electorate. Together, racial and ethnic minority groups constituted over one-fifth of the Northeastern voters, more than four times their number in the 1950s.

An even split among white voters, combined with the persistently strong Democratic preferences of increased numbers of African Americans, Latinos, and other ethnic groups, regularly generates large leads for Democratic candidates. These developments have relegated the Republicans to the status of a struggling minority party in a region where they once held the upper hand.

The Northeast was the first region in which white Protestants lost their dominant position in the electorate. Originally, white Protestants were a majority of Northeastern voters. Over time, however, extensive immigration, mainly from Europe, brought huge numbers of Catholics and smaller numbers of non-Christians (chiefly Jews) into the big cities of the Northeast.[3] The migration of Southern blacks accelerated during and after World War II, and more recently Latinos have also settled in the region. All of these population movements diversified the electorate and reduced the political leverage of white Protestants.

Pluralism still reigns in the Northeast, but very different groups of voters are now ascendant. The right-hand chart in figure 4.1 plots the changing sizes of white Protestants, white Catholics, and the combination of non-Christian whites and racial/ethnic minorities. It documents a continuing decline of white Protestants, a slight shrinkage of white Catholics, and a substantial increase in the size of racial/ethnic minorities plus non-Christian whites in the Northeastern electorate.

White Protestants dropped below white Catholics in the 1970s and fell behind minorities and non-Christian whites in the 2000s. In 2004 white Protestants were merely 29 percent of the electorate, 4 points lower than white Catholics. By contrast, minority groups plus non-Christian whites had more than doubled from 16 percent in the 1950s to 38 percent in 2004. A Northeastern electorate dominated fifty years ago by white Protestants and white Catholics has become a setting in which minorities and non-Christian whites now cast a plurality of the vote. These changes in the relative size of the principal voting groups greatly facilitate Democratic dominance.

Important shifts have also occurred in the partisanship of white Protestants and Catholics. Although white Protestants remain more Republican than Democratic, the Republicans' traditional advantage has withered. An even more fundamental change, in the opposite direction, has taken place among white Catholics. Once overwhelmingly Democratic, Northeastern white Catholics are now evenly divided between the parties. Declining Republican leads among white Protestants, decreasing Democratic attachment among white Catholics, and continuing Democratic strength among non-Christian whites produce the close partisan divisions among Northeastern whites.

Republican strength in the region peaked during the 1950s. Northeastern Republicans orchestrated Dwight Eisenhower's nomination and successful presidential campaign in 1952. Running as a moderate conservative, Eisenhower united Republicans and attracted support from independents and some Democrats. Under

Eisenhower's leadership, Republicans regained the presidency after five straight defeats. He carried every state in the Northeast by drawing upon the party's traditional support in rural areas and small towns as well as its new base in the suburbs.

Northeastern Republicans were strongest in the towns and countryside in the 1950s. These areas, however, produced just over one-quarter of the region's votes. Two-fifths of the Northeastern vote came from Democratic strongholds in big cities such as New York, Philadelphia, and Boston. The future of the Northeastern party battle lay in the rapidly growing suburbs. More than one-third of the region's voters resided there in the 1950s, and Republicans held a 48 percent to 32 percent lead. Republican victories in rural areas and suburbs, combined with greater-than-usual strength in the large cities, gave the Grand Old Party success throughout the Northeast.[4]

Despite these victories, the Republican advantage in the Northeastern electorate, 40 percent to 38 percent, was slim and precarious in the 1950s. By and large, the Northeastern Republican Party was the political instrument of white Protestants, 65 percent of whom remained loyal to the party of their ancestors. Only 14 percent of the region's white Protestants were Democrats. White Protestants—Congregationalists, Episcopalians, Methodists, Presbyterians, and members of other denominations—made up three-fourths of the region's Republicans. The Northeastern Republican Party was overly dependent upon a single voting group that was declining in size in the electorate. White Protestants were already less than half of the region's voters in the 1950s, and they have continued to shrink in subsequent decades.

Beyond white Protestants, the Northeastern Republican Party had scant appeal in the 1950s. Only one-fifth of white Catholics, one-tenth of non-Christian whites, and one-twentieth of racial/ethnic minorities were Republicans. Majorities of these social groups were Democrats. As the Northeastern electorate has continued to diversify, the negative consequences of the Republican Party's reliance upon white Protestants became more apparent.

During the 1960s (see figure 2.3), Democrats surged to a substantial lead over Republicans in the Northeastern electorate, 43 percent to 34 percent. "As liberalism and the New Deal institutions took firm hold," Kevin P. Phillips argued, "they gave rise to a new establishment in the Northeast and became vested interests themselves."[5] At the same time, the national Republican Party, increasingly influenced by Westerners like Arizona senator Barry Goldwater, became more conservative and thereby less attractive to Northeasterners. The new party leaders were far more conservative on a broader range of issues than the Northeastern Republicans who had once dominated the party.

In 1964 Northeastern Republicans permanently lost control of "their" party when the Arizonan won the Republican presidential nomination. Goldwater despised the Northeast. "Sometimes I think this country would be better off if we could just saw off the Eastern Seaboard and let it float out to sea," he once declared.[6] Although Richard Nixon, the party's presidential nominee in 1960 and 1968, had relocated from California to New York, Northeastern Republicans never accepted him as one of their own. "During the second Nixon candidacy," Phillips observed, "the GOP was no longer the Yankee party it once had been, and the lopsided partisan traditions and majorities of the Republicans' Yankee era were a thing of the past."[7] During the 1960s, according to Phillips, the Northeast had become "the most liberal and Democratic section of the United States."[8]

Today Democrats lead Republicans by a wider margin in the Northeast than in any other region. Furthermore, according to the 2000 exit poll, the Northeast was also the only region where a majority of voters (51 percent) wanted more government rather than less government. Eighty-one percent of African-American voters and 70 percent of Latino and other voters took this position. Their prefer-ences, when combined with the progovernment views of 47 percent of white voters, made the Northeast truly unique in its desire for ad-ditional government.

Non-Christian whites made up 16 percent of the region's voters in 2004 and were especially influential in the largest cities. They are the most liberal and pro-Democratic group of white voters in the Northeast. According to the 2000 exit poll, 59 percent of non-Christian whites wanted more government. In 2004 nearly half (49 percent) were liberals, and Democrats led Republicans by 52 percent to 16 percent. Jewish voters were the most Democratic (66 percent) of the non-Christian white groups. Democrats out-numbered Republicans among female Jewish voters by 75 percent to 10 percent, and Jewish men (58 percent to 15) were only slightly less pro-Democratic.

Catholics are the largest religious group among Northeastern whites. In 2004 they accounted for two-fifths of the region's white voters and one-third of all voters. Shifts in partisan strength among Northeastern Catholics constitute a major development in Ameri-can politics. As the Democratic Party took increasingly liberal posi-tions on a wide range of issues, many conservative Catholics began to abandon the party.

Reagan urged Catholics to rethink their partisan ties. One of his earliest campaign appearances in 1980 took him to "Liberty Island in New York Harbor with the Statue of Liberty as a backdrop," wrote George J. Marlin in *The American Catholic Voter.* It was an ideal set-ting to praise immigrants and speak "directly to the ethnic-Catholic voters."[9] Eight years later, nearing the end of his presidency, Reagan used a Columbus Day dinner in New York City to explain the re-vised political landscape in straightforward terms. "The secret is that when the left took over the Democratic Party, we took over the Republican Party," he told his largely Catholic audience. "We made the Republican Party into the party of the working people, the family, the neighborhood, the defense of freedom, and yes, the American flag and the Pledge of Allegiance to one nation under God. So, you see, the party that so many of us grew up with still exists, except that today it's called the Republican Party, and I'm asking all of you to come home and join me."[10]

According to Marlin, "Reagan also hit a chord with Catholics when he spoke fondly of New Deal programs and harshly about the Great Society social experiments."[11] In the 1980s, the Democratic advantage among white Catholics in the Northeast narrowed to about 10 points. By 2004, for the first time in the region's history, Republicans slightly outnumbered Democrats, 38 percent to 36 percent, among white Catholic voters.

Gender has also structured the political transformation of Northeastern white Catholics. White Catholic men have realigned their partisanship. Fifty years ago, Democrats led Republicans 50 percent to 21 percent among white Catholic men; in 2004 Republicans exceeded Democrats by a smaller but still impressive margin, 42 percent to 29 percent. Moderates (53 percent of white male Catholic voters) were evenly divided in partisanship in 2004, but the Republicans' huge advantage among conservatives swamped the Democrats' lead among the smaller group of liberals.

Democrats have continued to lead among Northeastern Catholic women, though by a much smaller margin than in the past. In the 1950s, Catholic white women were overwhelmingly Democratic, leading Republicans by 61 percent to 21 percent. By 2004 the Democratic edge had narrowed to 7 points, 41 percent to 34 percent. Unlike white Catholic men, among whom conservatives were twice as common as liberals, conservatives barely outnumbered liberals among white Catholic women. Moderates made up a majority (53 percent) of white Catholic females, and in this group Democrats led by 10 points. For white Catholic women, the Democratic lead among moderates and liberals exceeded the Republican advantage among conservatives.

Northeastern white Protestants, always the region's most pro-Republican group, fell from 45 percent of all voters in the 1950s to 29 percent in 2004. Unlike white Protestants in the Republican strongholds, Northeastern white Protestants are in no position to set the political agenda. To make matters worse for the GOP, fewer than half of the Protestants (46 percent) have remained Republicans, and more than three of every ten are now Democrats. Moderates (49 percent) constituted the largest ideological group, and conservatives made up only one-third of Protestant voters. A 50-point GOP lead among white Protestants in the 1950s dropped to a 16-point edge in 2004. A smaller lead from a smaller group of white Protestant voters leaves Northeastern Republicans in a very weak position.

The Republican problem among Northeastern white Protestants becomes much clearer when nonevangelicals and evangelicals are compared. By and large, nonevangelicals set the partisan and ideological tone of Northeastern Protestantism. They made up 71 percent of the region's white Protestant voters in 2004. Half of the nonevangelical Protestants were moderates, and the remainder split evenly between liberals (25 percent) and conservatives (24 percent). Even more damaging for the Republican Party, there were as many Democrats (37 percent) as Republicans (36 percent) in the group.

In 2004 nonevangelical white Protestants were quite liberal on social issues. More than four-fifths believed that abortions should usually or always be legal. Only 16 percent objected to any legal recognition of gay and lesbian couples. Forty-four percent favored civil unions, and another 40 percent supported legal marriage for gay and lesbian couples. Fifty-five percent of nonevangelical Northeastern white Protestants disapproved of the decision to go to war with Iraq. Only 53 percent approved of Bush's presidency. Among nonevangelical white Protestants in the Northeast, Kerry beat Bush by 54 percent to 46 percent.

In 2004 Protestant Republicanism thrived in the Northeast only among the small minority (29 percent) of evangelicals. Conservatives made up 55 percent of the evangelicals; only 35 percent were moderates; and only 10 percent thought of themselves as liberals. Republicans outnumbered Democrats 54 percent to 24 percent. Two-thirds of the region's white evangelical Protestants thought abortions should usually or always be illegal; 46 percent, a plurality, opposed any legal recognition of gay and lesbian couples; and three-fourths approved of the decision to go to war with Iraq. Four-fifths approved of President Bush's performance in office, and he won three-fourths of their votes. These conservative views, commonplace among white evangelical Protestants in the Republican strongholds, were voices in the wilderness among most Northeastern Protestants, voices that have eroded GOP strength among the much larger numbers of nonevangelical Protestants.

A national Republican Party strongly influenced by conservative evangelical Protestants—especially conservative evangelical Protestants from the South and the West—is a nonstarter in the Northeast. Such a party has virtually no appeal to non-Christian whites and racial/ethnic minorities, and quite limited appeal to many white Christians. Only 16 percent of white Christian voters in the Northeast described themselves as born-again or evangelical Christians—by far the smallest share in any region of the United States.

Since the 1950s, Democrats have strengthened their position everywhere in the Northeast—cities, suburbs, and small-town/rural areas. Democrats have continued to dominate the region's biggest cities. Large concentrations of racial/ethnic minorities, non-Christian whites, and liberal Catholics and Protestants in New York City, Baltimore, Boston, Philadelphia, and Pittsburgh provide Democrats with important geographical bases of one-party control. These areas typically generate Democratic leads in the hundreds of thousands (more than a million in New York City) of votes, margins that are exceedingly difficult for rural Republicans to overcome.[12] If the Democrats can carry the large cities by comfortable margins, they can easily win statewide elections simply by splitting the suburban and small-town vote with the Republicans.

Republican strength has deteriorated among the region's suburban and rural/small-town voters. The GOP enjoyed a lead in Northeastern suburbs during the 1950s but lost it in the 1960s, and the two parties now usually attract the same numbers of loyalists in the suburbs. More votes have been cast in the suburbs than in any other locale in the Northeast since the 1960s. In 2004, for example, the suburbs produced more than 60 percent of the total regional vote. The Republicans also lost their customary leads in the countryside and small towns in the 1970s.

Republican decay in the suburbs and small towns has devastated the party's prospects in statewide elections. Republican victories in the region now require candidates who have extraordinary appeal to small-town and suburban voters and who can also reduce the party's losses in the large cities. At present, the Republicans have no geographical strongholds from which they can generate huge leads to offset Democratic strength in the large metropolitan areas.

The 2004 election results illustrate Democratic domination in the Northeast. A highly diverse electorate helps perpetuate the Democrats' regional advantage. In 2004 the Democratic Party base (Democrats plus liberal independents) was much larger than the Republican Party base (Republicans plus conservative independents) among five important groups: minority women (77 percent to 15 percent), non-Christian white women (74 percent to 14 percent), minority men (69 percent to 19 percent), non-Christian white men (56 percent to 26 percent), and (by a modest margin) Catholic white women (46 percent to 40 percent). Northeastern Republicans had plurality leads among Catholic white men (47 percent to 33 percent) and Protestant white women (47 percent to 38 percent). Only among Protestant white men (56 percent to 30 percent) did the Republican base break 50 percent.

In the presidential election itself, John Kerry's home region exemplified the Democratic strategy: win overwhelmingly among African Americans (almost 9 to 1), carry the New Minorities of Latinos and other minorities by better than 2 to 1, and neutralize the large white vote. According to the aggregated state exit polls, Bush led Kerry 49.7 percent to 49.2 percent among all Northeastern whites. Kerry defeated Bush by 4 to 1 among non-Christian whites and split the votes of nonevangelical Christian women. Bush achieved a modest majority among nonevangelical Christian men and won decisively only among the small group of evangelical Christians. Neither income nor education divided the Northeastern white vote as sharply as religion. However, Kerry defeated Bush among low-income whites and among whites with graduate and professional training. Bush prevailed among whites with family incomes of $30,000 or higher and among whites with a college or high school education.

THE CHANGING NORTHEASTERN PARTIES

In the 1950s, Northeastern politics matched two closely competitive minority parties that attracted very different social groups. The Northeastern Republican Party was composed primarily of white Protestants (74 percent), supplemented by a small group of white Catholics (20 percent) and much smaller numbers of non-Christian whites and racial minorities (6 percent).

White Catholics dominated the Northeastern Democratic Party. Representative Joe Moakley, an Irish Democrat from South Boston, once summarized the cultural imperatives. " 'As soon as we're born,' " he told a *New York Times* interviewer, " 'we're baptized into the Catholic Church, we're sworn into the Democratic Party, and we're given union cards.' "[13] Nearly three-fifths of Northeastern Democrats were white Catholics. In no other region of the United States did white Catholics make up a majority of Democrats. So sizable and widespread were Catholic whites throughout the Northeast, and so cohesive were their Democratic loyalties, that they comprised majorities of Democratic voters in the region's large cities, suburbs, and rural/small-town areas.

Although Northeastern Democrats in the 1950s were mainly a party of white Catholics, they also attracted majorities of non-Christian whites and racial minorities as well as some white Protestants. The rest of the Democratic party consisted of non-Christian whites (18 percent), white Protestants (17 percent), and racial/ethnic minorities (8 percent).

Over time the Northeastern Democratic Party has been transformed in its group composition. White Catholics, for generations the single largest group of Democratic voters in the Northeast, no longer dominate the party. Because white Catholics now divide their political capital, the Northeastern Democratic Party has become a coalition of various minorities. In the 2002 and 2004 elections, on average, white Catholics made up only 31 percent of the party. Racial and ethnic minorities have expanded to 27 percent of the party. White Protestants, more Democratic today than fifty years ago, accounted for 22 percent of the Democrats, and non-Christian whites were 20 percent. The ability of Northeastern Democrats to assemble large coalitions based on a wide range of diverse groups makes them a truly formidable party.

Northeastern Republicans are now somewhat more diverse in their group composition. White Protestants no longer monopolize the party. They have declined from 74 percent of all Republicans in the 1950s to 45 percent in the early 2000s. During the same period, white Catholics have increased from one-fifth to almost two-fifths of the Northeastern Republicans. Minorities and non-Christian whites, groups who were only 5 percent of the Republicans in the 1950s, accounted for slightly under one-fifth of the GOP five decades later.

Figure 4.2 compares the changing weight within each party of white Christians vis-à-vis minorities plus non-Christian whites. In the 1950s, white Christians dominated both parties. In the Northeastern Democratic Party, they outnumbered minorities and non-

Figure 4.2
Transformation of the Northeastern Parties

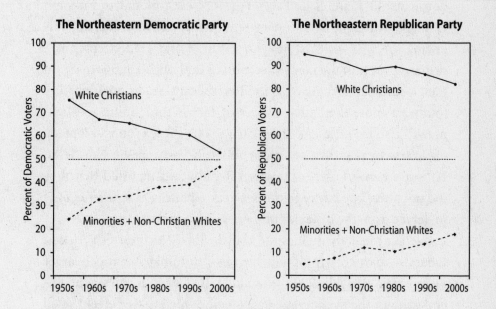

Christian whites by 3 to 1. Over the following fifty years, the gap between these two groups has steadily narrowed. As of the early 2000s, white Christians were only a small majority (53 percent) of all Democrats. The combination of non-Christian whites and racial/ethnic minorities accounted for 47 percent of Northeastern Democrats. The secularization of the modern Democratic Party is also clear. According to the 2004 exit poll, only one-third of Northeastern Democrats attended religious services on a weekly basis.

Northeastern Democrats have remained strong by simultaneously retaining many white Catholics and most non-Christian whites, while attracting minorities and many white Protestants. Greater support for government and opposition to a national Republican Party seen as far too wedded to conservatism and evangelical Christianity have solidified the Northeastern Democratic Party.

Republicans in the Northeast are fundamentally on the defensive. Although white Christians continue to dominate the party, the exit of moderate and liberal white Protestants and the entry of conservative white Catholics mean that white Protestants no longer dominate the Republican Party. Former New York mayor Rudolph Giuliani, who came to national attention through his leadership following the 9/11 terrorist attacks on the World Trade Center, is a prime example of the new generation of Catholic Republicans from the Northeast. Unchanged is the Republicans' traditional inability to attract more than small shares of racial/ethnic minorities and non-Christian whites. As of the early 2000s, those groups still made up less than one-fifth of the Republican Party in the Northeast. Fifty-five percent of Northeastern Republicans reported that they did not attend weekly religious services, a pattern that differed only in degree from the behavior of the region's Democrats.

Ideology acutely divides the transformed Northeastern parties. Liberals—particularly big-city liberals—dominate the much larger Democratic Party. In 2004 white liberals plus minorities—the liberal wing of the Democratic Party—amounted to 64 percent of all Democrats in the Northeast. White moderates were 31 percent, and the few white conservatives made up only 5 percent of the party. Within the smaller Republican Party, slightly fewer than three-fifths of the Republicans belonged to the party's conservative wing (white conservatives plus minorities). The Northeastern Republicans' conservative wing was smaller than the conservative wings of the Republican Party in the South and the Mountains/Plains.

The politicians and policies associated with the new Republican regional strongholds provide no realistic basis for Republican advances in the Northeast. The new Western and Southern Republican leaders are conservative on economic, racial, and national-security issues. In the 1980s, their influence soared when Reagan brought the social conservatism of evangelical Christians into the Republican Party. Reagan, Bush I, and Bush II have been the only Republicans to win national elections since 1980. This new Republican Party, however, is far too conservative on too many social, religious, and foreign-policy issues to succeed in the Northeast. Any revival of Republican strength in the region would require an image of Republican national leadership that emphasizes national security and policies to stimulate economic growth while deemphasizing conservative cultural and religious issues.

THE EMERGENCE OF THE PACIFIC COAST DEMOCRATIC STRONGHOLD

Consistent Democratic strength in national elections emerged later in the Pacific Coast than it did in the Northeast. During much of the past half century, Pacific Coast voters divided their political influence. While usually sending more Democrats than Republicans to Congress, they preferred Republicans for the White House. Republican presidential candidates won huge electoral majorities in nine of the ten contests for the White House from 1952 through 1988. In seven of these elections, a California Republican was on the ballot for president or vice president. The breakthrough in presidential elections for Pacific Coast Democrats occurred with Bill Clinton's victory in 1992. Since then, every Democratic presidential candidate has carried the region's electoral votes. Democrats began to dominate the region's elections for all three national institutions only after conservative Republicans won control of the House and the Senate in 1994.

Starting in the mid-1990s, Democrats have won massive proportions of the Pacific Coast's electoral votes as well as large majorities of its Senate and House delegations. The 2004 elections demonstrated continuing Democratic strength in the Pacific Coast. Kerry won 53 percent of the region's popular vote and 96 percent of its electoral vote. Democrats held seven of the ten U.S. Senate seats and fifty-two of the region's eighty seats in the U.S. House of Representatives. For the first time since the end of World War II, the Pacific Coast has become a highly reliable Democratic stronghold in battles for the presidency, the House, and the Senate.

Although falling short of a majority, Democrats have consistently outnumbered Republicans in the Pacific Coast electorate during the past fifty years. The Democratic Party has maintained a plurality advantage among the region's voters even as the key social groups who make up the party have changed. From the 1950s through the 1970s, a plurality of whites and a majority of nonwhites were Democrats. During Reagan's presidency, however, more white voters began to identify as Republicans than as Democrats (see figure 2.2). Since then the Pacific Coast party battle has aligned a small Republican plurality of whites against a much larger Democratic majority of nonwhites. Among all voters in 2004, Democrats led Republicans by 41 percent to 35 percent.

The Pacific Coast is the only region in the United States where the growth of pro-Democratic minorities has trumped a Republican realignment among whites. Figure 4.3 demonstrates extraordinary shifts in the composition of the region's electorate. The

Figure 4.3
Settings: Pacific Coast

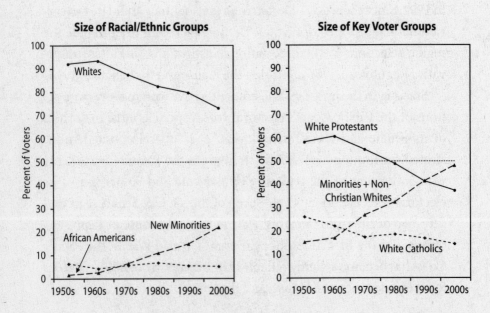

left-hand figure shows the changing sizes of white, African-American, and New Minority voters. As late as the 1960s, whites made up more than nine-tenths of all voters.[14] Since then whites have gradually declined as a percentage of the entire electorate. By 2004 the white majority amounted to 72 percent of Pacific Coast voters—about the same percentage as white voters in the South.

From the 1950s through the 1970s, Democrats averaged a 7-point lead over Republicans. A weak realignment of white voters during Reagan's presidency was the only positive development in the electorate in favor of Republicans in the Pacific Coast during the past fifty years. Realignment in the South generated a Republican lead among whites of nearly 30 percentage points by 2004. By contrast, the GOP edge among Pacific Coast whites in the same year was only 5 percentage points, 40 percent to 35 percent. It was a margin too small to overcome robust Democratic strength among nonwhite voters.

In 2004 nearly three-tenths of all voters in the Pacific Coast were racial or ethnic minorities. Fifty years ago, these groups totaled merely 8 percent of the region's voters. Latinos, Asians, and other ethnic groups, combined as the New Minorities, have been largely responsible for the more diverse electorate. During the past fifty years, these groups expanded from 2 percent to 24 percent of Pacific Coast voters. African Americans have consistently made up 5 percent to 6 percent of the region's voters. The Democratic Party has been the main beneficiary of increasing diversification. Among all nonwhite voters in the Pacific Coast, Democrats led Republicans 55 percent to 23 percent in 2004.

The right-hand chart shows the transformation of the electorate in terms of race, ethnicity, and religion. Historically, white Protestants dominated Pacific Coast politics. Accounting for three of every five voters in the 1960s, white Protestants have since fallen to less than two-fifths of the electorate. Their declining size is a central explanation of Republican weakness in the Pacific Coast. White

Catholics have also shrunk to 1 of every 6 voters. Thus white Christians (Protestants plus Catholics) declined from 84 percent of all Pacific Coast voters in the 1950s to 53 percent in 2004. In no other region have white Christians become such a small majority of the entire electorate.

Rapidly ascending in the West Coast electorate are groups that strongly favor the Democratic Party—racial and ethnic minorities plus non-Christian whites. Members of these combined groups began to outnumber white Catholics during the 1970s and surpassed white Protestants, on average, in the 2002 and 2004 elections. In 2004 minorities plus non-Christian whites made up 47 percent of all Pacific Coast voters, a much larger share than in any other region. The Pacific Coast is thus the prime example of Democratic gains driven by changing demographics.[15]

Fifty years ago, Democrats outnumbered Republicans among nonwhite *and* white voters in the Pacific Coast. Racial and ethnic minorities gave the Democrats a 50-point lead, but these groups were a very small portion of the entire electorate. Democrats enjoyed a smaller lead among white voters. A majority of white Catholics and a plurality of non-Christian whites were Democrats. Republicans held only a small lead among white Protestants. In the 1950s, therefore, Pacific Coast Democrats attracted a greater variety of supporters than did the Republicans, and they also benefited from partisan divisions among the large group of white Protestants.

White conservatives, of course, have led the modern Republican advance in the Pacific Coast. In the 2004 election, 3 of every 4 conservative whites were Republicans, just as more than 7 of every 10 liberal whites were Democrats. Moderates—43 percent of all white voters—were evenly divided between the two parties. Conservatives made up only one-third of the Pacific Coast white voters, and only among these voters have Republicans been able to attract majority support. Put differently, two-thirds of white voters in the Pacific Coast in the twenty-first century were not conservatives, a reality that severely constrains the growth of a purely conservative Republican Party in the region.

The Republican realignment of white Pacific Coast voters, such as it has been, has resulted from the party's increased strength among Protestants. As white Protestants have become a smaller portion of the entire electorate, they have become more Republican and less Democratic. White Protestants responded positively to Reagan's presidency. From 1984 to 1990, 50 percent were Republicans and only 31 percent were Democrats—a 19-point GOP lead. By 2004, Republicans outnumbered Democrats by 51 percent to 26 percent among these voters. Republicans led Democrats across a variety of white Protestant social groups: men and women; college educated and those who never attended college; and those of low, middle, and upper incomes.

Pacific Coast Protestants were separated, however, along evangelical/nonevangelical lines. Evangelicals made up nearly half (48 percent) of the region's white Protestant voters in 2004. Among this group, Republicans easily dominated Democrats, 57 percent to 17 percent. Conservatives outnumbered liberals by 57 percent to 7 percent, and only 37 percent thought of themselves as moderates. Evangelical Protestants in the Pacific Coast were not as conservative about abortion and the legal status of gay/lesbian couples as evangelicals in the Midwest and the Republican strongholds. However, very large majorities of the group supported the war with Iraq and approved of President Bush's performance in office. Seventy-nine percent of the region's evangelical white Protestants voted to reelect the president.

Republicans held a plurality advantage, 40 percent to 34 percent, among the slightly larger group of nonevangelical white Protestants in 2004. Moderates constituted a plurality (42 percent) of these voters, and liberals actually outnumbered conservatives by 32 percent to 27 percent. Most of the nonevangelical Protestant whites were cultural liberals: 88 percent believed abortions should usually or al-

ways be legal, and only 18 percent opposed legal recognition of gay
and lesbian couples. Forty-six percent favored civil unions, and another 36 percent supported marriage for gay or lesbian couples. The
group divided narrowly over the Iraq War. A large majority (57 percent) disapproved of President Bush's performance in office, and
Kerry won 51 percent of their vote.

White Catholics in the Pacific Coast have become considerably
less pro-Democratic during the past fifty years. Democrats are still
in the lead, but their advantage is much smaller. During the 1950s,
52 percent of Pacific Coast Catholics were Democrats. Only one in
five was a Republican, and Democrats enjoyed a 32-point advantage
in partisanship. Democrats still outnumbered Republicans in 2004
but only by 6 points, 43 percent to 37 percent.

The region's white Catholic women and men displayed different
patterns of partisanship in 2004. By 48 percent to 33 percent, white
female Catholics still preferred Democrats to Republicans. This
substantial lead was based on the Democratic Party's continuing
strength among moderate and liberal Catholic women. Republican
realignment was limited to conservatives, who made up only one-
fourth of all white female Catholic voters in the Pacific Coast. White
Catholic men, however, had abandoned the party of their birth and
upbringing: Republicans led Democrats 42 percent to 37 percent. In
addition to realigning the conservatives, the Republicans had neutralized the traditional Democratic advantage among moderate
white Catholic men. Democrats were relegated to a majority only
among the small group of liberal white Catholic men.

All in all, Republicans held leads among only three groups, all declining in size in the Pacific Coast electorate: white Catholic men
and white Protestant men and women. The result has been a widen-
ing Republican advantage among white Christians but a severe decline in the size of the white Christian majority in the Pacific Coast.

The enduring Democratic edge in the Pacific Coast has been
based upon the increasing numbers of non-Christian whites and

racial/ethnic minorities. They are the region's most liberal voters. When asked in the 2000 exit poll if they wanted more or less government, 60 percent of nonwhites and 55 percent of non-Christian whites opted for more government. By contrast, a huge majority of white Christians—70 percent—preferred less government.

Pacific Coast Democrats have benefited from increasing numbers of non-Christian white voters. Making up only 8 percent of Pacific Coast white voters in the 1950s, non-Christians rose to 29 percent of the white electorate by 2004—much higher than in any other region of the United States. Democrats led Republicans 47 percent to 23 percent. Forty-six percent in this group thought of themselves as moderates, 41 percent as liberals, and only 13 percent as conservatives. Non-Christian whites in the Pacific Coast are among the most culturally liberal voters in the United States: in 2004, 92 percent thought abortions should usually or always be legal, and a substantial majority (57 percent) thought gay or lesbian couples should be allowed to legally marry. Only 6 percent believed that gay or lesbian couples should have no legal recognition. Sixty-nine percent opposed the Iraq War, 70 percent disapproved of Bush's handling of the presidency, and 68 percent voted for Kerry.

By 2004 New Minority voters had risen to a quarter of the entire Pacific Coast electorate. As a group, the New Minorities favored Democrats over Republicans by 51 percent to 25 percent. Democrats attracted 70 percent of the group's liberals and also led Republicans 50 percent to 22 percent among the moderates. Only among conservative New Minority voters were Republicans able to attract a majority. Three-fifths of New Minority voters disapproved of Bush's handling of the presidency: Kerry beat Bush in a landslide, 62 percent to 35 percent, among the region's New Minorities.

African Americans were four percent of the region's voters in 2004, and in this group Democrats smothered Republicans, 75 percent to 10 percent. Huge majorities of liberal and moderate African Americans were Democrats, and even among conservatives, Democrats outnumbered Republicans. More than four of every five black voters in the Pacific Coast disapproved of Bush's presidency, and Kerry won 80 percent of their vote in 2004.

The larger Democratic base in the Pacific Coast is clear when party identification and ideology are combined for eight important subgroups of the electorate. In five of the groups, the Democratic base was larger than the Republican base. Two-thirds of minority women and non-Christian white women were Democrats or liberal independents, as were smaller majorities of minority men and Catholic white women. In addition, nearly half of non-Christian white men were in the Democratic base. Majorities of white Protestant men and women, as well as Catholic white men, were Republicans or conservative independents. White Protestant men were far and away the most pro-Republican group in the Pacific Coast, but they now made up only 17 percent of the entire electorate.

As in the Northeast, the location of Pacific Coast voters has changed over time. Suburbs and large cities together already accounted for 70 percent of the region's voters in the 1950s. According to the exit polls, on average nine of every ten votes in the Pacific Coast in the elections of 2002 and 2004 came from metropolitan areas. Large cities generated nearly two-fifths of all votes. In the large cities, the Democratic advantage in party identification has increased from less than 10 points in the 1950s to more than 20 points in the 2000s. Big-city Democrats benefited from a small plurality among whites and a majority among the increasing number of nonwhite voters. Los Angeles, San Francisco, Seattle, Portland, and other major Pacific Coast cities usually generate huge leads for Democratic candidates.

In the suburbs, where over half of Pacific Coast votes originate, whites and nonwhites preferred opposing parties. The Republican lead among the region's white suburbanites has increased from 6 to 15 points over the past fifty years, but whites have become a much smaller majority in the suburban electorate. Democrats claimed a majority among nonwhite suburban voters. The result was a virtual partisan draw in Pacific Coast suburbs, with Republicans ahead of Democrats by only 2 points, 39 percent to 37 percent. When Democrats neutralize Republicans in the suburbs, it is very difficult for Republican candidates to win statewide contests.

Small towns and rural areas have plummeted in size. In the early elections of the twenty-first century, only 10 percent of Pacific Coast votes came from the countryside and small towns. White voters in the region's rural areas and small towns have realigned their partisanship. Democrats held a majority in the 1950s, but Reagan opened a Republican lead in white partisanship that has proved to be durable. In 2004 Republicans led Democrats by 20 percentage points, 48 percent to 28 percent. These areas have also become more diversified in terms of race and ethnicity, a continuing plus for the Democrats. The result has been a modest Republican lead among all small-town and rural voters in the Pacific Coast, 42 percent to 34 percent. These voters, however, now produce only one-tenth of the region's votes.

The Democratic advantage in Pacific Coast politics results from huge Democratic margins in the major cities that overcome smaller Republican margins in the towns and suburbs. Democrats use their big-city strongholds to generate large leads. Republicans have no comparable strongholds. Only when Democrats split their vote or fail to vote is it possible for Republicans to win statewide elections.

THE TRANSFORMATION OF THE PACIFIC COAST PARTIES

In the 1950s, white Christians dominated both Pacific Coast political parties, accounting for more than 90 percent of Republicans and over 80 percent of Democrats (see figure 4.4). More specifically, white Protestants were the largest group in each party. Three-fourths of Republicans were white Protestants; the remainder was made up of relatively small numbers of Catholic whites, non-Christian whites, and racial/ethnic minorities. White Protestants did not dominate the Democrats to the same extent as they did the Republicans, but they still accounted for nearly half of the Democratic Party. The second largest group in the Pacific Coast Democratic Party—about one-third—was made up of white Catholics. The remaining one-fifth of the party's members were racial/ethnic minorities and non-Christian whites. Fifty years ago, the Democratic Party was considerably more diverse than the Republican Party.

Today the two Pacific Coast parties look very different. White Christians have plummeted in size among Pacific Coast Democrats. From over four-fifths of the party in the 1950s, they now constitute less than two-fifths of the region's Democrats. Racial/ethnic minorities and non-Christian whites now make up more than three of every five Pacific Coast Democrats—higher than any other regional

Figure 4.4
Transformation of the Pacific Coast Parties

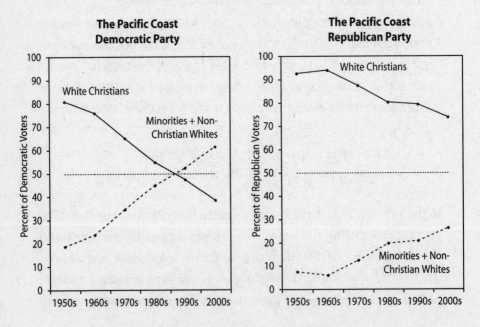

Democratic Party in the United States. The secularization of the Democratic Party is quite evident in the Pacific Coast. Three-fourths of Pacific Coast Democrats reported that they did not attend religious services on a weekly basis. Much less change has occurred in the region's Republican Party. White Christians continue to dominate the Pacific Coast Republican Party, and white Protestants still make up a majority of the party. Secularization is also apparent among Pacific Coast Republicans, with only 44 percent reporting weekly religious attendance.

Profound racial and ideological divisions separate the two major parties in the Pacific Coast. When the racial and ethnic minorities in each party are combined with liberal whites for the Democrats and conservative whites for the Republicans, the results highlight the ideological differences that separate the modern parties. The liberal wing of the Democratic Party is 64 percent, fifteen times the size of its white conservatives and considerably larger than its white moderates (26 percent). The conservative wing of the Republican Party (68 percent) overshadows its tiny group of white liberals (3 percent) and is much larger than its white moderates (30 percent).

The Northeast and the Pacific Coast are the regional foundations for a nationally competitive Democratic Party. In both regions (as of 2004), Democrats and liberal independents far outnumbered Republicans and conservative independents among all voters. Democrats had a 13-point lead in the Northeast (49 percent to 36 percent) and a 5-point lead in the Pacific Coast (46 percent to 41 percent). In their strongholds, Democrats were especially popular among African Americans, non-Christian whites, the New Minorities, white Catholic women, and white nonevangelical Protestant women. These five groups constituted 70 percent of the Pacific Coast electorate and 66 percent of the Northeast's electorate, giving the Democrats enormous size advantages. Republicans were left with impressive leads in party bases only among three groups of white voters: evangelical Protestants, nonevangelical Protestant men, and Catholic men. All in all, the pro-Republican groups were much too small to make the party truly competitive in the Democratic strongholds.

Stark regional differences are at the heart of modern American politics. The implicit Republican challenge to the Democrats' New Deal/Great Society heritage—initiated by Ronald Reagan in the 1980s and accelerated by George W. Bush in the 2000s—has produced mixed results in four regions. Republicans have successfully developed strongholds in the Mountains/Plains and the South, but their conservative challenge has more than met its match in the Northeast and the Pacific Coast. In response to Republican victories in presidential and congressional elections, Democrats have countered by consolidating their strength in the Northeast and the Pacific Coast. Because of their regional successes, Democrats remain a highly competitive minority party in the national electorate.

With two regional strongholds apiece, the Democratic and Republican parties have moved beyond Battlefield Sectionalism to a new alignment of regional conflict. The New American Regionalism generally produces competitive national politics. Yet neither Republicans nor Democrats can win national elections simply by doing extraordinarily well in their own regional strongholds. Their respective regional strongholds do not constitute national majorities. Hence the Midwest, as America's swing region, is the key to winning or losing in the modern American power struggle.

5

THE DIVIDED MIDWEST

THE MIDWEST IS THE HARDEST AMERICAN RE-GION to nail down. Long ago, political scientist Frank Munger addressed the heart of the matter. "The South is a self-conscious region with relatively fixed boundaries," he wrote, and "another group of states can be set off, identified as the Northeast, and associated with certain common features. No one can deny the physical existence of a Rocky Mountain West or entertain much doubt as to which states are included within it. The remaining section is more of a puzzle; it is the most difficult of all to define and to characterize; in one sense, the Midwest is simply what is left after all the other regions have been distinguished away."[1]

Even though the Midwest may be more of a residual than a "self-conscious" region, its two-party battle is crucial to understanding modern American politics. The divided Midwest is America's swing region. The ten states that we group together as the Midwest— Illinois, Indiana, Iowa, Kentucky, Michigan, Minnesota, Missouri, Ohio, West Virginia, and Wisconsin—represent the most volatile, evenly balanced, and reliably competitive geographical area in the United States.[2] Only in this large geographical area has neither party dominated recent presidential and congressional elections. After the 2004 elections, Republicans controlled a majority of Midwestern House seats, while Democrats held a majority of its Senate seats. George W. Bush narrowly carried the Midwest's popular and electoral votes. Success in the Midwest, combined with a sweep of the Republican strongholds, returned Bush to the White House.

As of 2000, some 64 million people resided in the Midwest, giving it a larger population than the Northeast, the Pacific Coast, or the Mountains/Plains. Only the South, with a population of 84 million, contained more people.[3] From the 1870s until the South overtook it in the 1980s, the Midwest was America's biggest region. Like the Northeast, its population growth has fallen below increases in the other three regions. The Midwest's House delegation has declined from 132 in 1950 to 100 in the 2000s. During this period, every Midwestern state lost congressional representation. The region's states contain twenty senators and produce 22 percent of the nation's electoral votes.

In many important ways, the Midwest lies squarely between the Republican and Democratic strongholds. The realignment of white Christians has propelled the Republican advance in the South and the Mountains/Plains. The common denominators of Democratic success in the Northeast and the Pacific Coast have been the party's strength among growing numbers of racial/ethnic minorities and non-Christian whites. In the Midwest, neither party has fully capitalized on these developments.

Based on the attitudes of white voters concerning religion, the Midwest presents an environment closer to the Republican strongholds than the Democratic strongholds. In ANES surveys conducted from 1992 to 2000, 61 percent of white Midwestern voters said religion had quite a bit or a great deal of importance in their lives—much higher than in the Democratic strongholds (46 percent) and only slightly lower than in the Republican strongholds

(65 percent). White Christians made up a larger share of all voters in the Midwest (71 percent) than in any other region, but they have not decisively shifted to the Republican Party. Republicans outnumber Democrats among Midwestern white Christians less than they do in the Republican strongholds.

Union strength in the Midwest has partially blunted Republican efforts to capitalize on religion. As Munger pointed out, "In the Midwest, the critical election that reshaped party loyalties was not 1928, when Catholic opposed Protestant, but 1936, when industrial workers were pitted against the group that President Roosevelt liked to describe as the 'economic royalists.' " Writing in the mid-1960s, he observed that "the party division in the Midwest today is a two-party division that closely follows class lines."[4]

Midwestern Democrats continue to benefit from organized labor. Although union membership today is much lower than fifty years ago, 18 percent of voters in the region were union members in 2004. According to the exit polls, union size in the Midwest was 1 percentage point higher than in the Democratic strongholds and two and one-half times larger than in the Republican strongholds (7 percent). Fifty-six percent of union members in the Midwest were Democrats, and union Democrats constituted one-tenth of all Midwestern voters.

A different problem has constrained Midwestern Democrats. Although the main pro-Democratic groups—racial and ethnic minorities plus non-Christian whites—are highly cohesive, they account for a much smaller share of the Midwestern electorate (29 percent) than they do in the Democratic strongholds (42 percent).

A Democratic lead in the Midwestern electorate fifty years ago has now narrowed to parity with the Republicans. In the 2004 election, Democrats and Republicans were tied: each party claimed 39 percent of the region's voters. Adding liberal independents to Democrats and conservative independents to Republicans, moreover, still produced a virtual dead heat. The Republican base expanded to 44 percent, while the Democratic base increased to 43 percent of all Midwestern voters.

In 2004 most of the states located in the Democratic or Republican strongholds had patterns of partisan advantage consistent with their regional classifications. Thirteen of the sixteen states in the Democratic strongholds, for example, had electorates with more Democrats and liberal independents than Republicans and conservative independents. The exceptions were the small states of Alaska, New Hampshire, and Oregon. Similarly, the Republican base exceeded the Democratic base in twenty-two of the twenty-four states that comprised the Republican strongholds. Arkansas and New Mexico were the only exceptions.

The situation is very different in the Midwest. No party dominates the entire region. The Democratic base was larger than the Republican base in five states (West Virginia, Illinois, Michigan, Minnesota, and Kentucky), but the Republican base exceeded the Democratic base in the other five states (Indiana, Ohio, Iowa, Wisconsin, and Missouri). Furthermore, in six of the region's states—Kentucky, Ohio, Minnesota, Michigan, Missouri, and Wisconsin—the partisan advantage among voters was smaller than 5 percentage points. These characteristics underscore the potential volatility of elections in the region. With many state electorates very closely divided between the parties, short-term events and controversies can quickly shift power from one party to the other.

Figure 5.1 displays the changing setting of politics in the Midwest. Whites continue to dominate the electorate. As the left-hand chart shows, whites comprised 95 percent of the region's voters in the 1950s. According to the average of the 2002 and 2004 exit polls, whites still made up 85 percent of the Midwestern electorate— similar to the percentage of white voters in the Mountains/Plains. Far greater declines in the size of white voters have occurred in the South, the Pacific Coast, and the Northeast.

Figure 5.1
Settings: Midwest

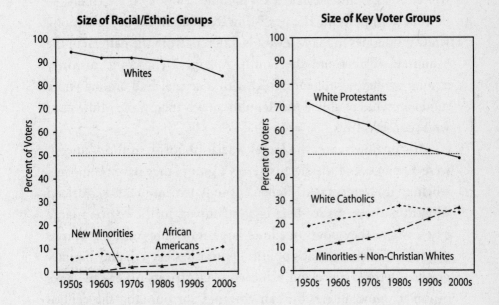

Relatively weak support from white voters is the biggest problem facing Midwestern Republicans. Fifty years ago, Democrats enjoyed a slight advantage among these voters (see figure 2.2). Both parties lost strength in the 1970s. By the 1980s, they were tied, and in the following decade, Republicans opened up a small lead. In 2004 Midwestern white voters gave Republicans a 7-point edge over Democrats, 42 percent to 35 percent, much smaller than the GOP lead among whites in the Republican strongholds.

The size of the three white ideological groups, combined with the Democratic preferences of white moderates, help explain Republican weakness among white voters. According to the 2004 exit polls, 35 percent of Midwestern whites were conservatives, much smaller than in the Republican strongholds. Liberals made up 18 percent of the region's white voters. Typical partisan patterns prevailed among these voters: 75 percent of conservatives were Republicans, and 70 percent of liberals were Democrats. The center of partisan gravity rested with moderates, who comprised 46 percent of the region's white voters. Democrats held a 9-point lead among these voters, 40 percent to 31 percent. The persisting Democratic advantage among white moderates in the Midwest is different from the pattern in the Mountains/Plains and the South. A large Democratic majority among white liberals, combined with a crucial lead among white moderates, has confined the Republican advance in the Midwest to white conservatives.

African Americans, the largest racial minority in the Midwest, were 10 percent of the electorate. As a group, they have been overwhelmingly Democratic (76 percent to 9 percent in 2004). African Americans have made their biggest impact in the region's large cities, where they now constitute large minorities and sometimes majorities of voters. Black political power has been mainly big-city power (Detroit, Cleveland, Chicago). As African Americans have begun to move into suburban counties surrounding the central cities, these areas have become Democratic, or their Democratic traditions have been reinforced. Latinos and other ethnic groups made up the remaining 5 percent of Midwestern voters. While not as strongly Democratic as African Americans, 50 percent of the New Minorities in the Midwest were Democrats, and only 26 percent were Republicans in 2004.

The right-hand chart in figure 5.1 tracks the changing size of white Protestants, white Catholics, and the combination of non-Christian whites and racial/ethnic minorities. The Midwest has relatively more white Protestants than the Democratic strongholds but fewer than the Republican regions. White Protestants, a large majority of all Midwestern voters in the 1950s, declined to less than half (47 percent) of the regional electorate in 2004. White Catholics made up about one-fourth of Midwestern voters, second in size only to the Northeast. Non-Christian whites and racial/ethnic minorities, less than 10 percent of the region's voters in the 1950s, now slightly outnumbered white Catholics.

In the 1950s, fewer than half of the region's white Protestants were Republicans, and they led Democrats by only a few points. In 2004, 49 percent of the region's white Protestants were Republicans, and 31 percent were Democrats. The Republican lead had widened to 18 points, but it was still less than half the GOP advantage—39 points—that white Protestants generated in the Republican strongholds. Partisan divisions, not unity, still characterize white Protestants in the Midwest.

To understand the partisanship of white Protestants, we shall first separate evangelicals from nonevangelicals, and then examine nonevangelicals by gender. Whereas Republicans led by 39 points among the region's evangelical white Protestants, Republicans trailed by 4 points among the region's nonevangelical white Protestants. Nearly half (48 percent) of the region's white Protestants were evangelicals, and they made up 22 percent of all Midwestern voters. Evangelical Protestants were thus a much larger group in the Midwest than in the Democratic strongholds but a considerably smaller force than in the Republican strongholds.

White evangelical Protestants were the most pro-Republican group in the Midwest. Sixty-one percent were Republicans; only 22 percent were Democrats. Conservatives swamped liberals, 57 percent to 8 percent. Two-thirds reported weekly church attendance. Most were conservative on social and religious issues. Seventy-eight percent thought abortions should usually or always be illegal. Seventy percent opposed any legal recognition of gay or lesbian couples. Nearly three-fourths supported the Iraq War, 79 percent approved of Bush's presidency, and 77 percent voted for his reelection.

A very different pattern of partisanship prevailed among the region's nonevangelical white Protestants: Democrats were ahead 41 percent to 37 percent. Fifty-four percent were moderates, and conservatives outnumbered liberals by only 8 points, 27 to 19 percent. Most of these white Protestants were occasional churchgoers. Two-thirds believed abortions should usually or always be legal. There was no consensus about the legal status of gay and lesbian couples, but only one-third of the group opposed legal recognition. Although 56 percent approved of the Iraq War and 53 percent approved of Bush's presidency, Kerry beat Bush by 52 percent to 48 percent among these voters.

Gender affected the party preferences of nonevangelical white Protestants. Men were slightly more Republican than Democratic, 40 percent to 36 percent. Conservatives outnumbered liberals (37 percent to 16 percent), but the largest group was moderates (47 percent). About three of every five were social liberals who supported the legality of abortions and some sort of legal status for gay and lesbian couples. Yet nearly two-thirds supported the Iraq War, and three-fifths approved of President Bush's presidency. Bush carried nonevangelical Protestant men in the Midwest by 8 points, 54 percent to 46 percent.

Nonevangelical Protestant women were far more Democratic than Republican, 45 percent to 34 percent. Only 19 percent of these Midwestern women thought of themselves as conservatives, and Democrats outnumbered Republicans among moderates and liberals. Sixty-nine percent wanted abortions to usually or always be legal, nearly three-fourths favored some kind of legal status for gay or lesbian couples, 52 percent opposed the Iraq War, and 53 percent disapproved of Bush's presidency. Kerry beat Bush by 14 points, 57 percent to 43 percent, among nonevangelical white Protestant women.

College-educated white Protestants have been an important social force behind the modern revival of the Republican Party in the region. Fifty years ago, four-fifths of all Midwestern white Protestants had not attended college, and Democrats outnumbered Republicans among these voters. College-educated white Protestants now account for 40 percent of the region's white voters and 35 percent of all voters. In 2004 Republicans led Democrats among this large group by 50 percent to 27 percent. In recent elections, noncollege white Protestants have shifted as well to the Republicans.

Midwestern white Protestants also split their partisanship according to union membership. Republicans led Democrats by more than 2 to 1, 54 percent to 26 percent, among the large majority of white Protestants who were not union members. Among the 18 percent of white Protestants who were union members, Democrats exceeded Republicans by 50 percent to 30 percent. The contrast with the Republican strongholds is instructive. In the South and the Mountains/Plains, merely 6 percent of white Protestants belonged to unions, and the Democratic lead among union members was only 15 points, 51 percent to 36 percent. Ninety-four percent of white Protestant voters in the Republican strongholds did not belong to a labor union, and Republicans led Democrats by more than 3 to 1, 62 percent to 19 percent.

Residues of past class divisions also appear when the partisanship of the region's white Protestant voters is related to their incomes. In 2004 Democrats held only a 1-point edge among those with incomes of less than $30,000. Republicans easily led, 51 percent to 29 percent, among the large group of middle-income white Protestants. Among those with incomes of $100,000 and higher, the Republican advantage over Democrats increased to 41 points, 61 percent to 20 percent.

Historically, white Catholics were a huge asset for the Democratic Party. Irish, German, Italian, Polish, and other ethnic groups with large numbers of Catholics settled in the Midwest in the nineteenth and early twentieth centuries. Democratic politicians welcomed the ethnic Catholics and encouraged them to vote. Often viewing the overwhelmingly Protestant Republican Party as hostile to their interests, Midwestern Catholics invested most of their political resources in the Democratic Party. Based on their average party identification in the 1950s and 1960s, 58 percent of the region's white Catholic voters were Democrats, and only 14 percent were Republicans. Democrats fell slightly below 50 percent during the period of 1972 through 1982, but few white Catholics—only about one in five—thought of themselves as Republicans. During the four elections from 1984 to 1990, the Democratic edge weakened to 41 percent to 28 percent, and it remained in this range during the elections of 1992 through 2000.

While many Midwestern white Catholics are no longer Democrats, there has been no sustained shift of the entire group to the Republican Party. Mixed patterns of partisanship among white Catholics appeared in the 2002 and 2004 exit polls. In 2002 Democrats still led by 8 points, 43 percent to 35 percent. In 2004, for the first time, the results were virtually a dead heat: 39 percent were Republicans, and 37 percent were Democrats. Averaging these two elections produces a Democratic lead of 3 points. Whatever the actual balance between the parties, these recent developments were not good news for Midwestern Democrats. Republicans were challenging Democrats among an important group of Midwestern voters whose parents, grandparents, and great-grandparents had almost exclusively chosen the Democratic Party to represent their values, interests, and priorities.

In 2004 white Catholic voters in the Midwest were deeply divided. The abortion issue helped Republicans among white Catholics in the region: 58 percent thought abortions should usually or always be illegal. Catholic whites were less traditional, though, concerning gay and lesbian couples. More than two of every five supported civil unions, nearly one-quarter supported marriage, and only one-third thought no legal recognition should be given to gay and lesbian couples. Fifty-five percent supported the Iraq War and approved of President Bush's performance as president. Bush defeated Kerry by 7 points, 53 percent to 46 percent.

Gender clearly separated the Midwestern white Catholic voters.

Catholic men, slightly more conservative and slightly less liberal than Catholic women, have realigned their partisanship. In 2004 Republicans led Democrats 44 percent to 31 percent among the region's white Catholic men. No realignment has appeared among white Catholic women. Among these voters, Democrats were still ahead of Republicans 42 percent to 36 percent. While Democrats predominated among liberal white Catholic women, their decisive advantage came from a substantial lead among the large group of moderate Catholic women.

Party identification also varied at the extremes of income for white Catholics in the Midwest. Democrats held a 20-point lead over Republicans among those with incomes of less than $30,000, while Republicans led Democrats by 30 points among those with incomes of $100,000 or more. Three-fifths of Midwestern white Catholics had incomes ranging from $30,000 to $99,999. Here the parties were virtually even: 38 percent Democrats, 37 percent Republicans. In every income range, white male Catholics were more Republican and less Democratic than white female Catholics.

Non-Christian whites are a growing Democratic presence in the Midwestern electorate. They constituted 13 percent of the region's voters in 2004, up from 3 percent fifty years ago. Nearly half (47 percent) were Democrats; only 22 percent were Republicans. Ideologically, moderates (45 percent) were the largest group of non-Christian whites. Liberals (39 percent) were more than twice as common as conservatives (17 percent). Most liberals and a plurality of moderates identified as Democrats. Republicans attracted a majority of partisans only among the few conservatives.

The Midwest's non-Christian whites were cultural liberals: 88 percent believed abortions should usually or always be legal, and only 11 percent believed that gay and lesbian couples should have no legal standing. Half favored gay or lesbian marriage, and another 39 percent supported civil unions for gay or lesbian couples. Sixty-nine percent opposed the Iraq War. Two-thirds of non-Christian whites disapproved of President Bush's performance in office, and less than one-third voted for his return to the White House.

In the 1950s, more votes in the Midwest were cast in small towns and rural areas (45 percent) than in cities (29 percent) or suburbs (27 percent). Over time, huge population shifts have altered the location of the region's voters, and many native Midwesterners have moved out of the region. Midwestern suburbs passed the large cities in size in the 1960s and moved ahead of the small-town/rural areas in the 1980s. In the 2004 election, 44 percent of the region's vote came from suburbs, 31 percent from small towns and rural areas, and 25 percent from cities.[5]

The most valuable Democratic asset in the Midwest is the party's steady strength in big cities. In 2004 Democrats led Republicans by 19 points, 48 percent to 29 percent. Whites were 94 percent of the Midwestern city electorate in the 1950s, and they still made up two-thirds of city voters fifty years later. According to the 2004 exit poll, white voters in the region's cities were only slightly more Democratic than Republican, 39 percent to 35 percent. African Americans, 23 percent of city voters, favored Democrats over Republicans 80 percent to 7 percent, as did Latinos and other ethnic groups, but by a much smaller margin. Cohesive support from racial and ethnic groups in Midwestern cities continues to produce sizable leads for the Democratic Party among all voters.

In the region's truly large cities (500,000 and higher), one-party Democratic rule remained even more firmly in place (61 percent to 20 percent). Because so few big-city voters are Republicans, the minority party seldom seriously contests elections. Democratic candidates routinely sweep the cities with margins well above their share of partisans. Two examples from the 2004 state exit polls illustrate enduring big-city Democratic strength: In Chicago, Democrats outnumbered Republicans by 64 percent to 13 percent, and Kerry defeated Bush by a whopping margin of 82 percent to 18 percent. In Detroit, the Democratic advantage in partisanship was even greater,

86 percent to 7 percent, and Kerry secured 96 percent of the vote. Although Detroit cast only 7 percent of Michigan's total vote, so overwhelming was Kerry's victory that he carried the city by nearly 286,000 votes, more than enough to overcome Bush's lead in the rest of the state.[6] Persisting Democratic strongholds in most of the other very large Midwestern cities usually put Republican candidates far behind in the battle for statewide victories and makes imperative a Republican sweep of the suburbs and rural areas for any hope of statewide victories.

Midwestern small towns and rural areas showed only a modest Republican advantage in partisanship, 41 percent to 37 percent, in 2004. Whites made up 95 percent of these voters, and Republicans held a 6-point lead. Seventy percent of conservatives were Republicans, and two-thirds of liberals were Democrats. The key Republican weakness lay among moderates, who were about half of white voters in the small-town/rural areas. Democrats enjoyed a 15-point lead among the white moderates. African Americans, Latinos, and other ethnic groups, while only 5 percent of all voters in small towns and rural areas, were strongly Democratic. Their presence narrowed the Republican advantage in the small towns and rural areas of the Midwest to only 4 points, much smaller than the Democratic advantage in the region's cities.

Suburbs have become the largest segment of the Midwestern electorate. In 2004 Republicans led Democrats in the Midwestern suburbs by 8 points, 43 percent to 35 percent. Indeed, in basic partisanship, Republicans led Democrats in the suburbs of every Midwestern state by margins that ranged from 29 points in Indiana to only 1 point in Ohio. Whites accounted for 89 percent of suburban voters in the Midwest. Republicans led among white voters 45 percent to 32 percent. Moderates (45 percent) made up the largest group of the region's white suburban voters, and Democrats led Republicans by 1 point, 36 percent to 35 percent. Majorities of liberals and conservatives identified with their respective parties. The Republican Party's lead among all white suburban voters was largely due to the fact that conservatives outnumbered liberals by nearly 2 to 1. African Americans, Latinos, and other ethnic groups constituted the rest of the suburban electorate. Their tilt toward the Democratic Party narrowed the Republican lead in the entire Midwestern suburban electorate.

Statewide elections in the Midwest turn on variations in the size and cohesion of city Democrats, as well as the degree to which Republicans can win sufficiently large margins in the rural/small-town areas and suburbs to offset Democratic leads in the cities.

THE TRANSFORMATION
OF THE MIDWESTERN PARTIES

The Midwestern Democratic and Republican parties have experienced less change in their social composition than parties in other regions. Fifty years ago, white Protestants were majorities in both Midwestern parties. In the 2002 and 2004 elections, on average, two-thirds of Midwestern Republicans were Protestant whites. White Catholics made up another one-fifth of the Republicans. Relatively few non-Christian whites and racial/ethnic minorities were Republicans. The Midwestern Democratic Party has become more diverse. White Protestants are still the largest group, but they have declined to less than 2 of every 5 Democrats. Racial and ethnic minorities are now the same size as white Catholics. Non-Christian whites remain less than one-tenth of Midwestern Democrats.

White Christians continue to be the largest group in both Midwestern political parties (see figure 5.2). The vast majority of Republicans—nearly 9 of every 10—remain white Christians. A more substantial erosion of white Christians has occurred among Democrats. A half century ago, almost nine-tenths of all Democrats were white Christians. While they still make up a large majority of the

Figure 5.2
Transformation of the Midwestern Parties

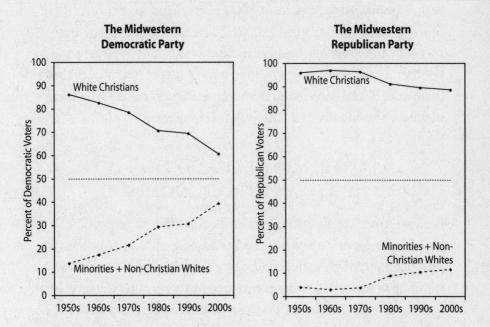

party, white Christians have fallen to six-tenths of the Midwestern Democrats. White Protestants are still the overwhelming majority of Republicans and remain the largest group of Democrats. Because white Catholics remain a sizable minority among Democrats and have increased their number in the Republican Party, the political resources of the region's white Christians are still divided between the parties in a way that does not occur in any of the other regions.

In terms of race and white ideology, the conservative wing dominates the Midwestern Republican Party: 65 percent of voters who identified themselves as Republicans in 2004 were either white conservatives or nonwhites. White moderates made up 32 percent of the party, and 4 percent were white liberals. Thus the Midwestern Republican Party appeared to be very similar to those in the other regions of the nation.

The Midwestern Democratic Party, on the other hand, was considerably less dominated by its liberal wing. White liberals plus non-whites amounted to 51 percent of the party, a smaller majority than in the Democratic strongholds. White moderates still made up 41 percent of the region's Democrats, and white conservatives added another 8 percent. In every other region except the Mountains/Plains, the liberal wing of the Democratic Party exceeded 60 percent of voters who identified themselves as Democrats.

THE MIDWEST AND THE PARTISAN STRONGHOLDS

Because American politicians are elected to office in geographically based constituencies, and because broad geographical areas tend to produce patterns favoring one party over the other, our understanding of national politics is enriched by recognizing the very different partisan tendencies that characterize different parts of the nation.

The crucial swing position of the Midwest appears in comparison with the Democratic and Republican strongholds. Table 5.1 shows the Democratic and Republican bases in 2004 among eight groups of voters classified by race, religion, and gender. Results are reported for the Democratic Party strongholds, the Midwest, and the Republican Party strongholds. Paying attention to the size and cohesion of the groups deepens our understanding of party politics in the United States.

In the 2004 election, the most overwhelmingly united groups in the Midwest, the Democratic strongholds, and the Republican strongholds were African Americans for the Democrats and white evangelical Protestants for the Republicans. Non-Christian whites and New Minorities were also pro-Democratic in each setting, but the size of the Democratic advantage differed across the three constituencies. Similarly, the Republican base exceeded the Democratic

Table 5.1
Democratic and Republican Party Bases in 2004 (%) *

Political Group	Democratic Strongholds			Midwest			Republican Strongholds		
	DB	RB	Size	DB	RB	Size	DB	RB	Size
African Americans	80	11	(9)	80	12	(9)	82	11	(16)
Non-Christians	61	22	(18)	58	25	(13)	52	31	(11)
New Minorities	60	28	(15)	56	31	(7)	48	42	(11)
Catholic women	47	39	(15)	45	41	(13)	34	52	(6)
Nonevangelical Protestant women	47	35	(10)	50	36	(14)	29	60	(11)
Nonevangelical Protestant men	37	46	(9)	38	46	(11)	25	61	(10)
Catholic men	35	48	(12)	33	50	(12)	27	61	(6)
Evangelical Protestants	23	67	(12)	22	68	(22)	21	72	(30)
All	48	38		43	44		39	50	

* DB (Democratic Base) = Democrats + liberal independents; RB (Republican Base) = Republicans + conservative independents; Size = size of group. New Minorities = Latinos + other minorities. Aside from African Americans and New Minorities, all other groups are categories of white voters. Percentages are rounded to the nearest whole number.
Source: 2004 exit polls.

base in every context among white nonevangelical Protestant men and white Catholic men, even though the size of the GOP advantage varied.

Two groups of white women—nonevangelical Protestants and Catholics—were the most important swing groups. For both groups, the Democratic base exceeded the Republican base in the Democratic strongholds and the Midwest. A very different pattern prevailed in the Republican strongholds, where majorities of

Catholic women and nonevangelical Protestant women were Republicans or conservative independents.

In the combined Democratic strongholds, the Democratic base exceeded the Republican base by 10 points (48 percent to 38 percent) among all voters. Because the size of the Democratic advantage varies among the states of the Northeast and the Pacific Coast, and because short-term electoral factors do not always benefit the party with a larger base, Democrats do not win all of the elections in their strongholds. But as long as their substantial advantage persists in the electorate, Democrats should win most elections for federal offices in the Northeast and the Pacific Coast—as they have done in recent cycles. In 2004 Democrats had huge victories in their two regional strongholds: 98 percent of the electoral vote, 69 percent of the Senate seats, and 63 percent of the House seats. Democrats and liberal independents in the Northeast and the Pacific Coast accounted for two-fifths of the nation's entire Democratic base.

For the combined Northeast and Pacific Coast electorate, the three most pro-Democratic groups—African Americans, non-Christian whites, and New Minorities—made up 42 percent of all voters. Large majorities of each group were part of the Democratic base. In addition, pluralities of nonevangelical white Protestant women and white Catholic women, another 25 percent of the voters, were Democrats or liberal independents. Of the three pro-Republican groups in the Democratic strongholds, the Republican base was a majority only among white evangelical Protestants, a group that cast only 12 percent of the vote. The Republican base outnumbered the Democratic base by much smaller margins among nonevangelical white Protestant men and white Catholic men. Republican weakness in the Democratic strongholds was striking: the GOP led the Democrats among groups that made up only one-third of all voters in the combined Northeast and Pacific Coast.

Very different patterns occurred in the Republican strongholds of the South and the Mountains/Plains, where the Republican base exceeded the Democratic base by 11 points, 50 percent to 39 percent. Bush won 100 percent of the electoral votes in the two Republican strongholds. In addition, the Republicans held 65 percent of the House seats and 75 percent of the Senate seats. Republicans and conservative independent voters in the South and the Mountains/Plains accounted for 45 percent of the entire Republican base in the United States.

The Republicans' advantage in their regional strongholds has been based on their strength among five of the eight groups presented in table 5.1. White evangelical Protestants—by far the most pro-Republican group—made up 30 percent of the voters in the Republican strongholds. Among the white evangelical Protestants, the Republican base outnumbered the Democratic base by 72 percent to 21 percent. They were two and one-half times as large in the Republican strongholds as they were in the Democratic strongholds. The Republican base also outnumbered the Democratic base among nonevangelical white Protestant men and white Catholic men. Together these three groups accounted for 46 percent of all voters in the Republican strongholds.

In the South and the Mountains/Plains, the two other groups of white Christian women (another 17 percent of the electorate) were also strongly disposed toward the GOP. Nonevangelical white Protestant women paralleled the partisanship of their male counterparts, and the Republican base was 18 points larger than the Democratic base among white Catholic women. By contrast, Democratic strength in the Republican strongholds was reduced to three groups: African Americans, non-Christian whites, and New Minorities. These groups included only 38 percent of all voters in the Republican strongholds. Only among African Americans did the Democrats do as well in the Republican strongholds as in the other regions of the nation. In the Republican strongholds, the Democratic margin among the New Minorities and non-Christian whites was considerably smaller than elsewhere.

Neither party has achieved a decisive advantage in the Midwest. Unlike the partisan balances in the Democratic and Republican regional strongholds, neither Midwestern Democrats nor Midwestern Republicans have established party bases that approach a majority of all voters. In 2004 the rival Midwestern party bases were virtually equal in size—44 percent Republican, 43 percent Democratic—according to the aggregated state exit polls. The leading party's base was 5 or more points greater than its rival in only four of the ten Midwestern states. Democrats held sizable leads in West Virginia and Illinois, as did Republicans in Indiana and Iowa. In the other six states, the party bases were more evenly balanced. Republicans had small leads in Ohio, Missouri, and Wisconsin; Democrats were slightly ahead in Michigan, Minnesota, and Kentucky.

For the entire Midwest, the Democratic base exceeded the Republican base among five of the eight groups of voters, which collectively made up 56 percent of the region's voters. Democrats drew large majorities from African Americans, Non-Christian whites, and New Minorities, but these three groups made up only 28 percent of the entire Midwestern electorate, far lower than their percentage in the Democratic or Republican strongholds.

Although Republicans had the advantage with only three groups of white voters (evangelical Protestants, Catholic men, and non-evangelical Protestant men), they collectively accounted for 45 percent of voters in the Midwest—about the same size as in the Republican strongholds and much larger than in the Democratic strongholds. The two key groups of white female voters—Catholics and nonevangelical Protestants—were closer to their counterparts in the Democratic strongholds than in the Republican strongholds. Together, these groups of white women accounted for more than one-fourth of the entire Midwestern vote.

Having identified striking regional variations in the strength of the Republican and Democratic parties, we can now show how America's political regions provide the basic framework for the national power struggle. Distinctive regional strongholds in the electorate have become the starting point for today's tight party battles to control the White House, the House of Representatives, and the Senate.

6

THE PRESIDENTIAL
POWER STRUGGLE

F AR AND AWAY, THE MOST SIGNIFICANT DEVELOP-
MENT in the modern presidential power struggle is the
reinvention of the Democratic Party as the implicit party of
the North. By adding the Pacific Coast and the upper Midwest to its
previous base of support in the Northeast, America's oldest major
party has reestablished itself as a consistently strong force in presidential elections. Although defeated in 2000 and 2004, the Democratic Party won more popular votes than the Republican Party in
2000 and was exceptionally competitive in the electoral college in
both elections.

The Democrats' impressive northern gains, when set against the
Republicans' own strongholds in the South, the Mountains/Plains,
and the lower Midwest, have revitalized presidential elections.
Landslide Republican victories have disappeared and are unlikely to
return. Overwhelming Republican triumphs in 1980, 1984, and
1988 at first yielded to easy Democratic wins in 1992 and 1996 and
were then replaced by exceptionally close battles in 2000 and 2004.

Recent elections reveal clearly the sectional and regional transformations of presidential politics.

PRESIDENTIAL TRANSFORMATIONS

Unlike the New Deal of Franklin Roosevelt, Lyndon Johnson's Great Society was an electoral failure for the Democratic Party. Roosevelt's leadership during the Great Depression and World War II produced four national victories, and the Democratic coalition was still sufficiently strong to elect Roosevelt's successor, Harry S. Truman, in 1948. Johnson's landslide victory over Barry Goldwater in 1964 did not produce similar results. By 1968 his own party was bitterly divided over the Vietnam War. Widespread domestic turmoil created a broad demand for law and order and put the Johnson administration on the defensive. Moreover, Johnson faced increasingly serious challenges from fellow Democrats (especially Robert F. Kennedy) for the party's nomination. Weighing his chances, Johnson decided not to seek reelection. His retirement testified to a political climate radically different from that of 1964. FDR had achieved his greatest triumph with his second-term victory in 1936, but the extraordinarily ambitious LBJ could not even afford politically to run in 1968.[1]

From 1968 through 1988, the Republican Party won five out of six presidential elections. For the Republicans, it was a performance surpassed only by their record of six consecutive victories from 1860 through 1880. A badly disunified Democratic Party gave the Republicans a windfall opportunity in 1968. Republican former vice president Richard Nixon defeated Democratic vice president Hubert Humphrey by 56 percent to 35 percent in the electoral college. Nixon became the first Californian to win the Presidency. He achieved his national victory by combining three-fifths of the Northern electoral vote with a plurality (45 percent) of the Southern electoral vote. Only in the Northeast did Humphrey trounce Nixon.[2]

Four years later, in a mismatch that was nearly as lopsided as Johnson's 1964 victory, Nixon easily defeated liberal Democratic senator George McGovern of South Dakota. Republicans carried the entire North except Massachusetts and the District of Columbia. In the South, for the first time ever, Republicans won all eleven states. Like Johnson, Nixon then squandered his national landslide. The Watergate scandal engulfed the White House, forced Nixon's resignation in 1974, and placed the Republican Party squarely on the defensive.

In 1976 former Georgia governor Jimmy Carter made a virtue of his outsider status and led the Democrats back into the White House against Nixon's unelected successor, Republican president Gerald Ford of Michigan. Carter's electoral college victory of 55 percent to 45 percent was based on unifying the South (91 percent) and securing a respectable minority share (44 percent) in the North. Outside the South, Carter carried the Northeast decisively and the Midwest narrowly. He completely lost the Mountains/Plains and every state in the Pacific Coast except Hawaii.

By 1980, however, the Democratic president was in serious trouble. A poor economy, American hostages in Iran, and general dissatisfaction with his performance in office jeopardized Carter's reelection prospects. Carter defeated a challenge for the nomination from Senator Edward Kennedy of Massachusetts, only to be routed in the fall election by Ronald Reagan, the former Republican governor of California.[3] Effectively attacking the Democratic president on the economy and the hostage situation, Reagan put a smiling face on his conservatism and achieved an electoral vote majority only slightly less overwhelming than Nixon's victory in 1972. In both the North and the South, Reagan won 91 percent of the electoral vote. Although some of Reagan's Southern victories were very close, the Californian defeated Carter in every Southern state except Georgia.[4]

Reagan's presidency transformed American politics. He was the first Republican president to challenge the big-government and

high-tax philosophy of the Democratic Party that began with Roosevelt's New Deal and was reinforced and extended by Johnson's
Great Society. Reagan's first term had a tremendous impact on the
national party battle. A superb communicator, the former actor
used the White House as a platform to advocate tax cuts and to de-
nounce the Soviet Union as an "evil empire" that the United States
needed to confront through greater military expenditures. By 1984,
with the economy again expanding, Reagan campaigned as a successful conservative, the restorer of national prosperity.

Reagan's opponent, Democratic former vice president Walter
Mondale of Minnesota, was a veteran Northern liberal who was ap-
palled by Reagan's conservatism and especially by his tax cuts. In his
televised speech accepting the Democratic nomination, Mondale
promised the nation that his first priority as president would be to
raise income taxes. It was a courageous but foolhardy gesture, en-
abling the Reagan campaign to use Mondale's own words to define
him as a sincere champion of higher taxes. Reagan swept the nation,
losing only Minnesota and the District of Columbia. Reagan's presidency reinforced Democratic loyalty among blacks but produced
net Republican gains among whites in both the South and the
North.

In 1988 George H. W. Bush, Reagan's vice president for eight
years, stressed his allegiance to Reagan as his main asset in securing
the Republican nomination. "No new taxes" became the central
pledge of Bush's acceptance speech. Democrats countered with
Massachusetts governor Michael Dukakis, a Northeastern liberal
inexperienced in the crosscurrents of national politics. The result
was another Republican national landslide—79 percent to 21 percent—in the electoral college. Bush carried the entire South and
won 72 percent of the Northern electoral vote. Like Mondale in
1984 and Carter in 1980, Dukakis lost all four Northern regions as
well as the South. Nonetheless, Dukakis was considerably more
competitive in the Northeast than his predecessors had been. The

Democrats' Northeastern gains in 1988 presaged their extensive Northern comeback four years later.

Bush's election terminated an extraordinarily successful Republican era in presidential politics. The six elections from 1968 through 1988 represented unprecedented Republican strength across the entire United States. For a political party founded explicitly as a Northern party, the two decades after the Great Society constituted the first time in American history that Republican presidential candidates had demonstrated truly impressive strength in the South as well as the North. By adding the South to their traditional base in the North, the Republicans achieved national landslides in 1972, 1980, 1984, and 1988. Four of America's five regions—the Mountains/Plains, the South, the Pacific Coast, and the Midwest—all furnished overwhelming Republican electoral majorities. Only the Northeast stood out as a center of relative Republican weakness, the only region where reliably Republican states did not dominate presidential elections.

BILL CLINTON LEADS THE DEMOCRATIC REVIVAL

For Democrats the two decades after the Great Society were disastrous in presidential politics. Beginning in 1992, though, Democratic resurgence has significantly reshaped presidential politics. By that year, George Bush was a tired and ineffective chief executive. Unlike Reagan, Bush could not communicate an energizing political vision. By rewarding his key campaign strategists, James Baker and Lee Atwater, with prestigious appointments outside the White House, Bush stripped himself of expert political guidance on a daily basis. In 1990 he shocked and badly disappointed millions of conservatives by agreeing to tax increases after making his unqualified opposition to any new taxes the central promise of his 1988 campaign. Reneging on taxes produced a challenge to his renomination from Pat Buchanan, a far-right conservative. Bush dispatched Buchanan in the Republican primaries, but his standing among fellow Republicans was severely damaged. As the leader of a minority party whose own decisions had undermined his partisan base, Bush was poorly positioned to win reelection.

Democrats seized the opportunity presented by Bush's weakness by nominating a different sort of Democrat, Arkansas governor Bill Clinton. Clinton brought to presidential politics the campaign style of a successful Southern Democrat. He did not run for president as a full-fledged liberal Democrat in the style of McGovern, Mondale, or Dukakis. Instead, Clinton campaigned as a New Democrat, one who sidestepped "meaningless" ideological labels while adeptly shifting his message back and forth between liberal and conservative positions. He would raise taxes on the rich and design a program to provide universal health care, but he would also reform the welfare system. As governor, Clinton had routinely balanced state budgets and occasionally authorized the death penalty. Unlike previous Democratic presidential candidates, Clinton could not be realistically attacked as an undiluted "liberal Democrat."

With a novel all-Southern ticket of Clinton for president and Tennessee senator Al Gore for vice president, Democrats saw an opportunity to win some of the Southern electoral vote as well as to compete in many Northern states. Clinton especially knew how to empathize with voters in a way that Bush could never match. Presidential debates enabled Clinton to demonstrate his energy, youth, and rhetorical skills to considerable advantage against the older and disengaged Bush.

To compound Bush's difficulties, maverick Texas entrepreneur Ross Perot mounted a third-party candidacy that carried not a single state but splintered the popular vote to Bush's disadvantage. Clinton's share of the national popular vote was actually 3 points lower than Dukakis's vote (43 percent versus 46 percent). In 1992 Bush's 37 percent was 16 points lower than his majority of 53 percent in 1988. In many states, Clinton's share of the 1992 vote was fairly close to the 1988 Democratic vote. Bush's percentages were generally much lower in 1992 than in 1988. In 1912, when Republicans split their vote between President William Howard Taft and former president Theodore Roosevelt, Democrat Woodrow Wilson had won the presidency with huge majorities in the South but only pluralities in most Northern states. Except for Arkansas and the District of Columbia, all of Clinton's victories were pluralities rather than majorities.

In the electoral college, Clinton trounced Bush 69 percent to 31 percent. Democrats have won many national landslides in presidential elections, but the sectional structure of Clinton's easy victory was unique. For the first time in American history, a Democrat won the presidency without carrying the South. Clinton combined 85 percent of the Northern electoral vote with only 27 percent of the Southern electoral vote. He carried every state in the Northeast, every state in the Pacific Coast except Alaska, and every state in the Midwest except Indiana. Although the Mountains/Plains region remained more Republican than Democratic, in that region Clinton carried Colorado, Nevada, New Mexico, and Montana. Arkansas, Tennessee, Louisiana, and Georgia accounted for the Democrats' Southern successes. It was a sweeping national victory. Clinton's fresh style revived the Democratic Party in presidential elections.

Once in office, Clinton initially stressed the liberal features of his New Democrat stance, most notably in his successful effort to raise taxes on wealthy Americans and in his unsuccessful attempt to reform health care. Both issues motivated Republican voters in the 1994 congressional elections. On Clinton's watch, the Republicans regained control of the House of Representatives and the Senate, control that was never relinquished as long as Clinton occupied the White House.

The Republicans' victory in the House of Representatives, largely unanticipated, placed a national spotlight on the new Republican

Speaker, Newt Gingrich of suburban Atlanta. Gingrich immediately became the symbol of the conservative Southern Republican, the other side of the ideological coin of the liberal Northern Democrat. Through his aggressive leadership of the House Republicans, Gingrich soon became the instrument of President Clinton's revival after the congressional defeats of 1994. Although Clinton ultimately signed the Republicans' welfare reform legislation, he exercised the presidential veto to minimize Republican legislative achievements. Gingrich's full-fledged conservatism allowed Clinton to reemerge as a champion of Democratic interests, especially when Gingrich overplayed his hand by briefly shutting down the government over appropriations bills.[5]

In 1996 Clinton used presidential incumbency to great advantage. California, by far America's largest state, became the central strategic target of the Clinton administration. Between 1952 and 1988, the Republicans had carried California in every presidential election except 1964. If California could be made reliably Democratic, the Republicans' advantage in presidential politics would be severely damaged. Clinton secured California for his party. In 1996, running against the former Republican Senate majority leader, Bob Dole of Kansas, Clinton repeated his electoral college landslide of 1992. Clinton portrayed himself as a Democratic centrist determined to contain the conservative Republicans as personified by Gingrich. Dole, a lackluster presidential candidate, was no match for Clinton as a campaigner.

The second Clinton administration was characterized by economic prosperity, on the one hand, and a White House scandal involving Clinton and an intern named Monica Lewinsky. The Lewinsky scandal encouraged Republicans to try removing him from office. House Republicans impeached Clinton, but the Senate refused to convict him. It was the American power struggle in action. The episode was thoroughly absorbing soap opera, but the net result was hardened grudges and animosities between conservative

Republicans and liberal Democrats. In the 2000 presidential election, the Lewinsky scandal created considerable tension between Clinton and Vice President Al Gore, who wanted to associate himself with the Clinton administration for economic good times while otherwise distancing himself from the Clinton White House.

Republicans, impressed by Texas governor George W. Bush's record (he convincingly defeated Democratic governor Ann Richards in 1994 and was easily reelected against token Democratic opposition in 1998), nominated the eldest son of former president Bush. The Bush-Gore battle produced an exceptionally close fight in the electoral college (50.4 percent to 49.4 percent in Bush's favor). Bush's narrow victory in Florida of 537 votes was not confirmed for weeks, and millions of Democrats sincerely believed that Gore had really carried Florida and hence should be the president of the United States. The fact that Gore won the national popular vote by more than a half-million votes further embarrassed Republicans and contributed to Democrats' anger over Bush's victory.

The 2000 presidential election revealed a political landscape radically different from that of the 1980s. Bush versus Gore clarified the new sectional and regional strongholds of both major parties. In 2000 the sectional structure of the electoral vote represented another first in American history. Never before had the Republican Party won the White House despite losing the North. Bush barely defeated Gore by combining the entire electoral vote of the South with a mere 32 percent of the Northern electoral vote. From the Democratic side, the sectional pattern of the Gore vote was also remarkable. Clinton had constructed his national landslides by uniting modest Southern support with overwhelming Northern success. Gore almost won the presidency without a single electoral vote from the South.

Even more revealing was the new alignment of regional support. Bush achieved his electoral victory by uniting the South and the Mountains/Plains, the two Republican strongholds. He carried every Southern state and every Mountains/Plains state except New

Mexico for a total of 207 electoral votes in the Republican strongholds. After winning 57 electoral votes in the Midwest, Bush was 6 votes shy of the 270 electoral votes he needed for a majority. Seven electoral votes from Alaska and New Hampshire pushed Bush's national total to 271.

Gore performed almost as well in the Democratic strongholds of the Northeast and the Pacific Coast. He won 193 votes in the two Democratic regions, and he carried the Midwest (68 more electoral votes) as well. Going into the Republican strongholds, Gore needed 9 more electoral votes to win the presidency. Winning New Mexico provided 5. All Gore really needed to do was carry his home state of Tennessee, which had 11 electoral votes. Had Gore fulfilled the most basic expectation of presidential politics—deliver your home state—he would have become president no matter what happened in Florida.

The 2000 presidential election was the final contest based on the apportionment of electoral votes after the 1990 census. During the presidential elections from 1992 through 2000, the Republican strongholds were only slightly bigger than the Democratic strongholds (212 to 201 electoral votes). The Midwest, the nation's swing region, contained the remaining 125 electoral votes. In 2000 Bush won slightly more electoral votes than Gore (98 percent versus 96 percent) from a slightly larger base (39 percent versus 37 percent). Because Bush did a better job of maximizing the potential of his regional strongholds, he did not need a Midwestern majority in order to win. Gore, on the other hand, needed a bigger majority in the Midwest than he actually won. Holding West Virginia (5 electoral votes), for example, would have given Gore the presidency.

THE 2004 PRESIDENTIAL ELECTION

George W. Bush's first term reinforced existing patterns of support and opposition, leaving the nation almost as evenly divided in 2004 as it had been in 2000. The terrorist attack on the United States on 9/11/01 was the defining event of Bush's presidency. Al Qaeda's attacks on New York City and Washington produced Bush's war on terror. Just as President Roosevelt had responded decisively to the Japanese attack on Pearl Harbor in 1941, Bush moved swiftly to find and destroy many terrorist leaders in Afghanistan. Then, despite widespread Democratic opposition, he went to war against Saddam Hussein's regime in Iraq. Domestically, on the important issue of tax cuts, Bush sought to reverse Clinton and return to Reagan. Here Bush won by persuading Congress to pass legislation that cut tax rates for the millions of Americans who pay federal income taxes.

Bush's leadership on terrorism and the economy produced intense criticism from most Democrats, and in 2004 Senator John Kerry of Massachusetts emerged from the Iowa caucuses and the New Hampshire primary as the strongest Democratic challenger. Kerry was a Vietnam veteran who first came to national attention as a vigorous opponent of that war. As an experienced Northeastern Democrat, Kerry's liberal voting record in the Senate positioned him to run very well in the Democrats' regional strongholds but doomed him in the Republican strongholds.

Above all else, the 2004 presidential election was a national referendum on George Bush. His decisions on terrorism, the war with Iraq, and the economy profoundly divided the nation. Because Republicans rely strongly on white support and because whites in every region cast the overwhelming majority of all votes, it is important to examine white opinion on these issues (see figure 6.1) [6]

The shock and horror of 9/11 brought America's response to terrorism to the forefront of presidential politics. When white voters were asked who they trusted to handle terrorism, "only George Bush" overwhelmed "only John Kerry" by 56 percent to 26 percent. On this crucial national-security issue, Bush's substantial lead commenced in the Northeast, increased in the Pacific Coast and the Midwest, and then broadened to well over 40 points in the

Figure 6.1
Regional Differences in White Opinion

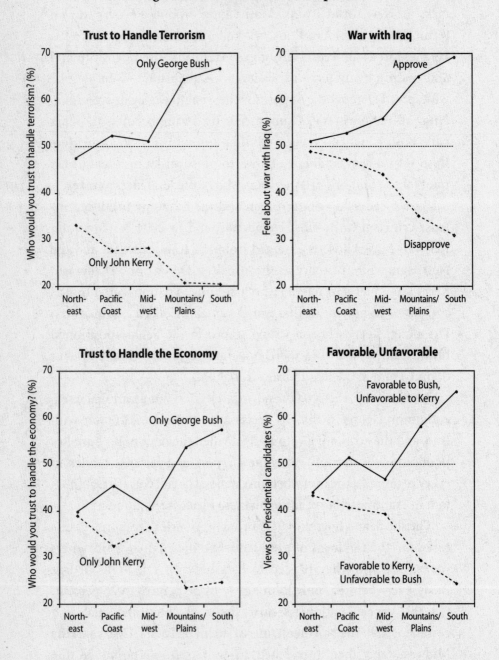

Trust to Handle Terrorism

Only George Bush

Only John Kerry

Who would you trust to handle terrorism? (%)

North-east · Pacific Coast · Mid-west · Mountains/Plains · South

War with Iraq

Approve

Disapprove

Feel about war with Iraq (%)

North-east · Pacific Coast · Mid-west · Mountains/Plains · South

Trust to Handle the Economy

Only George Bush

Only John Kerry

Who would you trust to handle the economy? (%)

North-east · Pacific Coast · Mid-west · Mountains/Plains · South

Favorable, Unfavorable

Favorable to Bush, Unfavorable to Kerry

Favorable to Kerry, Unfavorable to Bush

Views on Presidential candidates (%)

North-east · Pacific Coast · Mid-west · Mountains/Plains · South

Mountains/Plains and the South. Any Democratic presidential candidate with low numbers on the fundamental question of handling terrorism—ranging from a high of 33 percent in the Northeast down to one-fifth of white voters in the South and the Mountains/Plains—faces severe problems of credibility as a potential commander in chief.

When asked whether they approved or disapproved of the war with Iraq, white voters again split along regional lines, 59 percent to 41 percent. However, white opinion was much more evenly divided in the Democratic strongholds than in the Republican strongholds. On the central issue of "trust to handle the economy," Bush maintained a sizable advantage over Kerry only in the South and the Mountains/Plains. Northeastern whites were closely divided between the two candidates; Pacific Coast whites were more pro-Bush, and in the Midwest, where many states had experienced sizable job losses, white opinion was closer to the Northeast than any other region.

For white voters, the political bottom line concerning Bush and Kerry appears in the chart labeled "Favorable, Unfavorable." Here the percentage of whites favorable to Bush and unfavorable to Kerry is compared with the percentage of whites favorable to Kerry and unfavorable to Bush. On this matter, Bush led Kerry by 15 points, 53 percent to 35 percent, in the nation. Because Republicans run so poorly among minorities, they always need a huge advantage among whites to produce majorities among all voters. Only in the South and the Mountains/Plains were Bush so strong and Kerry so weak that—aside from Florida, New Mexico, Arizona, Colorado, and Nevada—the Democrats basically conceded the election. In the Northeast and the Pacific Coast, the Republicans' relative weakness among whites meant that they were compelled to do the conceding. Bush's modest white advantage in the Midwest highlighted that region as a true battleground in presidential politics. In all four of the key issues shown in the figure, sharp divisions are readily apparent between the Northeast and the Pacific Coast versus the South and the Mountains/Plains.

Bush's leadership of the war on terror, especially his decision to attack Iraq, intensified the sectional and regional cleavages established in 2000. Only in three states—New Mexico, Iowa, and New Hampshire—were the results of the presidential election different from those in 2000. America's power struggle thus remained exceptionally competitive. Bush defeated Kerry by 53 percent to 47 percent in the electoral college and 51 percent to 48 percent in the national popular vote.

Table 6.1 shows how Bush achieved his close victory in the electoral college. In the new American sectionalism, Republicans depend heavily on sweeping the South. In 2004 the South contained 6 more electoral votes than it did in 2000, and Bush won all 153 of these votes. Based on his Southern performance, Bush then needed only 117 (30 percent) of the 385 electoral votes found in the rest of the nation. By winning 133 (35 percent) of the North's electoral votes, Bush finished with a grand total of 286. Kerry's failure to carry any Southern state meant that he needed at least 270 electoral votes from the North. Although he won 65 percent of the Northern electoral vote, he needed 70 percent in order to offset his Southern defeats.

In 2004 as in 2000, the sectional imperatives for the two parties were the exact opposite of the old Battlefield Sectionalism of Northern Republicans versus Southern Democrats. The new American sectionalism aligns a Republican South versus a Democratic North. Even more important, America's old sectionalism has given way to a new American regionalism, a pattern of conflict in which Democrats and Republicans each possess two regional strongholds and in which the Midwest, as the swing region, holds the balance of power in presidential elections.

In 2004 President Bush won all 221 electoral votes in the combined South and Mountains/Plains. Because the Republican strong-

Table 6.1
Unity and Size: The Sectional and Regional Structure
of the 2004 Presidential Election*

Political Unit	Partisan Unity				Size	
	Rep	Dem	Rep	Dem	2004 EV	
United States	286	252	53%	47%	538	100%
South	153	0	100%	0%	153	28%
North	133	252	35%	65%	385	72%
Republican strongholds	221	0	100%	0%	221	41%
South	153	0	100%	0%	153	28%
Mountains/Plains	68	0	100%	0%	68	13%
Midwest	62	58	52%	48%	120	22%
Democratic strongholds	3	194	2%	98%	197	37%
Pacific Coast	3	77	4%	96%	80	15%
Northeast	0	117	0%	100%	117	22%

* Rep = Republican; Dem = Democratic; EV = electoral vote. Calculated by authors.

holds were a little larger in 2004 than in 2000 (they gained 9 electoral votes from the 2000 census), Bush emerged from the Republican strongholds needing only 49 more electoral votes to win the presidency. After taking 3 in Alaska, Bush needed 46 of the Midwest's 120 electoral votes (38 percent). He won 62. Bush's 51 percent to 49 percent victory in Ohio was the key to his national success. Without Ohio's 20 electoral votes, Bush would have lost the presidency by 4 votes. Ohio was the Republicans' only big-state victory outside the South.

As the resolutely anti-Bush option, Kerry easily unified the Democratic regional strongholds. By picking up New Hampshire, Kerry swept the Northeast (117 electoral votes). Kerry then won 77 more in the Pacific Coast for a grand total of 194 electoral votes in the Democratic strongholds. Yet because the Democratic base was slightly smaller in 2004 (losing 4 electoral votes compared to 2000), Kerry still needed 76 electoral votes in order to reach 270. Given Bush's total domination of the Republican strongholds, the Midwest was again the decisive battleground region. Kerry required a sizable majority—63 percent—of the Midwestern electoral vote in order to offset his defeats in the South and the Mountain/Plains. By winning only 58 votes in the Midwest, Kerry finished the election 18 votes shy. Had Kerry secured one more big state—either Florida in the South or Ohio in the Midwest—he would have defeated Bush. In both Ohio and Florida, the Bush campaign mounted impressive grassroots campaigns that produced close but solid Republican victories. Bush won Florida by more than 380,000 votes and Ohio by almost 120,000.

The 2004 exit polls show how Bush and Kerry fought such a close battle. The two parties obviously employ different starting points for constructing winning coalitions. Republicans begin with whites, and Democrats start with racial and ethnic minorities. The partisan unity and the number of white voters versus minority voters tell the national story. Republican strategists rarely speak in public about their party's strength among white Americans, but the general realities are well understood. Republicans always need a substantial white majority—in the high 50s—in order to be competitive nationally. Nonetheless, they do not attempt to win the presidency with white votes alone. As Republican strategists like Karl Rove fully understand, Republicans additionally need a sizable percentage of minority votes—in the neighborhood of the high 20s to low 30s—in order to secure overall national majorities.

Because Democrats typically win overwhelming majorities—

ordinarily in the 70s—of the total minority vote, they never need to win a majority of the white vote in order to achieve a majority among all American voters. Instead, what Democrats need is a sufficiently large minority of the white vote, generally in the mid-40s. In 1996, for example, Clinton won 44 percent of the national white vote. Although they do not draw public attention to their party's weakness among white voters, Democratic strategists are well aware that the party's loss of white support is central to the Democrats' narrow national defeats in 2000 and 2004.

In 2004 white voters outnumbered minority voters by 3 to 1 (77 percent to 23 percent). Bush got his 51 percent of the national vote by combining 58 percent of the very large white vote with 27 percent of the much smaller minority vote. Kerry achieved his 48 percent by attracting 71 percent of the minority vote but merely 41 percent of the white vote.

The competing party imperatives appear clearly when size is related to unity. Multiplying the size of the white vote by Bush's white share (77 x .58) produces Bush's white contribution of 45 points. Thus despite his emphatic success among whites, Bush was still well short of a national majority. Bush then secured his national victory by winning a modest share of the total minority vote (23 x .27 = 6 percent). Whereas Bush relied primarily on white support, Kerry's campaign started from the imperative to win as big a victory as possible from as many minority voters as possible. Kerry's minority contribution (23 x .71) yielded him 16 percent of the national vote. He therefore needed 34 more points from white voters to achieve a national majority. His weak performance among whites (77 x .41 = 32) resulted in his close national defeat.

The national perspective is important because it determines whether or not a president possesses the political legitimacy earned through overall national support. George Bush began his first term under the double burden of a razor-thin and fiercely contested electoral college victory, compounded by his defeat in the popular vote. In 2004 clear victories in the popular vote as well as in the electoral college gave Bush much greater legitimacy in his second term.

National imperatives, however, disguise contrasting regional dynamics of size and partisan unity. America's power struggle involves very different regional realities. In all five regions, whites constitute the vast majority of all voters, and in each region Democrats consistently win strong majorities from minority voters. Under these circumstances, the partisan division of the large white vote becomes a key factor in regional success or failure. Bush's close national victory was a composite of decisive Republican victories in the South and the Mountains/Plains, impressive Democratic victories in the Northeast and the Pacific Coast, and a tie in the Midwest.

In the Republican strongholds, overwhelming white support in the South (70 percent) and the Mountains/Plains (65 percent) combined with respectable minority support to produce Bush landslide victories. The deadlock in the Midwest resulted from a much smaller Republican advantage among whites (55 percent to 44 percent) plus a stronger Democratic vote among minorities (78 percent to 20 percent). Only the small size of the minority electorate (16 percent) prevented Democrats from winning a clear victory in the Midwest. And in the Democratic strongholds, the Republicans' dependence on large white majorities ensured their easy defeat. Any region in which Democrats can consistently neutralize the white vote while sweeping the minority vote is an automatic Democratic stronghold. Democrats remained much more competitive among white voters in the Northeast (50 percent) and the Pacific Coast (48 percent) than elsewhere in the United States.

Figure 6.2 shows the regional presidential vote in 2004 for whites, New Minorities, African Americans, and all voters. Consider first the chart labeled "Whites." When the five regions are aligned from the Northeast and the Pacific Coast on the left to the Midwest in the middle and the Mountains/Plains and the South on the right, the

Figure 6.2
Presidential Vote by Race, Ethnicity, and Region

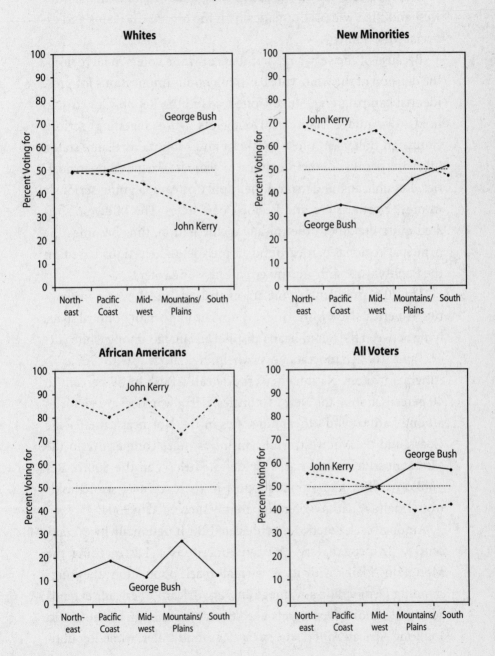

image of white voters appears as "the white funnel." A close division of white voters in the Democratic strongholds broadens in the Midwest and then widens dramatically in the Mountain/Plains and especially the South.

Because of the very large numbers of white voters in all regions, the division of the white vote has tremendous implications for presidential campaigning. Huge white leads in the Republican strongholds discourage national Democrats from investing serious campaign dollars in most Southern and Mountains/Plains states. Likewise, because of their inability to generate sizable white majorities, Republicans understand the futility of campaigning seriously in most Northeastern and Pacific Coast states. The Midwest, situated quite literally in the middle of the nation, thus becomes the principal regional battleground in presidential elections based on the Republicans' slim advantage among white voters.

The 2004 presidential vote among Latinos and Asians is instructive. America's New Minorities occupy the important political space lying between the Republicans' distinct advantage among white voters and the Democrats' overwhelming success with African-American voters. Nationally, Kerry defeated Bush by 59 percent to 40 percent among the New Minorities. Kerry won decisive victories among Latinos and other minorities in the Northeast, the Pacific Coast, and the Midwest, while Bush was more competitive in the Mountains/Plains and narrowly defeated Kerry in the South. Republicans' efforts to attract support in their regional strongholds from (mainly) Latino voters apparently succeeded in 2004.

Among black voters, Kerry defeated Bush nationally by 86 percent to 13 percent (see "African Americans"). Disregarding the Mountains/Plains with its very small black population, the longstanding Democratic advantage among African Americans extends across all regions. Democrats need to secure a margin of about 9 to 1 among African Americans in battleground states, while Republicans strive to expand their appeal from 10 percent to 12 percent into the mid-teens.

The chart for "All Voters" reveals the new regional bottom line of presidential elections. By sweeping the African Americans, winning impressive majorities among the New Minorities, and running even among white voters, Kerry achieved impressive victories in the Northeast (56 percent to 43 percent) and the Pacific Coast (53 percent to 45 percent). Bush won even greater victories in the Mountains/Plains (59 percent to 39 percent) and the South (57 percent to 42 percent). Large white majorities and competitive showings among the New Minorities enabled Bush to offset losses among African Americans in the two Republican strongholds. In the Midwest, Bush barely won (50 percent to 49 percent) among all voters.

Because of the Republicans' heavy dependence on white support, we need to examine Bush's white vote more closely. We begin with ideology because it has been the driving force in the Republicans' long-term strategy to become a much more competitive minority party. The Republican ideological strategy has been straightforward: ignore the white liberals, split the white moderates, and sweep the white conservatives. Nationally, Bush won 90 percent of the conservatives, 52 percent of the moderates, and 15 percent of the liberals. The Republican partisan strategy was similar: unify the white Republicans, neutralize the white independents, and attract more than one-tenth of the white Democrats. Across the nation, Bush won 94 percent of the Republicans, 51 percent of the independents, and 13 percent of the Democrats.

When conservative independents are added to Republicans to form the Republican base and liberal independents are added to Democrats to produce the Democratic base, the combined impact of party and ideology can be assessed. The Republican objective was to win more than nine-tenths of the Republican base, divide the moderate independents, and attract at least one-tenth of the Democratic base. In the 2004 election, Bush won 93 percent of the Republican base, 48 percent of the moderate independents, and 14 percent of the Democratic base. Kerry won 86 percent from his base, 50 percent from the moderate independents, and 6 percent from the Republican base.

Nationally, Bush did a better job than Kerry of unifying his partisan base, while Kerry narrowly defeated Bush among the white moderate independents. Party and ideology heavily structured the white vote for both candidates. Aside from modest fluctuations that usually favored Bush in his strongholds, the vote within each category was fairly stable across the five regions. A power struggle dividing whites by party and ideology consistently aligns white voters in every region.

The distinctive feature of the regions appears quite dramatically in the relative sizes of the white partisan bases. In the Northeast—and only in the Northeast—white Democrats plus liberal independents outnumbered white Republicans plus conservative independents. Here the Republican cause was indeed hopeless. A modest Republican size advantage first appears in the Pacific Coast and then broadens slightly in the Midwest. Only in the Mountains/Plains and the South did the Republicans secure truly large partisan and ideological advantages among white voters. In the South, to take the best example of Republican strength, 62 percent of white voters were Republicans plus conservative independents, while a mere 27 percent were Democrats plus liberal independents. The huge white Republican base in the South voted 96 percent to 4 percent in favor of Bush.

Republicans have established their two regional strongholds by leveraging ideology and party among the large white electorate. Absent a substantial Republican size advantage among whites, however, Republicans would not be competitive in presidential politics. In the Northeast, the Pacific Coast, and the upper Midwest, Democrats could combine overwhelming minority support with sizable white partisan bases and thereby produce their own strongholds.

Grouping white voters according to their religion and, when appropriate, their gender—evangelical Protestants, nonevangelical Protestant men and women, Catholic men and women, and non-Christians—further reveals areas of strength and weakness in the Bush vote. The national range in Bush's vote was very wide among different white religious groups. Among Protestants, the president's share of the vote ranged from 79 percent among evangelicals, to 59 percent among nonevangelical men, to 50 percent among nonevangelical women. A large majority of Catholic men (59 percent) voted for the president, as did a smaller majority (53 percent) of Catholic women. Bush lost decisively (30 percent) among non-Christians.

Evangelical Protestants voted overwhelmingly for Bush in every region. The Republicans' reliance on evangelical Protestants helps them dominate their strongholds and stay competitive in the Midwest. In the Democratic strongholds, however, such conspicuous support from evangelical Protestants is a surefire losing approach, one that puts the Republicans permanently on the defensive.

By smaller but still impressive margins, nonevangelical white Protestant men favored Bush everywhere except in the Northeast. Bush did especially well among these voters in the South, the Mountains/Plains, and the Pacific Coast. On the other hand, while the president won large majorities from nonevangelical Protestant women in the South and the Mountains/Plains, these voters rejected Bush by sizable margins in the Pacific Coast, the Northeast, and the Midwest.

White Catholics, once a mainstay of the Democratic Party, voted Republican in every region except the Pacific Coast. Large majorities of Catholic men voted for Bush in the South, the Mountains/Plains, the Midwest, and the Northeast. Only in the Pacific Coast did Bush narrowly lose. Substantial majorities of Catholic women in the Republican strongholds supported Bush over Kerry, as did a smaller majority in the Northeast. Midwestern Catholic women, however, evenly divided their votes, and in the Pacific Coast a large majority of female Catholics vote against Bush. Non-Christians in every region strongly preferred Kerry to Bush.

The profile of Bush's white support in 2004 was one of great strength in the Republican strongholds offset by considerable weakness in the rest of the nation. By making conservatism and evangelical Protestantism their leading edges, Republicans have implemented a strategy that is more likely to produce narrow national victories or defeats than landslides. The strategy works very well among whites in the South, Mountains/Plains, and the lower Midwest but is unlikely to succeed among whites in the Northeast, the Pacific Coast, and the upper Midwest. The Republican strategy implicitly concedes much of America to the Democrats.

How then did the Democrats make the presidential election close? Nationally, Kerry won decisive majorities from African Americans, non-Christian whites, and the New Minorities. In addition, he split the votes of white nonevangelical Protestant women. But Kerry trailed Bush by 7 points among white Catholic women and by 20 points among white Catholic men. Kerry became the first Catholic presidential candidate to lose Catholic voters. In addition, he ran behind Bush by 24 points among white nonevangelical Protestant men and by 58 points among white evangelical Protestants.

Despite losing white Catholics and evangelical Protestants in his home region, Kerry secured a comfortable victory in the Northeast by winning nonevangelical white Protestant men and women, African Americans, New Minorities, and non-Christian whites. In the Pacific Coast, by adding white Catholics (a majority of women and a plurality of men) as well as nonevangelical white Protestant women to his customary Democratic groups, he easily defeated Bush.

The Midwest was close. Kerry won African Americans, non-Christian whites, and New Minorities as well as nonevangelical white Protestant women. The white female Catholic vote divided evenly. The Democratic presidential candidate ran behind Bush among white evangelical Protestants, white Catholic men, and white nonevangelical Protestant men.

Kerry's defeats in the Republican strongholds were shaped in different ways. In the South, he ran ahead of Bush only among African Americans and non-Christian whites. Any Democratic candidate whose majorities are limited to these two groups is not competitive. In the Mountains/Plains, Kerry added Latinos and other ethnic groups to African Americans and non-Christian whites, but his weakness among the much larger groups of white Catholics and Protestants ensured his defeat.

The establishment of exceptionally strong Democratic bases in the Northeast and Pacific Coast is a momentous development in presidential politics. Unlike its situation in the 1980s, the Democratic Party has now forged a strong record of repeated successes in two key regions. No longer do Democrats face the Republican Party of Ronald Reagan, a party that routinely carried the Midwest, the Mountains/Plains, the Pacific Coast, and the South. Instead of a fight between a national Republican Party and a Democratic Party strong primarily only in the Northeast, the modern presidential battle gives both parties a big head start toward victory.

2008 AND BEYOND

Beginning in 1992 and continuing through 2004, the Democrats achieved a remarkable comeback in presidential elections. Political eras usually end when the dominant party squanders its advantage, is overcome by poor performance in office, and/or suffers overwhelmingly negative events that create opportunities for effective opposition. The GOP's national strength eroded significantly during George Herbert Walker Bush's presidency. Republicans were soundly trounced in the 1992 and 1996 presidential elections. Because Ross Perot's third-party campaigns in 1992 and 1996 contributed significantly to the Republicans' problems in the electoral college, we believe that the most realistic way to assess the presidential landscape in 2008 and beyond is to examine the party battle based on the 2000 and 2004 elections.

Table 6.2 summarizes the presidential battleground for 2008. It shows the sectional and regional structure of presidential politics in the United States. The results are based on a classification of the American states into three categories based on outcomes in the 2000 and 2004 elections: Republican states (those won twice by the Re-

Table 6.2
The Presidential Battleground in 2008 *

Political Unit	Partisan Unity				Size	
	Rep	Dem	Rep	Dem	2008 EV	
United States	274	248	51%	46%	538	100%
South	153	0	100%	0%	153	28%
North	121	248	31%	64%	385	72%
Republican strongholds	216	0	98%	0%	221	41%
South	153	0	100%	0%	153	28%
Mountains/Plains	63	0	93%	0%	68	13%
Midwest	55	58	46%	48%	120	22%
Democratic strongholds	3	190	2%	96%	197	37%
Pacific Coast	3	77	4%	96%	80	15%
Northeast	0	113	0%	97%	117	22%

* Rep = Republican; Dem = Democratic; EV = electoral vote. Calculated by authors.

publicans), Democratic states (those won twice by the Democrats), and swing states (those won once by each party).

America's presidential power struggle, examined according to electoral votes, is incredibly close. The twenty-nine consistently Republican states contain 274 electoral votes, slightly more than the 270 electoral votes needed to win the White House. Consistently Democratic jurisdictions (eighteen states plus the District of Columbia) total 248 electoral votes. Only Iowa, New Mexico, and New Hampshire—with 16 electoral votes among them—qualify as swing states. (Appendix 1 lists the fifty states and District of Columbia according to their presidential classification and electoral votes in 2008.) Such an even division of the electoral vote means that both Democrats and Republicans are in an excellent position to compete for the presidency. Only minor shifts would be necessary for a Democratic candidate to return to the White House.

The current sectional division between Democrats and Republicans has never before appeared in American politics. With its reliable Northern support limited to the Mountains/Plains and the lower Midwest, the Republican Party now depends disproportionately on Southern electoral votes to remain competitive in presidential elections. In addition, for the first time in the country's history, the most reliable Democratic states are located entirely in the North. Three clusters of Northern states—the Northeast, the Pacific Coast, and upper Midwest—give the Democrats their powerful new national base. Elections in California, Illinois, and New Jersey illustrate the Northern revival of the Democratic Party. These states went Republican six straight times from 1968 through 1988 before becoming consistently Democratic from 1992 through 2004.

In the 2000 and 2004 elections, the sectional division was stark indeed. The Democratic states contained 64 percent of the North's electoral vote, while the Republican states included 100 percent of the Southern electoral vote. Greater Republican unity in its sectional stronghold is offset by the huge size of the Democrats' Northern stronghold. Since there are 385 electoral votes in the North but only 153 in the South, the Democratic Party has entered the twenty-first century with realistic opportunities to win the White House without carrying a single Southern state.

From a purely sectional perspective, neither party has any real margin of error. In order to win presidential elections without the South, a Democrat must win 70 percent of the electoral vote in the rest of the nation. This Democratic Northern target can be met (Bill Clinton did so twice), but against strong Republican campaigners, it leaves Democratic presidential campaigns little room for failure. Assuming a Solid Republican South, Republicans now need only 30 percent of the Northern electoral vote to win the presidency. Since 1992, however, they have struggled to reach even that modest target. Persistent Republican weakness in the urban-industrial states of the North is one of the most important features of recent presidential elections.

Viewed in terms of regions, the Republicans operate with slightly larger electoral vote strongholds in the South and the Mountains/Plains than do the Democrats in the Northeast and the Pacific Coast. But the Republicans' slender edge in the total size of the respective strongholds (41 percent versus 37 percent of the electoral vote) still leaves it very dependent on splitting the Midwest. As a result, unless the Democrats can carry Florida, the Midwest will continue to be the principal region in play in presidential elections. Within the Midwest, Ohio has been and will continue to be the most important battlefield state. Neither party can afford to lose Ohio.

Democratic Presidential Priorities: Silent Northern Strategy?

Because of their enlarged Northern strongholds, Democratic presidential candidates are much more realistically positioned to win without any Southern electoral votes than they were in the 1980s. In 2004 Kerry occasionally speculated in public about this possibility. "Everybody always makes the same mistake of looking South,"

Kerry told a New Hampshire audience. In fact, Kerry argued, "Al Gore proved he could have been president of the United States without winning one Southern state, including his own."[7] Indeed, both Kerry and Gore came very close to winning the presidency despite losing the entire South.

The Democrats' electoral college strategy is simplicity itself. Secure the base is the first rule of presidential politics. Winning all of the states carried by Gore and Kerry is therefore the central priority of a Democratic nominee. The Northeast has become solidly Democratic in presidential elections. Only New Hampshire ranks as a swing state, and the trends in that state favor the Democrats. New York, Massachusetts, New Jersey, Pennsylvania, and Connecticut are especially important Democratic states because of their large size and great reliability. Among the Pacific Coast states, California, Washington, Oregon, and Hawaii have had perfect Democratic records from 1992 through 2004, leaving only Alaska as a small Republican enclave. In the Midwest, Illinois, Michigan, Minnesota, and Wisconsin have all been revived as important Democratic states. Iowa has been the sole swing state in the region, and it will be an important battleground.

If the Democrats continue to carry their core states, they will be very competitive in presidential elections. Sweeping the consistently Democratic states in the Northeast, the Pacific Coast, and the upper Midwest would leave a Democratic presidential candidate only 22 electoral votes short of victory. The three swing states offer several opportunities for Democratic gains. After all, Kerry won New Hampshire and almost carried Iowa and New Mexico. And Democrats will obviously target the two big states—Florida and Ohio—which they narrowly lost in 2000 and 2004. Florida, because of its 27 electoral votes and its competitiveness, is the most important battleground state; Ohio, with 20 electoral votes, ranks a close second.

A Democratic candidate who can hold the 2000 and 2004 base and win either Florida or Ohio will return the Democrats to the

White House. A Democrat who could hold the Democratic strong-holds but run more effectively in Ohio and elsewhere would be for-midable in 2008. New York senator Hillary Clinton, presumably guided at every step of the way by former president Bill Clinton, might be such a contender. Because the liberal wing of the Demo-cratic Party is much stronger in primary electorates than it was in 1992, the time may be ripe for the nomination of a full-fledged lib-eral candidate.

If Democrats wanted to penetrate beyond their regional strong-holds, a Democratic governor experienced in working effectively with a Republican legislature might have executive skills useful in the White House. Whether a more centrist Democrat could now win the party's presidential nomination or serve as a vice presidential candidate with the potential to bring some Southern and Mountains/Plains states into the Democratic coalition remains an open question.

Republican Presidential Priorities: Silent Southern Strategy?

For Republicans, the landslide elections of the 1980s have faded to a distant memory. Reagan reestablished the GOP as a highly compet-itive minority party, not as a new majority party. Among Reagan's many positive qualities for the Republican Party was his strength in California and other Pacific Coast states. Following his retirement, no California Republican has emerged as a major presidential can-didate, and California's changing demographics have undermined Republican prospects in presidential elections. Instead, Texas (the Bushes, father and son) and Kansas (Bob Dole) have supplied recent Republican presidential nominees. Kansas and Texas are safely Re-publican in presidential elections, giving the Republicans no addi-tional electoral votes.

Finding strong presidential candidates outside the South would be one way to regain competitiveness in the North. Former New York mayor Rudolph Giuliani and Senator John McCain of Arizona, for example, could be strong general election candidates provided that either could generate enthusiastic support in Republican presidential primaries dominated by conservative voters. Another Republican presidential nominee from the South would probably run stronger in Republican primaries than in the general election.

If the Democrats can almost win the presidency merely by securing their reliable states, the Republicans can actually do so provided that they continue to win all their reliable states. Whereas the Democrats' approach now amounts to a silent Northern strategy, the Republicans start with a silent Southern strategy. Unifying the Solid South is more vital to Republican success than ever before. With 153 electoral votes, the South is America's largest region. For the Republicans to win, they first need to carry all eleven Southern states. Although the Republicans should easily carry most of these states, Florida is obviously the South's most important competitive state. Depending on the Democratic ticket, other states, such as Virginia and Arkansas, might be brought into play as well. As a result, Republicans cannot simply assume that they can always unify the South.

Should Republicans again sweep the South, they still need 117 electoral votes from the North. Their second priority is to carry their areas of relative strength in the Mountains/Plains. Its small size is its main weakness in presidential politics. Together the two Republican strongholds contain 41 percent of the electoral vote.

Like the Democrats, Republicans must hold their regional strongholds and remain highly competitive in the lower Midwest. In the 2000 and 2004 presidential elections, Republicans won twice in Indiana, Missouri, Kentucky, West Virginia, and Ohio. As the most competitive big state in the Midwest, Ohio is the key to Republican hopes nationally. For Republicans to remain competitive, they need to redevelop their strength in the Great Lakes states of the Midwest. In 2004 the Bush campaign devoted much attention to Wisconsin, Minnesota, and Michigan, only to be defeated once again.

THE TRANSFORMATION
OF AMERICAN SECTIONALISM

Because of the winner-takes-all tradition, presidential elections reveal the sectional structure of American politics with the greatest clarity. Winning victories in particular states encourages implicit sectional (and state) strategies. Today the broad sectional imperatives of the two major parties have been reversed. In 1992 and 1996, the Democrats solved their Southern problem by unifying the North and winning several Southern states. They nearly did so again in 2000 and 2004 by simply unifying the North. Northern size and Northern unity have become key Democratic advantages in presidential elections. With 72 percent of the electoral vote located in the North, a Democrat who can win 70 percent of the 385 Northern electoral votes can indeed be elected president despite losing the entire South. Democratic gains in the Northeast, Great Lakes, and Pacific Coast make a silent Northern strategy much more realistic in the 2000s than it was in the 1980s. Doing only slightly better in the Midwest or in the South is the principal challenge for the Democrats in 2008 and beyond.

With the Democrats' Northern revival, Republicans face a far more daunting sectional landscape than they did in the Reagan era. The new Republican formula for victory is to win every Southern state plus 30 percent of the total electoral vote cast in the North. To a remarkable extent, the party of Lincoln has been reconstructed as the party of Reagan and Bush. In the 1980s, the Republicans kept the North, added the South, and thereby achieved three national landslides. George H. W. Bush's lackluster performance in office undermined Republican coalitions across the North, and Clinton demonstrated that Democrats could target particular Southern states as well.

Republicans responded with George W. Bush, a much tougher and shrewder politician than his father. In 2000 and 2004, Bush narrowly won the White House with a sectional division never before engineered by a victorious Republican. He unified the South but was beaten by around 2 to 1 in the North. For Republican strategists, the most sobering feature of the 2000 and 2004 elections was the GOP's poor showing outside the South. In 2000 the new American sectionalism almost defeated Bush. By carrying the South, Bush needed only 31 percent of the Northern electoral vote to win the presidency. He obtained 32 percent, for a national electoral vote total of 271.

Starting with the Great Depression, it was obvious that the Republican Party's traditional Lincoln Strategy of unifying the North and writing off the South was an unrealistic approach to winning the presidency. Since 1952 the Republicans have attempted to solve their historic inability to compete in the South. Ironically, overcoming their Southern problem has created a new strategic problem: a Republican "Northern problem." Finding ways to compete more successfully in the North while also continuing to dominate the South have become the main sectional challenges facing Republicans in presidential elections.

7

THE POWER STRUGGLE IN THE HOUSE OF REPRESENTATIVES

FOR MORE THAN SIX DECADES, FROM 1930 through the early 1990s, Democrats almost always controlled the House of Representatives. Against this background of virtually assured Democratic rule, the most important development in the modern House has been the Republicans' 1994 breakthrough to sustained majorities. During the heyday of Democratic dominance, members of both parties believed that Democrats would win a majority of House seats in practically every round of elections. The modern power struggle is radically different. Today, Republicans and Democrats are acutely aware that—given the right short-term issues and events—control of the House of Representatives can be won or lost every two years. Permanent Republican rule is not the automatic assumption of those who serve in the Congress or observe its elections.[1]

The Republicans' victory in 1994 was based on gains in all five regions of the United States. After their initial surge, Republicans have maintained slim national majorities by solidifying advances in three regional strongholds: the Mountains/Plains, the South, and the Midwest. Democrats have relied on their two regional strongholds—the Northeast and the Pacific Coast—to remain a highly competitive minority. The most significant factor in the Republican advance has been its rise in the South, a partisan realignment of such scope and depth that it propelled the party into majority status in the House. Shifts of great interest—as well as important continuities—have occurred in the other four regions. History provides the necessary perspective to appreciate the current power struggle in the House of Representatives.

THE NATIONAL PATTERN

As it did for the presidency and the Senate, the Great Depression destroyed the Republicans as a governing majority in the House of Representatives. Democrats immediately capitalized on the biggest political earthquake since the Civil War. After barely winning the House in 1930, Democrats then elected speakers in all but two of the Congresses before the 1994 elections. Landslide Democratic victories in the 1930s gave way to much closer party battles during the 1940s and much of the 1950s. Nonetheless, Republicans never regained their pre–Great Depression strength. Their rare House victories came in 1946 (the first contest after World War II) and 1952 (General Dwight Eisenhower's presidential coattails were helpful).

Steady Democratic control for three generations was an amazing achievement. The House of Representatives became America's most reliably Democratic institution. Apart from the mid-1940s and early 1950s, members of Congress whose judgment was guided by realism understood that Democrats would constitute the majority. Assured Democratic control moderated the partisan temperature of the chamber. Pitched battles between the parties did occur from time to time, but House Republicans could not afford to contest every conceivable issue and fight every possible fight. As members of an uncompetitive minority party, Republicans needed the good will of their Democratic counterparts to secure even sporadic benefits for their districts.

Nor was ideological purity a prominent feature of the congressional party system that emerged during the New Deal. The Democratic majority was ideologically diverse, ranging from Northern big-city liberals and moderates to rural and small-town conservatives from the South. Across the nation, Democrats were united by their support for popular New Deal programs that provided direct benefits to their constituents—like Social Security—as well as by their intense hostility to the GOP as the party of economic disaster.

Forced on the defensive by the economic collapse under their rule, Republicans were themselves split among conservatives, who opposed most of the New Deal; moderates, who began to accommodate a broader scope of legitimate governmental activities; and even a few liberals. Republicans who represented competitive districts were generally more practical, more apt to accomodate Democratic leadership, than were Republicans with truly safe seats.

In order to minimize fights within their own parties, Democratic and Republican leaders often acted to limit plain speaking on divisive issues. Democratic Speaker of the House Sam Rayburn, a Texan with a national perspective, came to believe that the Democratic caucus should be convened only for ceremonial duties. As Rayburn privately told former Speaker and vice president John Nance Garner in 1956, "You get in that [House Democratic] caucus, and a wild man from the North will get up and make a wild speech. Then someone from another section will answer him with a wilder speech. First thing you know, you've got the Democratic Party so divided that you can't pass anything."[2] Rayburn's solution was to separate his party's sectional adversaries. In the old days, neither liberal Democrats nor conservative Republicans could afford to insist on having their own way within their parties.[3]

Figure 7.1 tracks the national party battle in the House of Repre-

Figure 7.1
The National Party Battle, 1950–2004

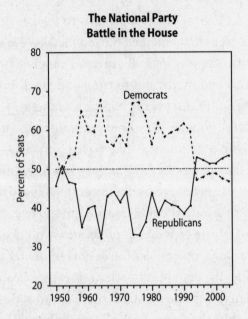

The National Party Battle in the House

sentatives from 1950 through 2004. This lengthy period of time provides the historical perspective needed to appreciate today's exceptionally competitive power struggle. In the early 1950s, the national party battle for the House was very close, and Republicans even held the majority in 1953–1954. Recessions during Eisenhower's presidency, however, revived doubts about Republican economic policy and ultimately produced impressive Democratic gains. In the 1958 elections, the Democrats' share of House seats rose to 65 percent. For the next thirty-six years, a period of eighteen consecutive elections, Democrats maintained highly comfortable national majorities in the House of Representatives.

Republican blunders—Barry Goldwater's disastrous presidential campaign and Richard Nixon's Watergate scandal had the greatest impact—periodically reinforced the Democrats' superiority. In 1964 Goldwater's abrasive conservatism temporarily gave Lyndon

Johnson the 2-to-1 Democratic majority he needed to pass his Great Society programs in the House of Representatives. Nixon's Watergate problems generated Democratic triumphs of similar magnitude in 1974 and 1976.[4] Between the late 1950s and the early 1990s, the national party battle in the House of Representatives was never really competitive. Republicans as well as Democrats generally took steady Democratic majorities for granted.

A new era commenced with the 1994 House elections. Benefiting from unusual circumstances, Republicans achieved their first national victory in forty-two years and their most impressive gains in a single election since 1946. Georgia congressman Newt Gingrich, a rising conservative leader, refused to accept permanent minority status for his party. Along with other conservative leaders such as Dick Armey and Tom DeLay, Gingrich engineered the Republicans' revival through their Contract with America. The contract was a set of conservative policy proposals—carefully selected for their popularity—dating back to Ronald Reagan's presidency. Nationalizing the House elections in a year of Democratic disillusionment, Republicans improved from 176 seats in 1992 to 230 in 1994. Their net gain of 54 seats was greater than the Democrats' advances of 48 seats between 1972 and 1974 and 49 seats between 1956 and 1958.[5]

Gingrich led the Republicans to power, but neither he nor his successor, Dennis Hastert of Illinois, expanded the initially slender Republican majority. Although Democrats failed to regain control of the House, they avoided the fate of the Republicans during the New Deal. The national party battle has remained exceptionally tight. Most House districts have been designed by state legislatures (or federal judges) to be very safe for a particular party. However, even if most representatives do not need to worry much about their own reelection, all House members have a vested interest in the success of their party. The current competitive party battle underscores the perpetually high stakes of every round of House elections.

Democratic defeat in the House of Representatives greatly intensified the American power struggle. The vast majority of Democrats and Republicans elected to the House now regularly vote as national partisans; that is, as conservative Republicans or as liberal Democrats. Because most congressional districts are safe seats, it is easier than before for representatives from both parties to sustain their House careers by voting and speaking in highly ideological and partisan terms. Neither party has many moderate partisans, and nominal partisans—whether conservative Democrats or liberal Republicans—have practically disappeared.[6] In Congress, ideology and partisanship are mutually reinforcing to a much greater extent than in the past.

SECTIONAL TRANSFORMATIONS

The intense national struggle to control the House of Representatives is the product, first of all, of very different trends in the North and the South. When comparing Democratic and Republican victory rates in the two sections, it is important to bear in mind that the North has historically contained approximately three times as many representatives as the South. In 1950 the North possessed 76 percent of all House districts. Population shifts have slowly diminished the North's size, but in the first decade of the twenty-first century, the thirty-nine Northern states still contained 70 percent of the 435 House districts. Southern representation has risen from 24 percent prior to the New Deal to 30 percent for the House elections of 2002 through 2010.[7]

Figure 7.2 compares the House party battle in the South versus the North. The Southern party battle has been gradually transformed from overwhelming Democratic domination—the truly Solid Democratic South of yesteryear—into a sizable Republican advantage (see "Southern Representatives"). As late as the 1950s, Democrats almost totally controlled the Southern House delegation. Nowhere else in the United States was one-party politics so

Figure 7.2
The Sectional Party Battle in the House, 1950–2004

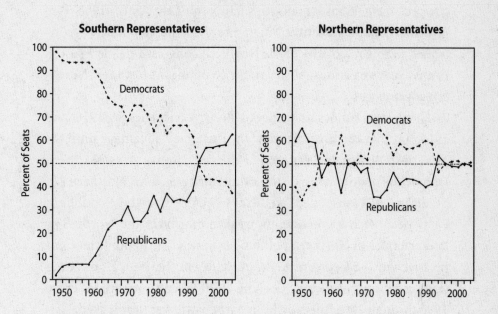

firmly established. With few Republicans in the electorate, and with Democratic state legislatures in charge of drawing House districts, two-party competition emerged very slowly in congressional elections. Even after the 1992 elections, Democrats still held over three-fifths of the Southern seats. Only in the final decade of the twentieth century did Republicans finally win a majority of the South's House delegation. In recent elections, Southern Republicans have consistently outnumbered Southern Democrats. The gradual reshaping of the Southern delegation continues to be a truly monumental development in American party politics.[8]

In contrast to the long-term Southern realignment, partisan volatility has characterized House elections in the North. The North was, of course, the traditional sectional home of the Republican Party. Huge Republican majorities in the 1920s disappeared in the face of sustained economic disaster. Yet despite the Great Depression, the Democrats' Northern surge was actually limited to the three elections of 1932, 1934, and 1936. Northern Republicans recovered their House majorities fairly quickly. Until 1958 (see "Northern Representatives" in figure 7.2) the Republicans controlled sizable majorities of the Northern congressional delegation. In that year's elections, however, the Republicans lost their Northern advantage.

Northern Democrats achieved decisive victories in 1958 and 1964, but they did not emerge with a sustained advantage until the 1974 post-Watergate election. For the next twenty years, Northern Democrats maintained a distinct superiority vis-à-vis Northern Republicans in House elections. Never before had the Republican Party been such a consistently weak minority in the North. The latest chapter in Northern politics began with the Republicans' impressive win—54 percent to 46 percent—in the 1994 House elections, a margin of victory that the GOP failed to maintain. From 1996 through 2004, the Northern party battle was deadlocked. Neither Democrats nor Republicans have yet found a way to regain comfortable majority status across the entire North.

Crucial sectional changes have occurred within each party. Beginning with the Great Depression, Democrats in the House of Representatives could always rely on their immense Southern megamajorities as a strategic hedge against any Northern weakness. In 1950, for example, Democrats won 54 percent of the nation's House districts. By winning 98 percent of the Southern districts (103 of 105 seats!), Democrats overcame their poor showing—a victory rate of merely 40 percent—in the North. A Solid Democratic South was the tacit starting point for sustained Democratic control of the House of Representatives. Starting in 1930, no Northern Democratic majority was ever required for a national victory so long as Democrats dominated the Southern delegation.

Southern supermajorities ensured Democratic control but compromised the national Democratic Party on the vital issue of civil rights. Historically, Southern Democrats in Congress offered strenuous and highly effective opposition to any Northern attempts to end racial segregation in the South. In the House of Representatives, segregationist white Democrats were not allowed to filibuster civil rights legislation. Nonetheless, their key positions in the party leadership and their numerous committee chairmanships offered many opportunities through the early 1960s to defeat the quest for racial freedom.

Passage of the 1964 Civil Rights Act and 1965 Voting Rights Act ended racial segregation in the public sector and expanded black political participation. These developments, combined with a growing white middle class, opened the way to two-party competition in Southern House elections.[9] Democratic state legislatures prolonged the Democratic advantage by drawing very few congressional districts that Republicans might win.

As time has passed, sectional tensions between House Democrats have diminished dramatically. Black Southerners became influential participants in Democratic primaries and general elections, compelling white Democratic politicians to accommodate to the desegregated public landscape. More recently, conservative whites have abandoned Democratic primaries. The ultimate result has been the disappearance of old-fashioned white conservative Southern Democrats in Congress. In the modern House, Northern Democrats and Southern Democrats have more in common than in the past. Fierce fights between Democrats and Republicans, not struggles between competing wings of a majority Democratic Party, characterize the new political landscape.

When the Democrats lost their House majority in 1994, they were defeated in the South as well as in the North. The Democrats' Southern surplus—a constant feature of House elections since 1874—vanished. It is unlikely to return. Since 1996 the Democratic Party has always won higher percentages of House seats in the North than in the South. In order for the Democrats to regain the House, sizable Northern Democratic surpluses will be required to offset the party's Southern deficits.

Republicans were historically a Northern party, and as late as 1950, that generalization was still literally true in the House of Representatives. With virtually no Southern Republicans, the GOP needed to win about two-thirds of all Northern districts in order to control the House. After the Great Depression, that Northern target was ordinarily an unrealistic objective. The 1952 House election, the Republicans' last national victory prior to 1994, illustrates the GOP's strategic sectional dilemma. Republicans won 51 percent of all House seats by combining 65 percent of all Northern districts with a mere 6 percent of the Southern seats.

At the midpoint of the twentieth century, Battlefield Sectionalism still remained the key to any Republican success. In 1952 Republicans emerged with a majority of the House delegation in twenty-seven Northern states. Democrats had majorities in every Southern state and six Northern states. Apart from Rhode Island, all of the Democrats' Northern strongholds bordered the South. Congressional delegations in the four remaining Northern states were evenly divided between the parties. Thus, nearly a century after the Civil War, classic American sectionalism continued to structure—and thereby severely restrict—Republicans' prospects in the House of Representatives. Their dependence on huge Northern majorities was at the root of the Republicans' inability to achieve national victories.

Beginning with their enormous Northern losses in 1958, the House Republicans entered a long period of permanent minority standing in the North as well as in the South. Penetrating the South became an even more urgent task for House Republicans once the party lost its capacity to generate sizable Northern majorities. Yet understanding the need to compete in the South was far easier for Republicans than actually defeating experienced Democratic incumbents. Four decades passed before the gap between Republican strength in the North and in the South was closed.

Unlike the situation in the North, the Republicans' tiny majority in the South in 1994 expanded in 1996 and grew to 63 percent of all seats in 2004. The Southern transformation, however, has not resulted in enormous Republican surpluses comparable to those produced by Southern Democrats in the one-party era. The modern South is far too diverse to produce a Solid Republican South similar in magnitude to the Solid Democratic South. Nonetheless, Southern Republican majorities have been vitally important to Republican control of the House of Representatives. Republican success in the South by no means guarantees Republican control of Congress. At the minimum, though, the partisan battles for the House of Representatives are highly competitive in every election cycle.

CHANGING REGIONAL SIZE: WINNERS AND LOSERS

Under the Constitution, the House of Representatives is reapportioned among the fifty states every ten years to reflect the changing distribution of the American population. To better understand the dynamics of the close national party battle in the House, it is essential to identify the regional winners and losers in congressional representation. Representation—and hence political power—has shifted quite dramatically among the five regions since the Second World War.

The South and the Pacific Coast have been the big regional winners (see figure 7.3). In the South, the number of House districts has risen from 105 in 1950 to 131 in the 2000s. Texas, the largest Southern state, now ranks second to California in the size of its congressional delegation. The Lone Star State has expanded from 21 in 1950 to 32 in 2002. During the same period, representation in the Pacific Coast states has more than doubled from 33 to 70. California is, of course, the giant of the Pacific Coast. Its delegation has grown from 23 to 53. The Mountains/Plains region has been essentially stable, its

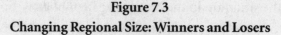

Figure 7.3

Changing Regional Size: Winners and Losers

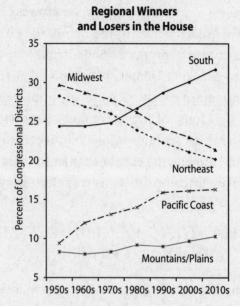

representation increasing only from 38 to 42 seats. Together these three regions, which possessed two-fifths of the House districts in 1950, now contain 56 percent of the nation's representatives.

America's great regional losers have been the Midwest and the Northeast. Since 1950 the Northeast has had 35 fewer House members (falling from 127 to 92), and the Midwest has lost 32 districts (declining from 132 to 100). New York, the nation's biggest state in 1950, with 45 districts, now possesses 29 seats. No other state has experienced such a severe loss in congressional representation. Gradual regional changes from decade to decade have accumulated to immense power shifts. In 1950 the combined Midwest and Northeast controlled three-fifths of the 435 seats in the House of Representatives. They now contain 44 percent of the districts.

When the regions are examined according to their size and partisan orientations, the most important generalization is that both political parties draw their strength from rising *and* falling regions. The Republican strongholds in the House of Representatives include the declining Midwest as well as the growing South and the slightly growing Mountains/Plains. The expanding Pacific Coast and the shrinking Northeast are the Democratic strongholds.

The 1980s marked a crucial transition in regional power shifts among the South, the Midwest, and the Northeast. For the first time, the South was slightly larger than either of the two Northern regions that were the historic bulwarks of Lincoln's Republican Party. In every subsequent decade, the gap between the South versus the Northeast and the Midwest has steadily increased. In the 2000s, the South is by far the largest American region. Projections for representation in the 2010s by the Washington research firm POLIDATA continue the trends of recent decades.[10] The reality of distinct regional winners and losers contributes to the intensity of the American power struggle.

REPUBLICAN STRONGHOLDS IN THE HOUSE

Within both parties, the enormous sectional gaps running from the 1870s through the 1960s have gradually narrowed to fairly modest differences. The Republican Party is no longer exclusively Northern, and the Democratic Party is considerably less Southern than in the past. Because of the North's immense size and internal variations, we need to move beyond sectional analysis to examine trends within the five American regions. We shall begin with the regional strongholds of the Republican Party.

In the House of Representatives, the Republicans' slim national majorities since 1994 have rested upon their success in *three* regions: the Mountains/Plains, the South, and the Midwest. Figure 7.4 charts

Figure 7.4
House Elections in Four Northern Regions, 1980–2004

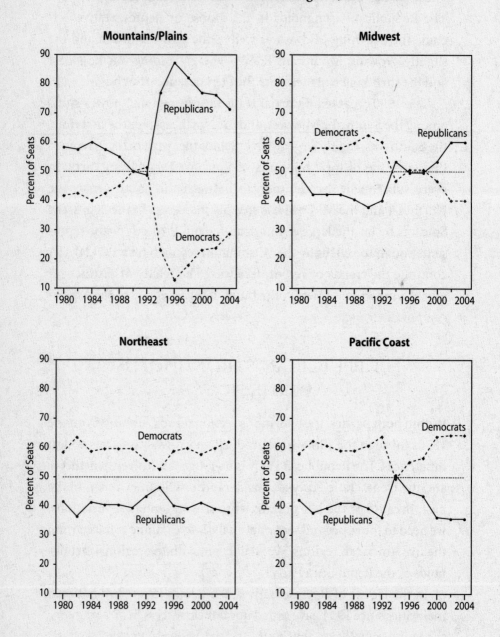

the party battle from 1980 through 2004 in the four Northern regions. Prior to the 1994 Republican breakthrough, the GOP was strong only in one region: the Mountains/Plains. Republican strength in this region dates back to 1942. After the Republicans reemerged during World War II as the region's majority party, they won 50 percent or more of its House elections except in 1948, 1958, 1964, and 1992, all bad years for the Republican Party nationally. Since 1994 the Mountains/Plains has consistently produced the most lopsided party battle of any American region. Yet with only forty-two districts, the Mountains/Plains is by far the nation's smallest region. None of the region's states has a large House delegation. After the 2004 elections, Republicans outnumbered Democrats in every delegation except North Dakota and South Dakota. They have been especially strong in the growing state of Arizona.

Developments in the South, of course, have been crucial to Republican success in the House of Representatives (see figure 7.2). During the 1980s, despite their tremendous success in presidential elections, Republicans remained a small minority of the Southern House delegation. After the 1990 election, they controlled only one-third of the Southern seats. In 1992, despite Republican weakness in the presidential election, Republican candidates made modest gains in the redrawn Southern districts. Two years later, with Republicans targeting Democratic incumbents in presidentially Republican districts, and with the Democrats placed on the defensive after the failure of President Clinton's health care initiative, Republicans achieved their breakthrough by winning 51 percent of the Southern districts. Republicans expanded their regional majority in 1996 and emerged in 2002 with victories in almost three-fifths of the Southern districts.

In 2004 House Majority Leader Tom DeLay of suburban Houston spearheaded an effort to redraw the Texas districts. He did so because Texas Republicans in the 2002 elections kept the governorship and the State Senate and—for the first time—won a majority of seats in the State House. After many ferocious battles (involving special legislative sessions and Democratic legislators leaving the state at various points to prevent legislative action), Republicans ultimately redrew the districts to maximum partisan advantage.

Ultimately, Texas Republicans engineered a heavy-handed but impressive advance. After the 2002 elections, the Texas House delegation consisted of seventeen Democrats and fifteen Republicans. Two years later, DeLay's hardball tactics produced a delegation where Republicans outnumbered Democrats by 21 to 11. Republican gains in Texas pushed the total number of Southern Republican representatives to eighty-two, the party's all-time high. The fallout from DeLay's redistricting battles continued in 2005, when DeLay was indicted in Texas for various irregularities connected to redistricting and forced to step aside as the Republicans' majority leader. In early 2006, confronted with eroding support within his own party, DeLay resigned his leadership position.

The national importance of the Southern transformation is obvious. Republican competitiveness in the South has made the GOP a national party and has given the party its firmest foundation in House elections since the 1920s. The destruction of the Democrats' long-standing Southern surpluses has reinvigorated the national party battle in the House of Representatives. After the 2004 House elections, Republicans were in the majority in eight Southern states: Florida, Texas, Virginia, Louisiana, Alabama, South Carolina, North Carolina, and Georgia. Democrats controlled the House delegations only in Arkansas and Tennessee. Mississippi's delegation was evenly divided.

Republican revival in the Midwest has been a third key element in the party's new national strength in House elections. The Midwest was, after all, a cornerstone of the Republican Party since its founding in the 1850s. Before the 1970s, Democrats had never controlled the Midwest's congressional delegation for more than three consecutive elections. Indeed, these landslide wins had come during the height of the New Deal's popularity, from 1932 through 1936. Democratic victories in 1948, 1958, and 1964 represented isolated spikes rather than the beginning of sustained Democratic advances.

The impact of the Watergate scandal, however, was quite different. Watergate profoundly damaged the Midwestern Republican Party. In 1974, following President Nixon's resignation, Democrats won 64 percent of the Midwestern House seats. More significantly, for the first time in the region's history, Midwestern Democrats continued to hold their impressive majorities—only 1980 was a fairly close election—for the next nine elections. Never before had the Democratic Party won majorities of Midwestern House seats for twenty straight years.

In 1994 Republicans reemerged with a regional majority of 53 percent. Unlike their counterparts in the Mountains/Plains and the South, however, Midwestern Republicans did not hold their gains. Not until 2000 did the party win another small majority of Midwestern seats. The decisive recent victories of Midwestern Republicans were achieved in the reapportionment and redistricting fights following the 2000 census. Republican legislatures and governors drew districts that produced net Republican gains. When the new district lines went into effect, Republicans emerged in 2002 with victories in 60 percent of the Midwestern seats. It was their strongest performance since the early 1950s. Republican strongholds as of 2004 included industrial as well as rural states: Ohio, Indiana, Kentucky, Michigan, and Iowa. Republicans achieved a modest advantage in Missouri, and they neutralized Minnesota and Wisconsin (both ties). Of the ten Midwestern states, Democrats controlled only Illinois and West Virginia.

DEMOCRATIC STRONGHOLDS IN THE HOUSE

Democrats have kept the national party battle for the House of Representatives closely competitive by winning impressive majorities in the Northeast and the Pacific Coast. In the Northeast, a region once as solidly Republican as the Midwest, Democrats have won majorities of the House delegation in every election since 1956. Northeastern Republicans have struggled to maintain a respectable minority presence. When the Republicans surged to their national victory in 1994, the Northeast was the only region in which Democrats held their majority of House seats (see figure 7.4). While the Northeastern Democrats' 1994 majority of 53 percent was their weakest performance since the early 1960s, they quickly recovered. Northeastern Democrats expanded their advantage in 1996 and emerged from the 2004 election with three-fifths of the region's seats.

After the 2004 House elections, Democrats outnumbered Republicans in seven of the Northeast's eleven state delegations. Democrats had commanding leads in Massachusetts, New York, and Maryland. In addition, Democrats held all the seats in Rhode Island and Maine and outnumbered Republicans slightly in New Jersey. Vermont's one independent representative caucused with the Democrats. Pennsylvania was the single large state in the Northeast with an impressive Republican majority, the result of a successful Republican gerrymander.[11] Elsewhere Republicans had small leads in three small states: New Hampshire, Connecticut, and Delaware.

The Pacific Coast also stands out as a source of reliable Democratic strength in the House of Representatives (see figure 7.4). Republicans controlled impressive majorities of the Pacific Coast delegation from 1946 (the year in which Richard Nixon began his national political career by winning a district based in suburban Los Angeles) through 1956. In 1958 the parties divided the Pacific Coast delegation. From 1960 through 1992, Democrats were consistently in the majority. The Republicans' share of the Pacific Coast delegation expanded from 36 percent in 1992 to 51 percent in 1994, only to decline sharply in later elections. In the elections from 2000 through 2004, Democrats held 64 percent of the House seats. All in all, the Pacific Coast produced in 2004 a Democratic surplus of 20 House seats (45 to 25). California, Washington, Oregon, and Hawaii gave the Democrats almost two-thirds of the Pacific Coast delegation in the early 2000s. Alaska, with a single representative, was the only Pacific Coast state with a Republican advantage in 2004.

The basic problem for Democrats in recapturing the House of Representatives is that the party has drawn large and reliable majorities from only two of the five American regions. Democratic success in the Northeast and the Pacific Coast has not been matched in the critically important Midwest. Republican success in the fierce reappointment and redistricting battles following the 2000 census is reflected in the declining Democratic shares of Midwestern House seats. In 2002 and 2004, Democrats won only 40 percent of the districts in the Midwest, their poorest showings in more than a half century.

DYNAMICS OF THE HOUSE PARTY BATTLE

Table 7.1 shows how the Republicans achieved their victory in 2004. The Republicans' national majority of 232 to 203 was due, first of all, to their strong performance in the South. A Republican Southern surplus of 33 seats offset its Northern deficit of 4 seats, thereby producing a national Republican surplus of 29 House seats. With their 82 Southern representatives, Republicans still needed a minimum of 136 seats in the rest of the nation in order to win a bare majority of 218. Republicans won 150 (49 percent) of the Northern districts.

Due to their weakness in the South, Democrats now require large Northern majorities to regain control of the House of Representatives. In 2004, because Democratic congressional candidates won

Table 7.1
The House of Representatives after the 2004 Elections*

Political Unit	Partisan Unity				Size	
	Rep	Dem	Rep	Dem	All Districts	
United States	232	203	53%	47%	435	100%
South	82	49	63%	37%	131	30%
North	150	154	49%	51%	304	70%
Republican strongholds	171	100	63%	37%	273	63%
South	82	49	63%	37%	131	30%
Midwest	60	40	60%	40%	100	23%
Mountains/Plains	30	12	71%	29%	42	10%
Democratic strongholds	60	102	37%	63%	162	37%
Pacific Coast	25	45	36%	64%	70	16%
Northeast	35	57	38%	62%	92	21%

*Rep = Republicans; Dem = Democrats. Calculated by authors.

only 37 percent of the Southern districts, they needed to win 56 percent—169 of 304 districts—of the North's House seats. The Democrats' actual Northern majority of 51 percent was 5 percentage points and 15 seats short of a national victory.

The distinctive feature of the modern congressional power struggle is the substantial Republican advantage in three regions. By adding the Midwest—a swing area in presidential elections and an area of Democratic strength in senatorial contests—to the South and the Mountains/Plains in congressional elections, the Republicans have enlarged their regional strongholds and left the Democrats with the Northeast and the Pacific Coast. In 2004 the two parties had identical congressional victory rates of 63 percent in their respective strongholds. Republicans won the national party battle because the South, the Midwest, and the Mountains/Plains together contain 273 House seats compared to 162 seats in the Northeast and the Pacific Coast.

As incumbents retire, we expect Republicans to make more advances in the South, and Democrats to win more seats in the Northeast. Fewer seats will probably shift in the Pacific Coast and the Mountains/Plains, leaving the Midwest as the region of greatest volatility in House elections. Although many Midwestern seats are now held by veteran incumbent Republicans with strong local ties and reputations for effectiveness that deter serious fund-raising by potential opponents, some of these districts could become intensely competitive in future elections. After the new redistricting goes into effect in 2012, Democrats may well be better positioned to expand their representation in the Pacific Coast because of favorable demographic trends.

LEADERS AND FOLLOWERS

The power struggle within the House of Representatives now routinely involves relentless confrontations between two large parties, parties whose leaders and followers are considerably more united by ideology than ever before. Very conservative Republican leaders preside over a conference populated mainly by very conservative Republican representatives. Likewise, very liberal Democratic leaders face a caucus of (by and large) very liberal Democratic members.

To place the modern Republican Party into perspective, it is instructive to consider the regional composition of the party fifty years ago. The 1952 House elections produced the final Republican victory guided by Lincoln's sectional strategy of uniting the North and—for nearly all practical purposes—writing off the South. All in all, the Republicans remained fundamentally a Northern party. Ninety-seven percent of the Republican House members represented Northern districts. The Republican Speaker in 1953 and

1954 was Joe Martin of North Attleboro, Massachusetts. Martin led a political party based mainly in the Northeast and the Midwest. Republicans from those two Northern regions accounted for nearly three-fourths of their entire party in the House of Representatives. Slightly less than one-quarter of House Republicans represented Mountains/Plains and Pacific Coast states. Of 106 Southern seats, Republicans managed to win only 6 contests.

After the 2004 elections, a transformed Republican Party maintained its modest national majority for the sixth consecutive election. Republicans from the South, only 3 percent of the party conference in 1952, accounted for 35 percent of the Republicans elected in 2004. Beginning with the 1992 House elections, the South had displaced the Midwest as the region with the most Republican representatives. Midwesterners, who accounted for nearly two-fifths of all Republicans in 1952, constituted only one-quarter of the House Republicans elected in 2004. In the Northeast, the Republican Party was a dramatically weaker presence. A region that had sent 79 Republicans to Congress in 1952 produced only 35 victors (just 15 percent of all Republicans) in 2004. The much smaller Mountains/Plains region elected only 5 fewer Republicans (30) than the entire Northeast. Only one-ninth of the Republicans came from the Pacific Coast. The South, the Midwest, and the Mountains/Plains together produced 74 percent of all Republicans elected in 2004.

The principal leaders of the new Republican majority originally came from the South. In the aftermath of the Republicans' 1994 breakthrough elections, Gingrich of Georgia was elected Speaker of the House, Armey of Texas became majority leader, and DeLay of Texas was chosen majority whip. House Republicans thus produced a leadership team drawn exclusively from very safe seats in the suburbs of (respectively) Atlanta, Dallas, and Houston. All three Republicans were very conservative in their philosophy of government, and all three ran in districts where their reelection was never in doubt. Inexperienced as leaders of a majority, together they put a highly "Southern" face on the new Republican majority.

When Gingrich became so controversial that he resigned the speakership in 1998, Republicans ultimately chose Dennis Hastert of Illinois as the new Speaker. Hastert was a low-key conservative from the distant Chicago suburbs. Avoiding the daily public controversies that Gingrich relished, Hastert put a calmer and more methodical face on the House Republicans. As political analyst Michael Barone has observed, "It has become apparent that for all his bear hugs, his penchant for listening to members, his Midwestern plainspokenness, Hastert is a formidable, aggressive, and partisan leader, of the kind often found in Illinois politics. Like a good coach, he has an appreciation for the talents of his players; but like a good coach, he wants very much to win." [12] Hastert's district, which gave George W. Bush majorities of 54 percent in 2000 and 55 percent in 2004, was far less overwhelmingly Republican than the districts of the Southern leaders. The 2000 Bush vote was much greater in the districts represented by Armey (72 percent) and DeLay (64 percent). Bush's majority was 65 percent in the district represented by Gingrich. In DeLay's new district Bush won 67 percent of the vote in 2004. [13]

Governing since 1994 with only tiny Republican majorities, Republican House leaders have put a premium on party discipline to support the leadership. We use *Congressional Quarterly*'s party-unity scores as a proxy for ideology. Representatives with scores of 80 to 100 are considered national partisans, those with scores in the 60 to 79 range are moderate partisans, and those scoring under 60 are nominal partisans. With Hastert as Speaker of the House and DeLay as the majority leader (Armey having retired), the Republicans were remarkably unified in their support of the party leadership. In 2004, 97 percent of the Republicans voted as national—that is, conservative—Republicans. Only 3 percent had voting records in the moderate range, and there were no nominal Republicans. [14]

Moderate Republicanism was limited mainly to a small minority of Northeastern representatives. Four of the thirty-five Northeastern Republicans—Christopher Shays and Rob Simmons of Connecticut, Michael Castle of Delaware, and Chris Smith of New Jersey—voted as moderate partisans. All represented districts (or a state for Castle) where emphatically conservative voting records would put their seats at risk. Like some of the Southern and Mountains/Plains Democrats (see below), survival at home required occasional departures from the leadership's wishes. With advancement within the Republican conference very dependent on party loyalty, and with plenty of highly conservative Republicans competing for committee and subcommittee chairmanships and leadership positions, moderate Republicans understood the difficulty of rising in the new Republican Party. Ideological purity reigned among most House Republicans.

Just as the rise of the Southerners and the decline of the Northeasterners have reshaped the Republican Party, so too have the House Democrats undergone remarkable regional transformations. Consider the regional structure of the House Democratic caucus in 1952. Sam Rayburn, of tiny Bonham, Texas, was the veteran Democratic leader. Rayburn's Texas delegation contained more Democrats (22 to 0) than any other state in the nation. Racially conservative white Southerners were almost a majority (47 percent) of all Democrats in the House of Representatives. By and large, the Southern Democrats were strenuously opposed to any serious federal intervention into Southern race relations. The Northeast and the Midwest each supplied one-fifth of the Democratic representatives. There were very few Democrats from the Mountains/Plains or the Pacific Coast (both 6 percent).

A half century later, the Democratic caucus was much less Southern, and the remaining Southern Democrats elected to the House were fully committed to civil rights. In 2004 there were more Democrats from the Northeast (28 percent) than from the South (24 percent). The Pacific Coast now contributed over one-fifth of the Democrats, while another fifth came from the Midwest. Only 6 percent represented Mountains/Plains states.

In 1952 the Northeast and the Pacific Coast accounted for only one-fourth of the House Democrats. Fifty years later, half of the Democrats represented districts in the Pacific Coast or the Northeast. Leadership fights have been revolutionized since Rayburn's era. Democrats from the most liberal American regions have been the main beneficiaries of the Republicans' Southern breakthrough. California (thirty-three) and New York (twenty), the two states with the biggest Democratic delegations to the House, together constituted one-quarter of the entire Democratic caucus. Sixteen percent of all House Democrats represent California districts.

When Richard Gephardt of Missouri announced his resignation as Democratic minority leader shortly after the 2002 House elections, California's enhanced power was demonstrated quickly and decisively. Nancy Pelosi, representing a San Francisco district that gave George W. Bush 15 percent of the vote in 2000 and 14 percent in 2004, easily became the most liberal Democrat ever selected as party leader in the House. (By comparison, Bush won 46 percent of the vote in Gephardt's district.)

The rise of a very liberal Democrat came at the expense of Texas Democrat Martin Frost. Both Frost and Pelosi had worked hard for years to become party leader. Although Frost was a staunch national Democrat, he was more concerned than Pelosi about putting too liberal a face on the Democratic Party. His Dallas district had produced a 2000 Bush vote of 48 percent, signifying a political environment much less completely Democratic than Pelosi's San Francisco district.

Brevity was the hallmark of the Pelosi-Frost confrontation. After conducting private soundings, Frost admitted defeat and withdrew his candidacy. The quick and decisive defeat of a liberal Texan by a highly liberal Californian symbolized a tremendous power shift within the Democratic caucus. Frost's humiliation continued as Texas Republicans obliterated his district. Forced to run in 2004 against Republican incumbent Pete Sessions in a Dallas district gerrymandered for the Republican, Frost was convincingly beaten.

Pelosi's easy victory was entirely consistent with the shift to an ideologically purer Democratic Party. Under her leadership in 2004, 89 percent of the House Democrats voted as national—that is, liberal—Democrats.[15] Only 10 percent voted as moderates, and 0.4 percent voted as nominals. National Democrats were especially concentrated in the party's regional strongholds. Ninety-nine percent of all Democrats elected from the Pacific Coast and the Northeast voted as liberals, compared to 72 percent of Democrats elected from the South and the Mountains/Plains. Midwestern Democrats were overwhelmingly (93 percent) national partisans. Moderate Democrats were relatively prominent (27 percent) only in the Mountains/Plains and the South. Like some of the Northeastern Republicans, a minority of the Democrats elected from those pro-Republican regions represented districts where it was good politics to distance themselves from the liberal leaders of their party.

Just as the parties in the modern House of Representatives differ in ideology, so too do they reflect very different patterns of religious, racial/ethnic, and gender diversity. According to information compiled from *The Almanac of American Politics, 2006,* 98 percent of House Republicans were white Christians. Nearly three-fourths of House Republicans were white Protestants, and almost one-fourth were white Catholics. The remaining 2 percent included three Latino Catholics from Florida, one Latino Baptist from Texas, and one Jewish representative from Virginia. There were no African-American Republicans in the House of Representatives, and women were merely a tenth of the Republicans.

House Democrats were more diverse in their racial, ethnic, religious, and gender makeup. Although white Christians remained a majority of House Democrats, they constituted only 55 percent of all members—much lower than in the past. White Protestants were 30 percent of the party, followed at 29 percent by racial and ethnic minorities. White Catholics were 25 percent, Jewish representatives made up 12 percent of the party, and those white Democrats who did not report a religious affiliation added a final 3 percent. Twenty-one percent of the House Democrats were women.

Thus many indicators show great differences in the ideology and social composition of the rival parties. House Republicans and House Democrats have more to argue about than ever before. The increasing diversity of the American population by race and religion multiplies the number of politically important groups with unique perspectives and thereby raises the stakes of controlling the House. Adding to tension within the chamber is widespread awareness that power can shift with the next election.

The Republicans' failure to increase their national majority since 1994 means that Democrats always have realistic fighting chances to retake the House. If Democrats can win considerably higher per-centages of seats in their regional strongholds, find ways to reduce their losses in the Republican strongholds, or do some of both, they can regain the majority in House elections. Whatever the outcomes of future elections, America's power struggle will continue full throttle in the House of Representatives.

8

THE POWER STRUGGLE
IN THE SENATE

FROM 1932 THROUGH 1980, DEMOCRATS GENER-
ally ran the United States Senate. During much of this time,
senators in both parties took Democratic control for
granted. The Democrats' success in the Senate was only slightly less
impressive than their record in the House of Representatives. In
the Senate, serious party competition commenced with the 1980
elections. Benefiting from Ronald Reagan's landslide presidential
victory, Republicans returned to the majority. Six years later, Democrats regained the Senate and kept it for eight years.

The 1994 Senate elections restored Republican majorities. Ever
since, with one brief exception, Republicans have retained formal
control of the Senate. Their post-1994 Senate majorities have rested
on an improved geographical foundation. In their 1980, 1982, and
1984 victories, the principal pro-Republican regions were the
Mountains/Plains and the Pacific Coast. Since 1994 Republicans
have been highly successful in the South as well as the Mountains/
Plains. Trading the smaller Pacific Coast for the bigger South has
been the key to improved Republican competitiveness.

In the Senate, neither party assumes continued Republican ascendancy. Partisan fights are based on ideologically driven disagreements over what constitutes wise public policy. These profound disagreements are given urgency by the realization that control of the Senate can in fact be won or lost in the next election. Unmitigated partisan politics thus permeates the modern power struggle between Republican and Democratic senators.

Achieving nominal majorities is one thing. Securing governing majorities is considerably more difficult. These observations apply with particular force to the Senate, a legislative institution whose rules and customs give much freedom of action to individual senators. Substantial Republican gains have not been converted into truly secure national governing majorities. Far from it. In fact, in neither branch of Congress have the Republicans been able to expand their initial victories into majorities reminiscent of Democrats' at the peaks of the New Deal or the Great Society, the sort of commanding majorities generally required to legitimize—not just enact—any bold agenda.

In the Senate, determined minorities have often blocked the legislative agenda of the party in power. The Senate filibuster has traditionally been the favorite weapon for exercising minority influence. Today the filibuster is the preferred tactic of the institution's minority party rather than of any particular minority within a party. In the modern Senate power struggle, the abiding objective of the party out of power is to frustrate the majority as often and as thoroughly as it can.

Leaders of the party in power usually need large majorities in order to pass controversial legislation. Although most senators typically vote as strong national partisans, neither party is completely made up of reliable members. Additionally, neither Democrats nor Republicans have come close in recent decades to securing truly impressive majorities.

The Senate's political arithmetic after the 2004 election illustrates the blocking process. Sixty votes are needed to defeat a fili-buster and bring an issue before the Senate. Assuming complete Republican unity, five Democrats would have to join fifty-five Republicans. On most truly controversial issues, of course, Republicans would not be completely united, and hence even greater support from Democrats would be required.

In 1994 Republicans surged to an impressive victory in the Senate. Nationally, the number of Republican senators rose from forty-three to fifty-three. The party advanced in the South, the Mountains/Plains, the Midwest, and the Northeast, and preserved a fifty-fifty split in the Pacific Coast. As time has passed, however, both parties have established two regional strongholds: the Mountains/Plains and the South for the Republicans versus the Northeast and the Pacific Coast for the Democrats. Neither party has secured a decisive advantage in the Midwest. As in presidential politics, the Midwest is the nation's swing region in Senate elections.

Just as in the House of Representatives, the Southern transformation was the principal element in the expansion of the Senate Republicans. After the 1994 elections, Republicans emerged with a clear majority of the region's delegation. Combined with long-standing majorities in the Mountains/Plains, the new strength in the South reestablished the Republicans as a competitive national party in the Senate. Although considerably weakened since the 1994 elections, Democrats have remained within striking distance of Senate majorities due to their growing strength in the Northeast and the Pacific Coast and their competitiveness in the Midwest.

THE NATIONAL PATTERN

The historical record makes plain the distinctive features of the Senate's current partisan battles. From the Civil War to the Great Depression, the Senate was the most reliably Republican institution in American government. The Grand Old Party controlled the Senate in all but five Congresses between 1860 and 1930. Apart from its brief efforts to elect senators from the South during Reconstruction, the Republican Party employed a purely Northern strategy to win the Senate. Taking advantage of the section's enormous size, Republicans could hold the Senate by winning around two-thirds of the Northern seats. Provided they met this target, Republicans could afford to concede all of the former Confederate states to the Democrats and still run the Senate.

For generations the Republican Battlefield Sectionalism strategy was extraordinarily successful. From 1858 through 1930, Republicans were *always* a majority of the Northern Senate delegation. On the rare occasions when the party lost the Senate, it never did so because it was defeated in the North. Instead, Republican defeats occurred only when the party failed to achieve the necessary 2-to-1 advantage in Northern Senate seats. Consistent success with this strategy vanished in the Great Depression. Winning two-thirds of the North's senators now became an utterly unrealistic target. From 1932 to 1940, Democrats won five straight Northern majorities. Even when Republican senators returned to the majority in the North from 1942 to 1956, their majorities were sufficiently large to produce national victories only in 1946 and 1952.

Under the combined impact of the Great Depression and President Franklin D. Roosevelt's popular leadership, Democrats emerged in 1932 as the Senate's normal majority party. Except for two isolated losses, Democrats held power until the 1980 elections. The Solid Democratic South was an invaluable cushion against any temporary Democratic weakness in the North. Liberal Northern Democrats and conservative Southern Democrats tacitly recognized that the Democrats' strength in the South was a huge advantage in controlling the Senate. The South's twenty-two safe seats always gave the Democratic Party a formidable head start toward national majorities. The party needed only to elect slightly more than one-third of the senators in the rest of the country to control the Senate.

Democratic control of the Senate for nearly fifty years was a truly impressive feat. Aside from a brief competitive period after World War II, the partisan balance in the Senate was not close. Republicans gradually accustomed themselves to the status of a permanent minority. Fighting (and losing) over every issue would simply irritate powerful Democratic Party leaders and committee chairmen, the very politicians whose support would be needed to bring home any tangible benefits to the Republican senators' states.

In the Senate, the Democratic Party's New Deal majority was ideologically diverse. Northern liberals and moderates wedded to Franklin D. Roosevelt's leadership joined Southerners to constitute large national majorities. The Southern Democrats, uniformly conservative on racial issues, were quite supportive of those New Deal programs that sent Yankee dollars to the region under terms that did not threaten the interests, values, and prejudices of local white Democratic elites.

Southerners loved the New Deal. "President Roosevelt's New Deal programs paid for Social Security, old-age assistance, and farm programs, and put unemployed Southerners to work," we have argued. "Millions of dollars helped to construct dams, reservoirs, harbors, highways, and airports. Federal money was political magic, a regional free lunch. It cost the South little because most Southerners did not earn enough money to pay federal income taxes."[1]

Senator Richard B. Russell's campaign in the 1936 Georgia Democratic primary illustrates the New Deal's great popularity in the South. Russell praised President Roosevelt and the New Deal to the skies. As he reminded one audience, "for the first time we have a government which is fair to the south, and the best friend this state and the south ever had."[2] Whites received explicit reassurance that Roosevelt's New Deal posed no threat to Southern racial traditions.

"This is a white man's country, yes, and we are going to keep it that way," Russell promised voters. "We are going to re-elect a president who won't put negro [*sic*] officers in the south. There are none in Georgia and there never will be with a democratic president in the White House."[3]

Russell's anti–New Deal opponent, Governor Gene Talmadge, had called for "the abolishment of the federal income tax," but the senator argued that eliminating income taxes would "take away all the farmers' benefit payments, drop all drought relief, cripple the postal service, disband the army and navy, and take away every dollar of compensation now being drawn by the disabled soldiers of this state."[4] In addition to these disastrous effects upon Georgians, Russell emphasized that "the big income taxpayers of the wealthy states" would pay most of the federal income tax. Not many Georgians were affected. "There are 16,000 persons who pay income tax in Georgia, paying $7,000,000," Russell asserted. "In return, there is paid into the state $66,000,000." As he explained to another audience, "New York pays in $27 per head and Georgia pays $2.70 per head, and that surplus money comes to us." In conclusion, Russell emphasized, "We'd be lost without the money which comes from the wealth of New York."[5]

Under these exceedingly favorable terms for Southern white Democrats—increased material benefits for the many at little direct cost (except for the wealthy few) combined with no direct challenges to white supremacy—the New Deal and President Roosevelt remained extraordinarily popular across the South. Russell beat Talmadge by nearly 2 to 1 in the Democratic primary. *The Atlanta Constitution* headlined the results: "Talmadge Crushed by New Deal Vote Throughout State."[6]

By the late 1930s, as the Republican Party revived in many Northern states, conservative Democrats from the South were positioned to exert tremendous positive and negative influence in the

Senate. Unlike many Northern Democrats, they never had to worry about Republican competition. As a group, they acquired tremendous seniority at a time when seniority really meant power on key committees and in the leadership. The size and unity of the Southern Democrats gave them extraordinary leverage. Twenty-two Southern Democratic senators, all of them racial conservatives, and many of them increasingly conservative on economic issues after the Depression ended, made up a formidable bloc inside the Democratic Party. They could vote with Northern Democrats to fund popular New Deal programs that brought tangible benefits to their states. And as circumstances warranted, conservative Democratic senators could align with conservative Northern Republicans to block or weaken Roosevelt's domestic agenda if his proposals were viewed as too liberal.[7]

Southern conservatives could thus exercise real power within the majority Democratic Party. Across the nation, Democrats were united by their hostility to Republicans and their general approval of Roosevelt's New Deal. Republicans, discredited by the Great Depression, were themselves split between conservatives and moderates. Neither liberal Democrats nor conservative Republicans could afford to insist on having their own way within their respective parties.

The vigorous modern power struggle to control the Senate appears in sharp relief when the national party battle is charted over the last half century (see figure 8.1). From 1950 through 1956, neither party had comfortable majorities in the Senate. Although Republicans had recovered from their Great Depression lows, they could never achieve impressive national victories. In 1958, against the backdrop of economic recession blamed on the Eisenhower administration, Democrats reasserted themselves as a dominant majority party in the Senate. Democrats gained sixteen seats, giving them an advantage of almost 2 to 1 in the entire Senate. For the next

Figure 8.1
The National Party Battle, 1950–2004

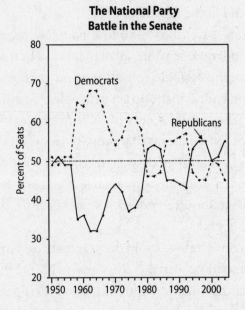

**The National Party
Battle in the Senate**

twenty years, Republicans did not seriously challenge the Democrats' majority. Starting in 1980, however, Democratic dominance yielded to a new pattern of much closer two-party competition. With Ronald Reagan heading the Republican ticket, Republicans reclaimed the Senate and held it for the next six years. Democrats regained the majority in 1986, and eight years later, in the 1994 elections, Republicans returned to power.

Since 1994 the national party battle for the Senate has remained very close. Republicans have retained their majorities except in 2001 and 2002. The 2000 elections produced a 50-to-50 tie, which subsequently gave way to a 51-to-49 Democratic advantage when Jim Jeffords of Vermont left the Republican Party, declared himself an independent, and then voted with the Democrats to elect Tom Daschle of South Dakota as the new Democratic majority leader. It was a rare example of a power shift produced by party switching rather than winning elections. In the 2002 elections Republicans reclaimed the Senate with a 51-to-49 majority, which expanded to a 55-to-45 advantage after the 2004 elections.

The modern Senate seesaw, while favoring Republicans more than Democrats, left no senator in any doubt that power could easily be won or lost with the next election. As in the House of Representatives, in the Senate the stakes of the next election remain permanently high. Under such circumstances, leaders of the party out of power are always on the attack, searching for the right combination of issues and events that will shift enough seats at the next election to defeat the majority party.

THE NEW SECTIONAL PARTY BATTLE IN THE SENATE

At the midpoint of the twentieth century, Battlefield Sectionalism still continued to limit Republican success in the Senate. The Republicans' inability to compete in the South and their unchanged dependence on huge majorities of Northern seats were the roots of their failure to achieve more than sporadic national victories. Such a total dependence on sustained 2-to-1 margins outside the South could not possibly serve as a realistic national strategy. If Republicans were going to compete for Senate victories on a routine basis, they had to become a genuinely national party.

Why has the Senate become such a highly competitive institution? In sectional terms, the simplest explanation of renewed national competitiveness is the collapse of the Solid Democratic South and the emergence of a Republican South. For well more than a century, Southerners had anchored the Democratic Party in the Senate. When the Southern Democratic surplus disappeared, the Republican Party no longer needed to win huge majorities of Northern Senate seats.

Figure 8.2
The Sectional Party Battle in the Senate

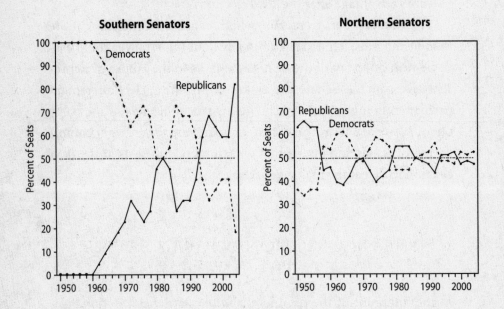

The modern tight national battle in the Senate is the product of strikingly different trends in the South and North (see figure 8.2).[8] Dramatic changes in the Southern delegation present a vivid contrast with much narrower partisan fluctuations in the North. The Southern party battle has gradually shifted from total Democratic domination in the 1950s to a distinct Republican advantage starting with the 1994 elections (see "Southern Senators").

Historically, of course, disproportionate Southern strength in the Democratic Party had tremendous negative implications for liberal public policies. Until the mid-1960s, the power of the South's Democratic senators made it impossible for Congress to legislate an end to racial segregation in the public sector. The favored weapon of Southern Democratic senators was the filibuster. At that time two-thirds of all senators were needed to end a filibuster and thereby bring significant civil rights legislation to the floor of the Senate. A solid bloc of Southern Democrats thus needed only twelve North-ern allies to kill civil rights.

Through the early 1960s, Russell, the leader of the Southern Democrats, had easily defeated attempts to outlaw racial segrega-tion in the South. Passage of the Civil Rights Act and the Voting Rights Act in the mid-1960s finally ended racial segregation in the public sector and, combined with a growing white middle class, opened the way to two-party competition in Southern Senate elec-tions.[9] By the mid-1970s, the South's Democratic senators by and large began to reposition themselves from anti–civil rights to pro–civil rights.[10]

A few breaks in the region's completely Democratic delegation began to occur in the 1960s, and by the 1970s the South was no longer monolithically Democratic. The 1994 elections relegated the Democrats to a minority of the Southern delegation and marked the disappearance of the Southern Democratic surplus. Since 1994, in fact, the Democratic Party has always been stronger in the North than in the South. After the 2004 elections, the Senate Democrats consisted of forty-one Northerners (including Jeffords) and a mere four Southerners, a truly unique sectional pattern. In order for Democrats to regain the Senate, sizable Northern Democratic sur-pluses will be required to offset the party's new Southern deficits.

From their totally dormant position in the 1950s, Southern Re-publicans made very slow progress in winning Senate elections. A century after Lincoln's election, his party remained an exclusively Northern institution. The Senate contained not a single Republican from the South in 1960. A bitterly divided Democratic Party in Texas was needed to produce the South's first Republican senator. John Tower, benefiting from factional divisions among Texas Dem-ocrats, won a 1961 special election to fill the seat vacated by Lyndon Johnson when he became vice president.

After that fluky beginning, Republicans made only occasional gains in the South before surging in 1980 behind Ronald Reagan's presidential coattails. Two years later, for the first time, Republicans evenly divided the Southern delegation. The initial GOP advance, however, involved inexperienced politicians riding Reagan's popularity. It did not last. Democrats recovered in 1984 and held even larger Southern majorities from 1986 through 1992.

A new era of Southern Republican office holding began with the 1994 elections. Taking advantage of Reagan's realignment of Southern white voters, Republicans finally achieved their first decisive majority in the Southern Senate delegation. Since then, operating with a much larger base of grassroots partisans, Republicans have sustained and even enlarged their advance. In the 2004 elections, Republicans capitalized on five Democratic retirements and expanded their majority to an unprecedented eighteen to four seats. The growing Republican surplus from the South enabled the national party to increase its lead in the Senate.

In the North, the partisan battle for the Senate has been filled with zigs and zags over the past half century. Republicans led Democrats in the early and middle 1950s, but in 1958 the Republicans again lost their Northern advantage (see "Northern Senators" in figure 8.2). Northern Democrats achieved decisive victories in 1958, 1962, 1964, 1974, and 1976, but from the early 1980s onward, the Northern party battle has shifted back and forth. In 1994 the Republicans' Northern majority was only 51 percent to 49 percent, substantially less than their performance in the North in the 1994 House elections. The long-term trend for Northern senators has been a fairly close division between the two parties, with Democrats holding slight leads in the early 2000s.

Not until 1994 did the Republicans achieve higher victory rates in the South than in the North. After 1994 the traditional sectional balance between Northern and Southern Republicans was reversed. In the North, Republicans hovered around the 50 percent line, while the South now provided the sectional surplus that usually produced Republican majorities.

REPUBLICAN STRONGHOLDS

Republican competitiveness for the Senate is based on the two regions—the Mountains/Plains and the South—where the GOP has best implemented its strategy of realigning white conservatives and neutralizing white moderates. In the aftermath of the Great Society, the Mountains/Plains emerged as the only region in which the Republican Party was consistently strong (see figure 8.3). Its durable majorities of senators and its large size—the thirteen Mountains/Plains states alone contain one-fourth of the entire Senate—have made the region especially crucial to Republican success. After losing ground in the 1986 elections, Republicans reemerged in 1994 with a substantial lead and subsequently expanded their majorities into a 2-to-1 advantage.

In many of the Mountains/Plains states, presidential and Senate politics are mutually reinforcing. Following the 2004 elections, Republicans held both Senate seats in Oklahoma, Kansas, Arizona, Utah, Wyoming, and Idaho. All six states were consistently Republican in the 2000 and 2004 presidential elections. Only in North Dakota was there a mismatch between presidential and Senate elections. North Dakota's two Democratic senators served in a presidentially Republican environment. Elsewhere the Republicans failed to capitalize fully on their presidential success. Nevada (the home of Democratic leader Harry Reid), Colorado, Nebraska, South Dakota, and Montana all sent one Republican and one Democrat to the Senate. Thus, within a clear Republican stronghold, the political skills of individual Democrats like Max Baucus in Montana and Kent Conrad and Byron Dorgan in North Dakota enabled them to survive despite the white realignment. New Mexico, the region's only swing state in presidential elections, also had a split Senate delegation.

While the Mountains/Plains contain more senators than any other region, Republicans needed to develop reliable support else-

Figure 8.3
The Party Battle in the Senate: Northern Regions

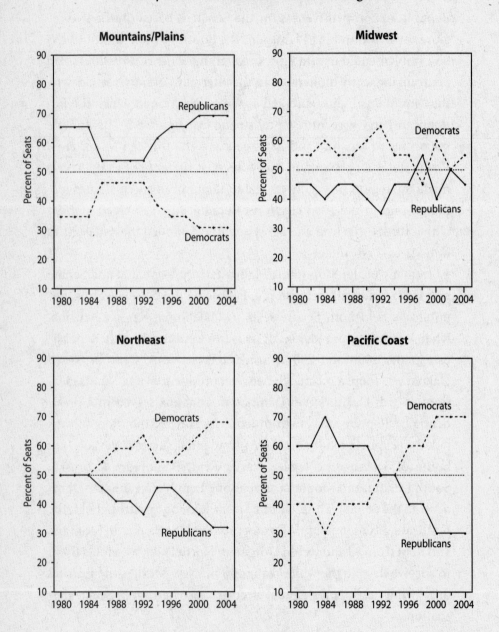

where in the nation to become consistently competitive. The South offered far better prospects for Republican gains than any other region. In 1980 Reagan's presence at the top of the Republican ticket helped elect four new Republican senators from the South. None of the newcomers lasted for more than a single term. In 1994, with much larger grassroots bases because of the Reagan realignment, and with President Bill Clinton's failed heath care proposals energizing Republicans and demoralizing many Democrats, Republicans for the first time emerged with a solid majority (13 to 9) of the Southern delegation. The Republicans' Southern breakthrough, when added to their renewed strength in the Mountains/Plains, positioned the GOP to win the Senate.

In 2004 five of the nine Southern Democratic senators—Fritz Hollings in South Carolina, Bob Graham in Florida, John Breaux in Louisiana, Zell Miller in Georgia, and John Edwards in North Carolina—decided not to seek reelection. It is, of course, an extraordinary event when a majority of a party's regional delegation voluntarily leaves the Senate. The unforced Democratic retirements, coming in a presidential election year in which President George W. Bush was expected to carry all the Southern states, gave Southern Republicans a tremendous windfall opportunity to increase their numbers in the South's Senate delegation. Republicans won all five open seats and emerged with an unprecedented fourteen-seat surplus of eighteen Republicans to four Democrats. Whether or not the Republicans can sustain their 4-to-1 advantage, their victories in 2004 signaled a powerful consolidation of Republican grassroots strength in the South.

After the 2004 elections, there were two Republican senators in eight of the eleven Southern states: Texas, Virginia, Tennessee, North Carolina, Alabama, South Carolina, Mississippi, and Georgia. All of these states went Republican in the 2000 and 2004 presidential elections. Arkansas, the only Southern state with two Democratic senators, stood out as the single regional mismatch between Senate and presidential outcomes. Florida and Louisiana, both presidentially Republican, had divided delegations.

The thoroughness of the Republicans' victories in 2004 could only demoralize many Southern Democrats. The national importance of the Southern transformation is readily apparent. Gains in the South have given the Republican Party its firmest foundation in the Senate since the 1920s. With the destruction of the Democrats' Southern surpluses and the creation of huge Republican surpluses from the South, the national party battle in the Senate has become extraordinarily competitive.

DEMOCRATIC STRONGHOLDS

Just as Republicans rely on two regional strongholds, Democrats have developed their own regional Senate strongholds in the Northeast and the Pacific Coast. In the Northeast, the long-term trend after the Second World War has been the conversion of a reliably Republican area into a region increasingly safe for Democrats. From 1946 through 1972, Republicans ordinarily constituted sizable majorities of the Northeastern Senate delegation. After a period in which neither party dominated, the Democrats emerged in 1986 with an advantage that has grown over time.

Reagan's conservatism played poorly in many Northeastern states, and Bush's conservatism has played even worse. The Democratic majority weakened but survived the Republicans' national surge in 1994. In the initial elections of the twenty-first century, Northeastern Democrats established a 2-to-1 lead over the Republicans in the Senate delegation. Increased Democratic strength in the Northeast has enabled the party to counter Republican growth in the South. Both regions contain twenty-two senators.

In the Northeast, Democrats have consolidated their power in a manner similar to Republicans in the South. Presidential Republicanism having collapsed in the Northeast, this region is steadily moving toward greater Democratic ascendancy. Grassroots politics (see chapter 4 on the Northeastern electorate) gives the Democrats enormous practical advantages throughout the region. After the 2004 elections, seven of the eleven Northeastern states—all of them presidentially Democratic in 2000 and 2004—sent two Democrats to the Senate: New York, Massachusetts, New Jersey, Maryland, Connecticut, Delaware, and (counting Jeffords) Vermont. Veteran Democratic senators Edward Kennedy and John Kerry of Massachusetts, along with the transplanted New Yorker Hillary Clinton, are the most visible national symbols of staunch Northeastern liberalism.

Republican senators in the Northeast face a bleak future. Pennsylvania and Maine, where two Republican senators in each state serve in presidentially Democratic environments, were the regional mismatches. In Democratic Rhode Island, Republican Senator Lincoln Chafee occupied a seat that left him vulnerable to challenges from conservative Republicans as well as liberal Democrats. Even in New Hampshire, where the Republicans held both Senate seats, the state was trending Democratic in presidential politics. Republican performance in the 2002 and 2004 Senate elections—the party held on to only one-third of the region's seats—was even weaker than it had been during the Great Depression. A Solid Democratic Northeast cannot be ruled out in the years ahead.

The Pacific Coast is the second Democratic stronghold. Stable Democratic strength in this five-state region represents a return to an earlier pattern of Democratic Senate majorities from 1954 through 1978. The recent transformation of Senate elections in the Pacific Coast appears vividly in figure 8.3. Aside from Alaska, the electorates in the other Pacific Coast states provide excellent foundations for Democratic victories. Republican strength during Reagan's presidency gave way to a regional tie in the 1992 and 1994 elections, which were a prelude to increasingly strong Democratic majorities from 1996 onward.

As is the case in the Northeast, Democratic strength in the Pacific Coast is mutually reinforcing in presidential and senatorial elections. Following the 2004 elections, California, Washington, and Hawaii were all presidentially Democratic states with two Democratic senators, and Oregon was a presidentially Democratic state with one Democratic senator. Alaska, a presidentially Republican state with two Republican senators, was the only Pacific Coast state where the GOP retained an advantage.

California's emergence as a solidly Democratic state is one of the most important changes in modern American politics. Republicans can no longer use California to groom prospective presidential nominees. Reagan and Richard Nixon, both of whom emerged from southern California to become national leaders, achieved their success in California electorates quite different from those of the early twenty-first century. California's demographic transformation now provides a firm foundation for liberal Democrats—especially female liberal Democrats with national aspirations. Senators Barbara Boxer (San Francisco) and Dianne Feinstein (Los Angeles) are the best examples of pronounced Pacific Coast liberalism in the Senate. Along with Hillary Clinton, Boxer and Feinstein illustrate the growing importance of women as leaders of the modern Democratic Party.

THE MIDWEST

In Senate elections, the Midwest has been a swing region. Thus far neither party has established a sustained stable majority—on the order of 60 percent or better—in this ten-state region. As it does in presidential politics, the Midwest therefore invites the keen attention of strategists in both parties. Based on past performance, Democrats are better situated than Republicans to win Midwestern Senate elections. The Republicans' failure to forge Senate majorities in the Midwest comparable to their House majorities makes them especially dependent on winning very large shares of Senate elections in their two strongholds.

Originally, of course, the Midwest and the Northeast were the two regional pillars of the Republican Party in the Senate. Between 1858 and 1930, Republicans lost their Midwestern majorities only four times. Crushed by the Great Depression, Midwestern Republicans regained the majority in 1942 and kept it through the mid-1950s. Beginning with the 1958 elections, however, the Democrats established a substantial advantage in the Midwest. They were able to sustain their lead until the 1998 elections.

The Senate party battle in the Midwest, unlike the trends in the Northeast and Pacific Coast, reflects transient partisan advantage rather than the emergence of a stable Democratic superiority. The 1994 elections narrowed the Democrats' advantage but did not terminate it. Only in 1998 did the Republicans achieve a majority; and only in 2000 did the Democrats control three-fifths of the Midwestern delegation.

In this swing region, both parties have performed best in their presidential states. After the 2004 elections, Democrats outnumbered Republicans in the Midwestern senatorial delegation 11 to 9. The presidentially Democratic states of Illinois, Michigan, and Wisconsin all sent two Democrats to the Senate. Likewise, each of the presidentially Republican states of Ohio, Missouri, and Kentucky had two Republican senators. West Virginia was the conspicuous mismatch. Robert Byrd and Jay Rockefeller were the two veteran Democratic senators in a state that Bush carried twice. Both parties had one state—Minnesota for the Democrats and Indiana for the Republicans—in which presidential strength did not prevent the election of one senator from the opposing party. Iowa, a swing state in presidential elections, was also divided in its Senate delegation.

DYNAMICS OF THE SENATE PARTY BATTLE

Table 8.1 reveals the sectional and regional structure of the Republican Senate majority following the 2004 elections. Nationally, the Republicans had an advantage of 55 to 45. Growing Republican strength in the South was critical to the party's national success. Republicans overcame their deficit of four senators in the North by producing a surplus of fourteen seats in the South. With their large Southern majority, Republicans needed only thirty-three of the seventy-eight Northern Senate seats—42 percent—in order to create a bare majority of fifty-one senators. They actually emerged with thirty-seven senators, or 47 percent of the Northern delegation. If

Table 8.1

The Senate after the 2004 Elections*

Political Unit	Partisan Unity				Size	
	Rep	Dem	Rep	Dem	All Senators	
United States	55	45	55%	45%	100	100%
South	18	4	82%	18%	22	22%
North	37	41	47%	53%	78	78%
Republican strongholds	36	12	75%	25%	48	48%
South	18	4	82%	18%	22	22%
Mountains/Plains	18	8	69%	31%	26	26%
Midwest	9	11	45%	55%	20	20%
Democratic strongholds	10	22	31%	69%	32	32%
Pacific Coast	3	7	30%	70%	10	10%
Northeast	7	15	32%	68%	22	22%

* Rep = Republicans; Dem = Democrats. Calculated by authors.

the Republicans keep electing four-fifths of the Southern delegation, they will remain highly competitive in the battle for the Senate. The last time Republicans failed to hold at least 42 percent of the Northern senators occurred in the post-Watergate election of 1974.

Losses in the South have made the Democratic Party increasingly dependent on success in the North. The Democrats' Northern target—the percentage of Northern senators they need to elect to create their own bare majority—has risen to levels not achieved by the Democratic Party since the early 1960s. In 2004, with only four Southern senators, the Democrats' Northern target rose to a new high of 60 percent. Winning three-fifths of the Northern Senate seats is certainly not impossible, but even a modest Democratic recovery in the South would make it much easier for the party to regain the Senate.

The size and unity of the Republican and Democratic strongholds are keys to understanding the Republicans' modest advantage after the 2004 elections. Republicans enjoy a huge advantage in the number of Senate seats located in their strongholds. The South and the Mountains/Plains together contain nearly half (forty-eight) of all senators, whereas the Northeast and the Pacific Coast include only one-third (thirty-two) of the Senate. Moreover, Republicans benefited in 2004 from slightly higher victory rates than Democrats—75 percent versus 69 percent—in their respective strongholds.

In the attempt to secure fifty-one senators in the 2004 elections, Republicans used their strongholds to gain a decisive advantage going into the Midwest. They produced thirty-six senators from their regional strongholds and another ten senators from the Democratic strongholds. Hence they needed only five of the Midwest's twenty seats in order to hold the Senate. The much smaller size and the slightly lower unity of the Democratic strongholds meant that the Northeast and Pacific Coast together yielded only twenty-two Democratic senators. Adding the twelve seats the Democrats held in the Republican strongholds still left them far behind the Republicans as they (figuratively speaking) approached the Midwest. At this point, Democrats needed to secure seventeen of the twenty Midwestern seats in order to organize the Senate. In short, they needed a higher victory rate in the Midwest—85 percent—than they actually achieved in the Pacific Coast or the Northeast. The end result—an 11-to-9 Democratic advantage—reaffirmed the Midwest as a swing region in Senate elections.

Unless the Democrats can convert the Midwest into a Democratic stronghold, the Republicans will continue to operate from a considerable size advantage. Higher victory rates in Democratic strongholds—the Northeast offers more opportunities for Democratic gains than the Pacific Coast—may be needed as well to return the Democrats to the majority. At the same time, it must be emphasized that Republicans do not have a secure majority. While Republicans currently have larger strongholds, they depend on very high victory rates to offset their sustained weakness in the Democratic strongholds and their middling performance in the Midwest.

LEADERS AND FOLLOWERS

The Senate's power struggle resembles that of the House of Representatives in the stark images it produces of harsh confrontations along partisan and ideological lines. With only a few exceptions, leaders and followers within each party generally agree with one another about the preferred direction of public policy. Very liberal Democratic senators want to be led by very liberal Democratic leaders. Very conservative Republican senators expect their leaders to represent their ideological stances. Each party pursues lines of attack that resonate with greatest force among supporters in their respective regional strongholds.

By and large, leaders of both parties work with colleagues who are predisposed to vote as strong national partisans (a score of 80 percent or higher on *Congressional Quarterly* "party unity" roll-call votes). Yet complete agreement within each party on all controversial issues is rare. Neither Senate party has been totally unified in recent years. When members of the party in power fail to support the party position, leaders are faced with immense practical problems of producing majorities on the floor and even greater difficulties in creating supermajorities of sixty votes to end filibusters. Democrat Thomas Daschle of South Dakota faced such challenges from some of his fellow Democrats when his party was in the majority during 2001 and 2002, and Republican leaders have faced similar problems in more recent Congresses.

At the time of the Republican Party's 1994 breakthrough, Robert Dole of Kansas was the majority leader. Dole's conservatism was primarily focused on economic and national security issues. When he left the Senate to run for president in 1996, his successor was Trent Lott of Mississippi. Lott had risen in the leadership of the House Republican Party before winning a Senate seat in 1988. His election as majority leader in the summer of 1996 stamped a Southern face on the Senate Republicans similar to the one assumed by the House Republicans after the 1994 elections.

Any prominent Republican conservative from Mississippi could expect intense media scrutiny whenever he discussed any issue connected to race. In late 2002 Lott took the occasion of South Carolina senator Strom Thurmond's retirement to praise Thurmond's 1948 presidential campaign. The brunt of Thurmond's 1948 states' rights candidacy was an explicit defense of southern racial segregation. By associating himself with the Dixiecrats, Lott wounded himself so badly as a national spokesman for the Republican Party that the Bush White House criticized his remarks and signaled that it wanted a new leader.[11]

In short order, Tennessee senator Bill Frist emerged as President Bush's choice to lead the Republicans in the Senate. Frist, a political newcomer, had made a national impression when he soundly defeated incumbent senator James Sasser as part of the Republican breakthrough in 1994. From the outset of his career, Frist had said that he did not wish to serve more than two six-year terms in the Senate. From the standpoint of the White House, Frist did not have Lott's liabilities and was perceived as much more of a team player than Lott.

During his tenure as majority leader, Frist has experienced the fundamental problem of all recent Senate leaders: leadership of a small-majority party in an institution where small majorities have usually been insufficient to pass ambitious agendas. Based on their 2004 voting records, forty-five of the fifty-one Republican senators (88 percent) consistently supported the position of the Republican majority on votes that divided the parties.[12] Six Republicans, however, departed from the positions of their colleagues on one-fifth or more of these votes. Frist could not depend upon the votes of all Republican senators on all issues. The Republicans, in short, did not have a governing majority over the entire range of issues that split the parties.

Much of the lack of cohesion was rooted in the different partisan environments of the senators' states. Lott and Frist presided over Republican conferences in which conservative Southern and Mountains/Plains senators made up two-thirds of the Republican senators, and these conservatives usually set the tone of the national party. Less than one-fifth of the Republican senators came from the Democratic strongholds. All Republican senators from the South and the Pacific Coast behaved as national partisans, as did 94 percent of the Republicans from the Mountains/Plains and 90 percent of the Midwestern Republicans. The only mavericks were John McCain of Arizona, whose convictions about policies and presidential ambitions have periodically set him apart from his fellow Republicans, and Mike DeWine of Ohio.

The story was very different among the seven Northeastern Republicans. Four of these Republicans scored in the 60 percent to 79 percent range of *CQ* party support. Lincoln Chafee of Rhode Island, Arlen Specter of Pennsylvania, and Maine's Olympia Snowe and Susan Collins represented presidentially Democratic states in the Northeast. All of them came from states where voting as a moderate Republican, particularly on cultural and environmental issues, was crucial to political survival. Three senators, Judd Gregg and John Sununu of New Hampshire and Rick Santorum of Pennsylvania, behaved as national Republicans. New Hampshire had a mixed record in presidential elections, but a Northeastern Republican like Santorum, who voted as a die-hard partisan, invited serious opposition in a presidentially Democratic state like Pennsylvania.

On the Democratic side, the Senate party leaders have been liberal stalwarts. One of the differences between the parties is that recent Democratic leaders have not represented Democratic strongholds. In 1994 opportunity beckoned for Tom Daschle of South Dakota. George Mitchell of Maine, the Democratic leader, retired to the private sector, and Tennessee's Sasser, Mitchell's apparent successor, was unexpectedly beaten for reelection. Daschle then defeated Christopher Dodd of Connecticut to become minority leader. For ten years he combined a mild-mannered persona with tough partisan politics.

In the aftermath of 9/11, Daschle and President Bush increasingly clashed over most aspects of politics, foreign and domestic. Although Daschle had been easily reelected in the 1990s, his prominence as a national liberal Democrat left him vulnerable in South Dakota. Bush persuaded ex–Republican representative John Thune—himself barely defeated for the Senate in 2002—to challenge Daschle. In a very tight election, Bush indirectly settled scores with Daschle by engineering his defeat. A Democratic leader running in a presidentially Democratic state would have been much harder to beat.

Democrats then promoted Harry Reid of Nevada from whip to minority leader. Reid's experience in the leadership (and in Congress generally) enabled him to maintain the disciplined opposition to the Bush White House that had been Daschle's hallmark. Reid was much less open to serious electoral challenge. He was easily re-elected in 2004, and Nevada was a considerably safer environment for a national Democratic liberal than South Dakota. Just as Frist faced a Republican conference composed mainly of fellow conservatives, Reid reported to a Democratic conference dominated by fellow liberals.

The Senate Democrats were, of course, transformed geographically in the opposite direction from the Republicans. After the 1952 elections, almost half of the entire Democratic Party in the Senate consisted of Southerners. Following the 2004 elections, only four of the Senate's forty-five Democrats were Southerners, making the South the weakest region within the party.

The Northeast, which contributed only one-tenth of the Senate Democrats fifty years ago, had become the Senate's largest Democratic region after 2004, accounting for one-third of the party's senators. In the Pacific Coast, California's prominence now provides an important platform for ambitious Democrats and (just as important) frustrates ambitious Republicans. Liberal Democrats from very safe states—Edward Kennedy and John Kerry of Massachusetts, Hillary Clinton and Charles Schumer of New York, Barbara Boxer and Dianne Feinstein of California, and Dick Durbin of Illinois are probably the best known—define the national face of the Democratic Party. Half of the Senate Democrats came from the party's two regional strongholds. Only one-quarter of them represented states in Republican regional strongholds.

In 2004, forty-three of the forty-nine Democratic Senators (88 percent) voted as national partisans.[13] All twenty-two Democrats from the Northeast and the Pacific Coast behaved as national Democrats. In fact, all but two of these Democrats voted with their party on at least 90 percent of the roll calls. Nine of the ten Midwestern Democrats were also party regulars. Relatively less support for

Democratic Party positions appeared in the Mountains/Plains and the South, though majorities of these Democrats were also national Democrats.

The six exceptions are instructive. Five of the defecting Democrats came from Republican strongholds. Zell Miller of Georgia and Ben Nelson of Nebraska voted as nominal Democrats. Miller's voting record was extraordinary: he was present for 96 percent of the *Congressional Quarterly* party-unity roll calls, and he voted with the Democratic majority on only 2 percent of them. Nelson remains an example of a Democrat acutely aware that he is elected from a conservative Republican state. Once a large faction in the Democratic Party, the nominals have almost vanished. Blanche Lincoln of Arkansas, John Breaux of Louisiana, and Max Baucus of Montana, who also represented presidentially Republican states, voted as moderate Democrats. Evan Bayh was the only Midwestern Democrat who behaved as a moderate. Breaux and Miller retired in 2004 and were replaced by Republicans.

The two Senate parties show different profiles in terms of race/ethnicity, religious affiliation, and gender.[14] As of 2005, non-Hispanic whites made up fifty-four of the fifty-five Senate Republicans (98 percent); the other Republican was Mel Martinez of Florida, a Latino. White Protestants made up 76 percent of Republican senators. Another 18 percent were white Catholics. Two Jewish Republicans, Specter and Norm Coleman of Minnesota, accounted for another 4 percent of the party, and Martinez completed the membership. Non-Hispanic white Christians made up 95 percent of the Senate Republican Party. Only 9 percent of the Republican senators were women.

Senate Democrats were somewhat more diverse in race and ethnicity. Non-Hispanic whites accounted for forty-one of forty-five Democrats (91 percent). The other four Democrats were Daniel Inouye and Daniel Akaka, two Asian Americans from Hawaii; Barack Obama, an African American from Illinois; and Ken Salazar, a

Latino from Colorado. Although now a minority of the entire party (44 percent), white Protestants were the largest religious group among Senate Democrats. The realignment of Southern white Protestants from the Democrats to the Republicans is presumably one of the most important factors in accounting for the declining size of white Protestants in the Senate Democratic Party. White Catholics made up another 27 percent, and Jews were one-fifth of the Senate Democrats. Non-Hispanic white Christians made up 71 percent of Senate Democrats, still a large majority, but considerably less than Senate Republicans. Women were 20 percent of the Democrats.

THE RESTORATION OF SENATE COMPETITION

In the first decade of the new century, the Senate of the United States is an arena in which the American power struggle proceeds on a daily basis. The Senate is relatively insulated from short-term forces in American politics due to six-year terms and staggered elections. Only one-third of senators are chosen in each election year. Many senators, from both parties, have presidential ambitions and are not shy about maneuvering to promote their candidacies. Senate traditions generally make the body exceptionally hard to control from the standpoint of party leaders.

On the other hand, as the two parties have moved toward ideological purity, Republican and Democratic senators in general have less in common with each other than before. Partisanship and ideology are mutually reinforcing, especially for Democrats elected from the Democratic regional strongholds and Republicans from the Republican regional strongholds. Republicans from Democratic strongholds and Democrats from Republican strongholds occasionally face harder choices in deciding how to vote on controversial issues because they are compelled more frequently to balance party demands against home-state realities. Thus Democratic senators, whether or not they publicly present themselves as liberal Democrats, have more in common with one another than was the case in the past. In a similar fashion; Republican senators usually present themselves as conservative in varying degree.

Continuing Republican control of the Senate will probably depend upon the party's ability to win larger shares of Senate seats in its regional strongholds. The Mountains/Plains states may hold more opportunities for expansion than the South, where the party already holds more than four-fifths of the seats. The most problematic region for the Republicans is the Midwest, where they must defend seats in states that do not have consistent Republican strength in the electorates.

For Democrats to regain the Senate, the most plausible scenarios involve a much greater consolidation of party strength in the Northeast, where a number of Republican senators represent states that are strongly Democratic in presidential elections, and a slight expansion in the Pacific Coast. In the Republican strongholds, the Democrats need to play defense with the goals of denying Republicans supermajorities of the Senate seats. Above all, the battleground for competitive state elections will be the Midwest. If the Midwest should become a Democratic stronghold in Senate elections, the party would neutralize its size disadvantage in Senate contests.

Because only small net shifts are needed to reverse the party balance, the modern Senate is safe for neither party. In every election cycle, we should see both parties competing with experienced, well-funded candidates in a relatively small number of states that have the potential to alter the Senate. An intensely competitive power struggle to control the Senate is likely to remain an enduring feature of the American political landscape.

9

THE AMERICAN POWER STRUGGLE

POLITICS IN THE UNITED STATES INVOLVES TWO intensely competitive minority parties, each of which is always on the verge of winning or losing the next round of elections. America's two-party system has been remarkably durable. For one and a half centuries, the Republican and Democratic parties have dominated American political life. Nowhere else in the world have the same two political parties opposed each other over such a long period of time. In assessing the modern power struggle, it is instructive to ponder history's impact on America's major political parties. Two cataclysmic events—the Civil War in the 1860s and the Great Depression of the 1930s—molded the nation's central political options for generations.

The Civil War preserved the American Union and ended slavery. These monumental achievements profoundly shaped the original battle between Republicans and Democrats. Slavery was America's historic evil. The United States Constitution has many virtues, but it provided no realistic way to end slavery. Supermajorities of two-thirds, required in both the House of Representatives and the Senate to amend the Constitution, could not be achieved against the united opposition of the slave states. Slavery's abolition could not possibly be accomplished through peaceful means.

Abraham Lincoln's election in 1860 demonstrated forcefully the political power of a united North. Southern reaction was swift and uncompromising. The purely Northern victory of the nation's first Republican president triggered secession and then full-fledged civil war. Eventually, of course, the Civil War between the Union North and the Confederate South concluded with the political and military triumph of the North. While the slave states were out of the Union, Republicans in Congress followed Lincoln's Emancipation Proclamation with the Thirteenth Amendment to the Constitution. That amendment prohibited slavery throughout the United States. Accepting the Thirteenth Amendment then became a condition for the eventual readmission of the former Confederate states to the Union.

Preserving the Union, eradicating slavery, and actively promoting Northern economic development gave the new Republican Party genuine achievements that ensured its future throughout the North. Likewise, the Confederacy's defeat turned the South into the sectional stronghold of the Democratic Party. Civil War and Reconstruction produced Battlefield Sectionalism, the political alignment of the victorious North versus the vanquished South. For some seventy years, the Republican Party leveraged its extensive Northern strength into routine control of American politics.

National Republican success flowed directly from underlying sectional realities. Northern size was the principal Republican advantage. Generally, the North contained about three times as many electoral votes, House seats, and Senate seats as did the South. Given the North's enormous size, Republicans did not need complete Northern unity in order to achieve national victories. If they could win about two-thirds of the North's electoral votes, House seats, and Senate seats, Republicans could afford to write off the former Confederate states. Lincoln's strategy of uniting the North and conceding the South became the standard model for Republican dominance.

Following the Civil War and Reconstruction, America's Democrats always started their national campaigns with a Solid South in presidential and congressional elections. With the South permanently unified, the Democrats' Northern targets were one-third of the presidential electoral votes or seats in Congress. Yet despite this seemingly modest target, the Democratic Party was so thoroughly discredited in so many Northern states as a disloyal party that it rarely achieved national victories. The superior size of the Republican North ordinarily trumped the greater unity of the Democratic South. Within the smaller Democratic Party, Southern senators and representatives—racially conservative white men who publicly pledged to defend the segregated South against any threat of national intervention on civil rights—held tremendous negative power for generations.

The Great Depression destroyed Battlefield Sectionalism in the North but reinforced it in the South. Northern Democrats under Franklin D. Roosevelt's leadership regained their competitiveness vis-à-vis the Republicans, whereas economic calamity simply reconfirmed Southern Democrats in their traditional hatred of Republicans. By adding much of the North to its Southern base, Democrats emerged in the 1930s as the nation's undisputed majority party. Because the Republicans had no standing in the South, their Lincoln strategy of relying exclusively on Northern supermajorities reduced them to an uncompetitive minority party. Just as Democrats needed generations to overcome their reputation as the "party of rebellion," decades would be required for the Republicans to live down their image as the "party of Depression."

Not until the 1980s did the Republicans successfully redefine themselves. Under Ronald Reagan's leadership, Republicans positioned themselves as a conservative party emphasizing national security, economic growth, lower tax rates, and traditional stances on cultural and religious matters. The modern Republican advance, coupled with a substantial decline in Democratic identification, occured during Reagan's presidency. When Reagan defeated Democratic President Jimmy Carter in 1980, the Democratic Party still enjoyed a sizable lead in the entire electorate. A plurality of white voters preferred Democrats to Republicans, and majorities of African Americans and New Minorities were Democrats. By the 1988 election, the national political landscape had been transformed. Democrats still outnumbered Republicans, but the difference had narrowed to only a few percentage points. Indeed, in the 2004 election, according to the exit polls, Republicans had drawn even with Democrats. Thus for more than two decades, American politics has been characterized by fierce battles between two minority parties in the electorate, each capable of winning national contests.

Increased white support propelled the Republican advance. Beginning with the 1984 election—Reagan's triumph over liberal Minnesota Democrat Walter Mondale—more white voters began to identify themselves as Republicans than as Democrats. The Republican realignment has involved attracting huge majorities of white conservatives and neutralizing the long-standing Democratic advantage with white moderates. In 2004 Republicans led Democrats among all white voters by 45 percent to 31 percent, their biggest advantage in modern times. Nonetheless, Republicans still fell short of attracting a *majority* of white voters, and their success with white voters did not generate a wide lead in the *entire* electorate. The Democratic Party remains highly competitive. Support from a minority of whites, combined with majorities among African Americans and New Minorities, has kept the Democrats within striking range of national victories.

At the beginning of the twenty-first century, American voters were as distant in time from the Great Depression as their ancestors in the 1930s had been from the Civil War of the 1860s. With neither a civil war nor a sustained national economic catastrophe to reshape the two-party system, America's close party battle is the product of many gradual changes over several decades. The Democrats' New Deal majority has deteriorated, but Republicans have not achieved any clear ascendancy in the national electorate.

Broadly considered, the most important structural change in American party politics has been the collapse of Southern Battle-field Sectionalism. As we concluded in 2002, "A newly competitive South means a newly competitive America."[1] The disappearance of enormous Democratic surpluses from the South—surpluses that were a steady feature of elections for president and Congress for more than a century—has reshaped national politics.

Rising Republican strength in the South has transformed the GOP from a sectional party to a national party and has thereby compelled Democrats to compensate for their Southern losses by cultivating greater strength in the North. The ancient sectional imperatives for the two parties are now totally reversed. Having lost their Southern advantage, Democrats now require large Northern majorities in order to win national elections. Republicans no longer need to win majorities of Northern electoral votes or seats in Congress. Yet because the South is far too small to produce national victories on its own, Republicans still need considerable support in the North.

In this book, we have analyzed the close national party battle by dividing the North into four regions and recasting the South as a fifth region. Electorates and institutions have then been examined according to the new American regionalism. Widely divergent patterns and trends in the five regions have netted out to ferocious and evenly divided battles over the entire range of American national institutions. Democrats rely on their strongholds in the Northeast and the Pacific Coast; Republicans count on their strongholds in the South and the Mountains/Plains. The Midwest generally functions as a swing region, typically providing the margin of victory in national elections. Because national winners and losers can shift with the next presidential or congressional election, the power stakes in American politics are permanently high. Activists, financial donors, and politicians—millions of people across the nation—routinely interpret personalities, issues, and events in relentlessly dire and sensational terms.

THE CHANGING ELECTORATE

Distinctive regional patterns among voters offset one another and thereby generate the tight national party battle. The central dynamic in reviving the Republican Party has been its attempt to realign white voters. Because Republicans have so little standing among America's minority voters, they always need white majorities to win national elections. In this final chapter, we shall begin by examining the regional white realignment according to age. Our initial focus will be on the size of the white party bases—Republicans plus conservative independents vis-à-vis Democrats plus liberal independents—among older and younger white voters as of the 2004 benchmark election.

White realignment, however, is only part of the story of sharpened national competitiveness. Increased participation by minorities has been the main trend favoring and sustaining the Democratic Party. An electorate historically dominated by whites has been transformed into one in which America's various minority groups are truly major forces. The entry of African Americans and the New Minorities has enabled Democrats to offset the Republicans' white realignment.

The top charts in figure 9.1 show the Democratic and Republican party bases for older (forty-five and above) and younger (eighteen to forty-four) white voters. In each chart, the regions are aligned from the Northeast and the Pacific Coast through the Midwest and then to the Mountains/Plains and the South. Important regional differences are readily apparent. Older white voters, people who

Figure 9.1
2004 Party Bases by Age

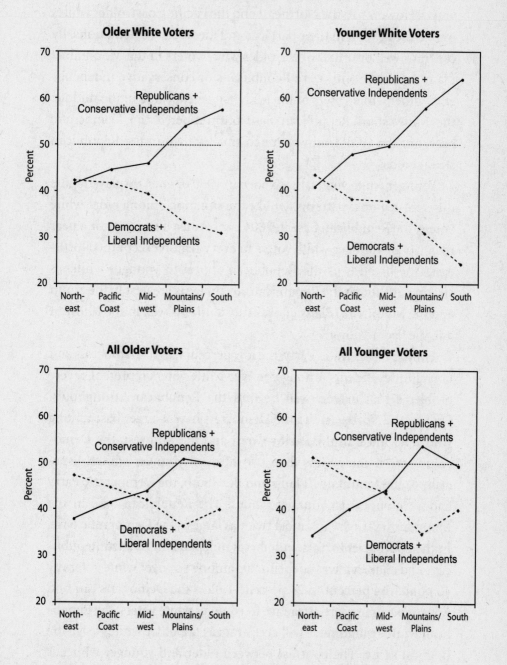

were born before 1960, follow intriguing regional patterns. In no region did the Democratic Party base approach a majority of white voters. However, in the Northeast and the Pacific Coast, older whites were basically tied in their partisan and ideological orientations. By contrast, well over half of the older white voters in the Mountains/Plains and the South were Republicans or conservative independents. Older white voters in the Midwest were located in the middle: the Midwestern Republican base outnumbered the Democratic base, but the GOP lead was much smaller than in the Republican strongholds.

Younger white voters, those born in 1960 or later, displayed quite different regional patterns. Unlike the situation among older white voters, the Republican base in 2004 constituted a majority or a near majority of younger white voters in every region except the Northeast. The breadth of the Republican appeal to younger whites is striking. Although the Republican advantage is greatest in the South and the Mountains/Plains, it was substantial as well in the Midwest and the Pacific Coast.

For the Democratic Party, the low percentages of Democrats and liberal independents among younger white voters represent severe problems that extend well beyond the Republican strongholds. Only in the Northeast did the Democrats have a larger base among younger whites. In the Pacific Coast and the Midwest, the Democratic base included less than two-fifths of younger whites. Especially in the Mountains/Plains and the South, the Democratic Party had little appeal to younger whites. The Republican base in the Mountains/Plains was almost twice as large as the Democratic base. In the South, Democrats and liberal independents trailed Republicans and conservative independents among younger white voters by 40 points, 64 percent to 24 percent. Unless the Democrats can find ways to become more attractive to younger white voters, the Republican white realignment will accelerate as the older whites leave the political scene. The contrast between older and younger whites is particularly important in the Midwest. Democratic traditions dating back to the New Deal appear to be giving way to a distinctive Republican advantage among younger white voters.

The Republican edge in 2004 shrinks or disappears, however, when attention shifts to the entire electorate (see the lower charts in the figure). Among all older voters, Republicans have bigger leads in their regional strongholds than do Democrats in their strongholds. In the Midwest, the Republicans have no more than a slender advantage. For all younger voters, the regional strongholds are even more distinctive. Democratic Party bases are larger vis-à-vis the Republican Party bases in the Northeast and the Pacific Coast, while the opposite is true in the South and the Mountains/Plains. The Midwest remains the single region in which neither party has a clear lead.

Highly distinctive regional patterns culminate in a closely divided national electorate, an electorate separated profoundly by race and ethnicity, religion, and gender. Figure 9.2 presents the American divide, the emerging social basis of competitive party politics in the United States. Voters in 2004 have first been separated into white Protestants, white Catholics, non-Christian whites, and all minorities. Each of these four groups has then been divided by gender. The resulting eight groups of voters have then been ranked (from left to right) according to the relative size of Democratic versus Republican party bases.[2]

From a national perspective, Democrats operate with huge majorities in four key groups: minority women (73 percent to 21 percent), non-Christian white women (66 percent to 21 percent), minority men (63 percent to 25 percent), and non-Christian white men (50 percent to 30 percent). Among these groups, who together constituted 36 percent of all voters in 2004, there was much support for a liberal Democratic Party but very little interest in a Republican Party dominated by conservative white Protestants.

White Catholic women, once overwhelmingly pro-Democratic,

Figure 9.2
The American Divide

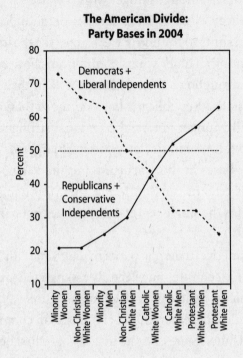

**The American Divide:
Party Bases in 2004**

were essentially tied: 44 percent were in the Democratic base compared with 42 percent in the Republican base. Republicans had succeeded in neutralizing this important group as a reliable Democratic asset. One of every nine voters in 2004, white Catholic women will assuredly be prime targets for both parties in the future. Nationally, they are the only group of white Christians that has not moved decisively toward the Republican Party.

Republican strength was concentrated in three groups of white Christians. In 2004 majorities of white Protestant men (63 percent to 25 percent), white Protestant women (57 percent to 32 percent), and white Catholic men (52 percent to 32 percent) were Republicans or conservative independents. Support for a conservative Republican Party and opposition to a liberal Democratic Party was greatest among these three groups, which accounted for 54 percent of the entire national electorate.

White Christians were a smaller percentage of American voters than in the past, but in 2004 they still made up 64 percent of all voters and were more Republican in their politics than ever before. Fifty-six percent of white Christians were Republicans or conservative independents, while only 32 percent were Democrats or liberal independents. Greater partisan unity among white Christians has offset their diminished size in the electorate. The Republican Party has thus been transformed from a Northern party historically dominated by white Protestants into a national party based primarily— but certainly not entirely—on white Christians.

In the 2004 benchmark election, the close national fight between Democrats and Republicans involved heightened ideological cleavages between groups divided by race and ethnicity, gender, and religion. These sharp divisions—all filtered through the leading politicians, issues, and events as reported and interpreted by newspapers and newsmagazines, network television, cable news, talk radio, and Internet commentary—are mutually reinforced on a daily basis in the unending search for partisan advantage. Such a two-party system cannot be other than a permanent power struggle.

NATIONAL INSTITUTIONS AND THE NEW AMERICAN REGIONALISM

Regional strongholds in the electorate translate directly into regional strongholds in national institutions. The new American regionalism gives each party realistic opportunities to win the presidency, the House of Representatives, and the Senate. Unlike the historical situations of Republican dominance after the Civil War or Democratic dominance following the Great Depression, in modern

Figure 9.3
Regional Outcomes for President, House, and Senate in 2004

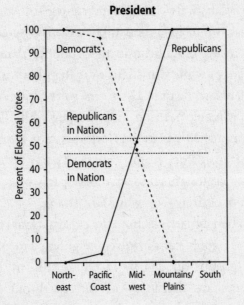

President

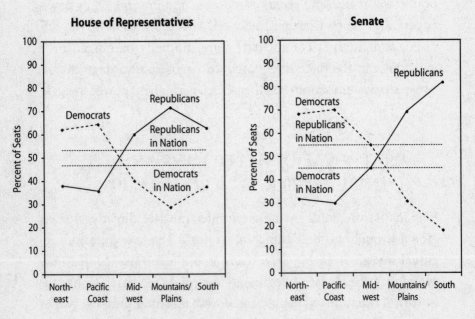

House of Representatives

Senate

American politics neither Republicans nor Democrats operate with any "lock" whatsoever on the presidency, the House, or the Senate.

The 2004 elections were fiercely contested for every institution of the national government. We shall use them as benchmarks to illustrate how the regional party battles culminate in close national outcomes. Figure 9.3 shows the results by region and nation for the presidency, the House of Representatives, and the Senate. Because presidential politics is based on the winning party taking all of a state's electoral votes, partisan strongholds can be won or lost in their entirety. Thus in 2004 (see "President"), John Kerry led the Democrats to a complete sweep of the Northeast's electoral votes and to a near sweep (Alaska was the Republican exception) in the Pacific Coast. Likewise, George Bush won all of the electoral vote in both the South and the Mountains/Plains. The Midwest divided its electoral vote, with the Republicans narrowly edging the Democrats.

Because the Republican strongholds contained slightly more electoral votes than the Democratic strongholds, Democrats needed 76 electoral votes from the Midwest to reach 270. Instead, Kerry won only 58, leaving him 18 electoral votes short of victory. Bush's win in Ohio, with 20 electoral votes the most competitive big state in the Midwest, was thus decisive for his close victory in the electoral college.

Persistent Republican weakness in the Great Lakes states of the upper Midwest—in contrast to Republican success in the 1980s—means that neither party has any margin of error in presidential elections. Specifically, any Democratic presidential candidate who can match Kerry's successes and win Ohio can reclaim the White House for the Democratic Party in 2008. And even if the next reapportionment slightly enlarges the Republican strongholds and modestly diminishes the Democratic strongholds beginning in 2012, Ohio will remain the single most important swing state in the Midwest. Unless momentous events, cataclysmic policy failures, and/or the nomination of a conspicuously flawed candidate give one party a decisive advantage, the close presidential power struggle will continue for the foreseeable future.

The 2004 House elections were the second wave of elections held in districts drawn after the 2000 census. Americans increasingly appear to sort themselves out in their decisions about where to live in ways that make many localities relatively safe for particular parties. Allowing for exceptions, of course, Democrats usually dominate large cities. Suburban areas are mixed in elections for the White House and Congress, while exurban areas and rural/small-town areas are generally Republican. Such geographical variations in partisan strength within states, combined with advances in computer technology, make it far easier than in the past to create House districts that greatly facilitate straight-ticket partisan voting from the top to the bottom of the ticket.[3]

Because most congressional districts in the United States are deliberately shaped to favor one party or the other, and because state legislatures and federal courts do the shaping, most Democratic and Republican incumbents emerge with fairly safe House seats. In state after state, the dominant political party obviously seeks to devise as many winnable districts for its fellow partisans as possible, a task that usually involves conceding some seats to the opposition party. (Of the larger American states, only in Massachusetts has the dominant party made every single House district safe for itself.) In 2004, for example, the same party's candidates won both the presidential and congressional contests in the vast majority of congressional districts (376 of 435). According to Michael Barone, only forty-one House Democrats won districts that Bush carried, and only eighteen House Republicans were victorious in districts that Kerry won.[4]

In 2002 Republicans retained their national majority and added the Midwest to their strongholds in the South and the Mountains/Plains. Structurally, the Republicans' slim advantage in the House of Representatives was thus based on three rather than two regional strongholds. Democrats maintained their clear dominance in the Northeast and the Pacific Coast. Results for 2004 reaffirmed the patterns established in 2002, except that Texas Republicans, led by House Majority Leader Tom DeLay of suburban Houston, redrew the Texas House districts to maximum Republican advantage and thereby increased the Republican Party's majority in Texas, the South, and the nation.

Because the Republican strongholds contain far more House seats (63 percent) than do the Democratic strongholds (37 percent), Democrats came out of the 2004 elections facing greater obstacles than before in reclaiming the House of Representatives. The Democrats' difficulties, however, are not insurmountable, should short-term events work to their advantage in a fairly small number of districts now held by Republicans. Democratic net gains in the mid-teens would be sufficient to elect a Democrat as Speaker of the House.

The new American regionalism is as evident in the Senate elections as it is for the House and the presidency. Democratic strength in the Northeast and the Pacific Coast declines to a more modest advantage in the Midwest, only to be replaced by Republican strength in the Mountains/Plains and the South. The Republicans' national majority after the 2004 elections was the product of slightly higher victory rates in the Republican strongholds (due to the South) and, more important, the much greater size of the Republican strongholds. In the Senate, the Midwest is the only region in the swing category. Should the Democrats convert the Midwest into a stronghold, the power struggle in the Senate would be even tighter than it is now. Modest Democratic net gains would restore the party to the majority.

Apart from the Midwest in House elections, the regional structure of the party battle for the presidency, the House, and the Senate is highly similar across the elected offices of the national government. The unique features of the regional electorates produce distinctive outcomes in the five regions. For each institution, the national consequences are very close battles. Because most politicians are thoroughly convinced that their party can win or lose power in the next election, and because every institution can in fact change hands in the next election, full-throttle partisanship is always the order of the day.

Based on the results of the 2004 elections, there were nine states in which Democrats won the presidential election, held a majority of the House delegation, and controlled both Senate seats. The staunchest Democratic states were New York, New Jersey, Massachusetts, Maryland, and Vermont in the Northeast; California, Washington, and Hawaii in the Pacific Coast; and Illinois in the Midwest. In seven more states, Democrats combined a presidential victory with control of either the House or the Senate delegation: Connecticut, Maine, Delaware, and Rhode Island in the Northeast; Oregon in the Pacific Coast; and Michigan and Wisconsin in the Midwest. Not a single state in the South or the Mountains/Plains qualified as a pro-Democratic state in terms of elected officials.

For the Republicans, sixteen states voted Republican for president, sent two Republicans to the Senate, and elected a Republican majority to the House of Representatives. Judged by elected officials, the staunchest Republican states were Texas, Virginia, North Carolina, South Carolina, Georgia, and Alabama in the South; Arizona, Oklahoma, Kansas, Utah, Wyoming, and Idaho in the Mountains/Plains; Missouri, Kentucky, and Ohio in the Midwest; and Alaska in the Pacific Coast. In another nine states, Republicans won the presidential election and controlled the delegation to one chamber of Congress. These Republican states were Florida, Tennessee, Louisiana, and Mississippi in the South; Colorado, Nebraska, Nevada, and Montana in the Mountains/Plains; and Indiana in the Midwest. Only Alaska qualified as a Republican state in the Pacific Coast. There were no Republican states in the Northeast.

THE TRANSFORMED REGIONAL PARTIES

In region after region, the group composition of the Democratic Party has been greatly transformed from its heyday during the New Deal. Historically, most Democrats in every region were white Christians—Protestants and Catholics in the North but mainly Protestants in the South. Increasingly, the center of gravity within the Democratic Party has shifted from white Christians to minorities and non-Christian whites. According to the 2004 exit polls, minorities and non-Christian whites constituted sizable majorities of all self-identified Democrats in the South (63 percent), the Pacific Coast (61 percent), and the Northeast (53 percent). In the Mountains/Plains, minorities and non-Christian whites were more numerous than either white Protestants or white Catholics; and in the Midwest, minorities and non-Christian whites were tied with white Protestants.

In the increasingly diverse American electorate, the Democratic Party has become the principal political home for African Americans, Latinos, Asians, and other ethnic and racial minorities, as well as the preferred party of non-Christian whites. White Christians remain a majority of Democrats only in the Midwest (61 percent) and the Mountains/Plains (56 percent). A long-term challenge for the Democrats is to reclaim support among white Christians—especially white Christian men—while remaining a highly attractive option to minorities and non-Christian whites.

The Democratic reaction to the Reagan realignment has been the establishment of a party in which the liberal wing—defined as the percentage of white liberals plus all minorities among Democrats—is by far the preeminent force in each region. Ideological purity (not limited, of course, to the Democrats) lends intensity and an atmosphere of permanent crisis to the American power struggle over and above the normal tensions produced by merely partisan considerations. Within the Democratic Party, white conservatives are rapidly disappearing across the nation. White moderates account for around one-third of Democrats in each region, making them a smaller force than was historically the case. White liberals plus racial and ethnic minorities are large majorities of the Democratic Party in every region except the Mountains/Plains. When Georgia Democratic Senator Zell Miller broke with his party to support George Bush's reelection, he presented himself as a conservative Democrat highly critical of his party's liberal wing. Miller's appeal was directed to a vanishing ideological tradition in his party. Most of the Reagan Democrats from the 1980s had long since left the party.[5]

Just as the regional Democratic parties have been dramatically transformed in recent decades, so have the regional Republican parties changed in important ways. A party originally composed largely of Northern white Protestants has now become a national party with a strong appeal to white Protestants and—increasingly—white Catholics. White Protestants are by far the largest group of Republicans in every region except the Northeast, where white Catholics are almost as numerous. In comparison with the Democratic Party, the modern Republican Party is overwhelmingly dominated by white Christians rather than just white Protestants.

Minorities and non-Christian whites make up only a small fraction—one-sixth or so—of all Republicans across the five regions. They are, in relative terms, a smaller component of the Republican Party than are Christian white men in the Democratic Party. If Democrats need to regain their traditional support from white Christians, Republicans face an even greater challenge to broaden their appeal to minorities and non-Christian whites. Here conservative ideology and the visibility of evangelical Protestants are major obstacles to Republican growth.

Ideological purity within the Democratic Party is matched by ideological purity within the Republican Party. In all five regions, white conservatives plus minorities are the dominant force within the Republican Party. (We assume that minority voters who identify with the Republican Party agree with the conservative philosophy of Republican elites.) White moderates represent a large but secondary element within the Republican Party. White liberals are as scarce within the Republican Party as white conservatives are in the Democratic Party.

THE TRANSFORMED
NATIONAL PARTIES

The changing composition of the national Democratic and Republican parties is one of the most important stories of modern American politics. A brief comparison of key groups in the 1950s versus 2004 highlights remarkable changes, especially within the Democratic Party. In the 1950s, there were far more Democrats than Republicans in the United States, and the Democratic Party was evenly balanced between women and men. A half century later, a relatively smaller Democratic Party contained far more women than men (60 percent to 40 percent). Gender imbalance is a defining feature of the modern Democratic Party. In contrast, the Republican Party has shifted from an institution with more women than men in the 1950s (55 percent to 45 percent) to one in which men and women were as evenly balanced in 2004 as Democrats were in the 1950s.

Dramatic shifts have also characterized the racial and ethnic composition of the Democratic Party. Whites have declined from over nine-tenths of all Democrats in the 1950s to less than two-thirds in 2004. African Americans have expanded to one-quarter of all self-identified Democrats; and the New Minorities of Latinos, Asians, and others constituted 12 percent of the Democratic Party in the 2004 election. Declining Democratic strength among white Americans primarily reflected losses among men. In the 1950s, white men were 46 percent of all Democrats. Their relative strength in 2004 was down to 25 percent. White women also lost ground as a percentage of all Democrats, but they still accounted for about two-fifths of the party in 2004.

Far more modest changes have occurred in the Republican Party. An overwhelmingly white party remains an overwhelmingly white party. In 2004 African Americans were only 2 percent of all Republicans, down 1 point from the 1950s. Republicans had more success among the New Minorities, who accounted for about one-tenth of the party in 2004. Unlike the wide gap in size between white women and white men in the Democratic Party, white women only slightly outnumbered white men in the Republican Party.

Truly profound changes in party composition appear when white Christians are compared to the combination of all minorities plus non-Christian whites (see the top half of figure 9.4). In the 1950s, white Christians dominated both parties. The net result of two contrasting strategies—Republican efforts to realign whites and Democratic efforts to mobilize minorities—has been fundamental changes in the social bases of the major parties. As the American electorate has become increasingly diverse, the Democratic Party has become the political home of racial/ethnic minorities and non-Christian whites. These voters, who together accounted for slightly more than one-tenth of Democrats in the 1950s, have expanded to half of all Democratic voters in the first decade of the twenty-first century. In fact, 2004 marked the first presidential election in which racial/ethnic minorities plus non-Christian whites formed a majority—53 percent—within a major American party.

Democratic strength among minorities and non-Christian whites has offset Republican gains among white Protestants and white Catholics and thereby enabled the Democratic Party to remain exceptionally competitive nationally. The other important Democratic trend is the steadily declining proportion of white Christians among all Democrats. For a party in which white Christians amounted to almost nine-tenths of all Democrats in the 1950s, the contemporary profile of the Democratic Party is remarkably

Figure 9.4
Transformation of the National Parties

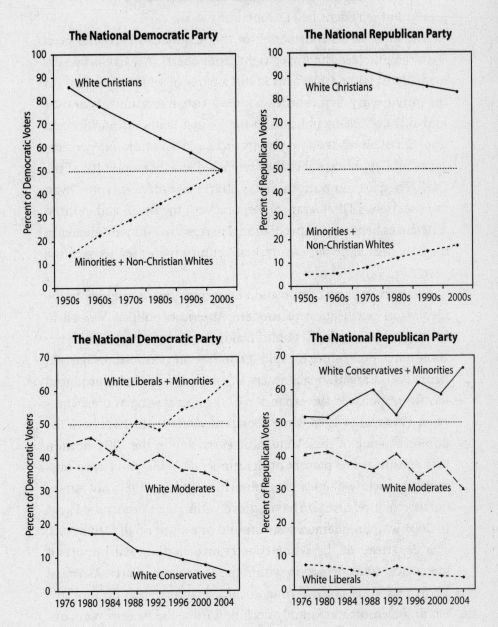

different in the early twenty-first century. In the 2004 election, for the first time in party history, white Christians were a minority (47 percent) of self-identified Democratic voters.

The internal transformation of the Republican Party has been less dramatic (see the upper right-hand chart). A party originally made up of white Christians is still a party of white Christians. In the early twenty-first century, white Christians accounted for over four-fifths of all Republicans in the United States. Minorities and non-Christian whites have slightly increased over time as a percentage of all Republicans, but they remained less than one-fifth of the GOP. The partisan bottom line is clear. For American voters who call themselves Democrats or Republicans, the social and cultural differences between the two national parties are infinitely greater in the first decade of the twenty-first century than they were in the past.

Changes in party composition have contributed mightily to the ideological purification of modern American politics. Viewed in ideological terms, the Republican and Democratic parties have become much purer since the mid-1970s (see the two bottom charts in figure 9.4). Reagan's realignment of white conservatives produced its own response in the expansion of the liberal wing of the Democratic Party. Since 1988 white liberals plus minorities have been the dominant wing of the Democratic Party, and in the 2004 election they constituted 63 percent of all Democrats. White moderates outnumbered white liberals plus minorities through 1980, but subsequently their relative size has declined within the Democratic Party. In 2004 white moderates were around one-third of all Democrats. The departure of the white conservatives is the final important ideological transformation within the Democratic Party. As late as 1976, this conservative wing included almost one-fifth of the nation's Democrats. Steadily declining from the Reagan years onward, it was down to one Democrat in twenty in 2004. Conservative

Democrats are now as insignificant within the Democratic Party as liberal Republicans are within their party.

In 1976 white conservatives plus minorities were already a majority of Republicans. The Republicans' conservative wing expanded during Reagan's presidency, fell in 1992 because of widespread disappointment with the first President Bush, and then rose to two-thirds of all Republicans in the high-turnout election of 2004. Within both parties, the white moderates have declined over time. Ideological polarization between the Republican and Democratic parties was greater than ever before.

AMERICA'S RELENTLESS POWER STRUGGLE

America's permanent power struggle, a fight between two evenly balanced minority parties, generally results in frustration on all sides. Temporary losers strive energetically to limit the achievements of temporary winners, while victorious partisans—especially the strongest partisans—frequently expect policy achievements that are highly unrealistic in view of narrow national victories and incomplete ideological cohesion in the parties. Most Republicans are conservatives, and most Democrats are liberals; but not all Republicans are conservatives, and not all Democrats are liberals. Thus the inability of Democratic President Bill Clinton to reshape the American health care system when he faced a Democratic Congress in the first two years of his presidency, and the failure of Republican President George W. Bush to reform Social Security despite Republican control of Congress after the 2004 elections. In both cases, nominal partisan majorities in Congress were too small for presidents and party leaders to consistently form governing majorities.

Just as Democrats and Republicans are minority parties in the entire American electorate, so too are conservatives and liberals both minority ideological orientations among the nation's voters.

Conservatives always outnumber liberals, according to the exit polls, but conservatives are themselves outnumbered by moderates. Short of truly powerful shocks that could create either a conservative Republican majority or a liberal Democratic majority in the electorate, attempts to govern completely from the right or completely from the left are obviously unlikely to succeed.

At the opening of a new century, America's two parties have less in common in their composition, values, and objectives than was the case after World War II. Because they are minority parties in the electorate, neither Democrats nor Republicans can secure national majorities simply by appealing to their most committed supporters. Hence it is essential to recognize—indeed, it is necessary to emphasize—the importance to each party of winning as many votes as possible from groups they ordinarily lose. Republicans manifestly need more support from minorities and non-Christian whites, and Democrats need to improve their performance among white Christians.

America's power struggle is rooted in the very different values and priorities advocated by the leading groups in each party's distinctive regional strongholds. The national and international problems facing American leaders transcend partisan imperatives, but the new regionalism encourages continuous battles between ideologically driven partisans—conservative Republicans and liberal Democrats—who represent minorities of the entire electorate. Under such conditions, governing the United States will remain an extraordinarily difficult challenge.

10

AFTERWORD: THE AMERICAN POWER STRUGGLE INTENSIFIES

The name of the game in American elections is to maximize the unity and turnout of partisans while also carrying sufficient numbers of independents and dissatisfied members of the rival party. The 2004 elections took place on a level partisan playing field. According to the national exit poll, 37 percent of voters were Republicans, 37 percent were Democrats, and the remaining 26 percent were independents or aligned with minor parties. George W. Bush won the White House and Republican candidates carried the Congress by attracting more votes from their partisan base than Democratic candidates were able to extract from their supporters. Independents slightly preferred John Kerry for the presidency and Democrats over Republicans for Congress, but these Democratic leads (2 to 3 points) were much too small to overcome the GOP advantage from its partisan base.

Democrats regained control of both houses of Congress in 2006 by sweeping their partisans and carrying independent voters by a huge margin. According to the 2006 exit polls, Democrats enjoyed a slight lead over Republicans in the electorate, 38 percent to 36 percent. Democrats backed their party's congressional candidates at a slightly higher rate than Republicans did for their party's nominees. Even more important, the Democrats' lead among independent voters expanded to *18* points. GOP congressional candidates ran well in 2006 only among their partisans.

The Democrats' victories in the 2006 congressional elections drew upon overwhelming support from the three principal racial/ethnic and religious minorities in the electorate: African Americans, the New Minorities of Latinos, Asians, and other ethnic groups, and non-Christian whites. Together these groups accounted for 35 percent of all voters. Each of these important groups produced landslide majorities for Democratic House candidates: 89 percent from African Americans, 72 percent from non-Christian whites, and 66 percent from the New Minorities. Democrats especially gained ground among the increasing number of New Minority voters. A Democratic lead of 11 points in partisanship in 2004 jumped to 27 points in 2006. After the debacle of the immigration fight in the Senate in 2007, Democrats will enter the 2008 election cycle even more strongly positioned among Latino voters.

Because of their weakness among African Americans, New Minorities, and non-Christian whites, Republican candidates require massive support from white Christians to win national elections. Although still a large majority (65 percent) of the total electorate, white Christians do not behave as a highly cohesive bloc of voters. In 2006 less than half (46 percent) were Republicans, 29 percent were Democrats, and the rest were independents or followers of minor parties. GOP House candidates won 57 percent among white Christian voters, a much smaller majority than Democratic candidates elicited from their strongest groups of supporters.

Only one large group of white Christians—evangelicals—displayed a high level of Republican identification and produced landslide support for GOP House candidates in 2006. White evangelicals made up 24 percent of the United States electorate, and Republicans outnumbered Democrats, 61 percent to 21 percent. Republican House candidates won 71 percent of their votes.

Between 2004 and 2006 the Republican Party experienced substantial losses among nonevangelical white Christians. Among these male voters, Republicans outnumbered Democrats by only 10 points, 40 percent to 30 percent, in 2006. Republican House candidates ran only 6 points ahead of their Democratic opponents. Among nonevangelical white Christian women, a 2-point Republican lead in 2004 changed to a 3-point Democratic lead in 2006, 38 to 35 percent. These female voters favored Democratic congressional candidates by six points.

Democratic victories among African Americans, New Minorities, and non-Christian whites thus overwhelmed the Republicans' strength among evangelical white Christians, while the different partisan choices of nonevangelical white Christian men and women offset each other in 2006. The basic Republican predicament is clear: a party that can elicit majority identification and landslide support from only one single large social group will seldom win national elections.

In 2004 only 53 percent of voters approved of President Bush's performance in office. Approval from three fifths of white voters overcame dissatisfied minority voters. By 2006, Bush's job approval had dropped to 43 percent in the entire electorate, and majorities of both whites and nonwhites disapproved of his presidency. Since the 2006 election, the president's approval numbers have fallen much lower. In poll after poll, sizable majorities of Americans have voiced disapproval of his performance.

The Iraq War especially poisoned Bush's second term. Voters had been narrowly divided over the war in 2004, but approval outnumbered disapproval by 53 percent to 47 percent. Two years later, public opinion had gone south on the war. A substantial majority of voters—57 percent—disapproved of the administration's conduct of the war, and 63 percent believed that the war had not improved the nation's long-term security. On all of the Iraq questions, majorities of American voters—nonwhites *and* whites—took antiwar positions in 2006.

National victories are constructed from geographical areas of strength. The consequences of the 2006 election become more vivid when we analyze the results in the five regions. In House elections, Democrats added to their already large majorities in the Northeast and Pacific Coast while reducing Republican majorities in the Midwest, South, and Mountains/Plains. In Senate elections, Democrats strengthened their majorities in the Northeast and Midwest, maintained their huge majority in the Pacific Coast, and lowered Republican majorities in the South and Mountains/Plains.

INCREASING DEMOCRATIC STRENGTH IN THE NORTHEAST

Political developments in the Northeast deserve special emphasis. The most consequential partisan developments in 2006 occurred here. Once the most Republican area of the nation, the Northeast is now the most Democratic region. In the 2006 House elections, Democrats rose to 68 seats while Republicans collapsed to merely 24 seats. The huge Northeastern Democratic surplus—a 44-seat advantage—was nearly twice as large as the 23-seat Republican surplus from the South. Never before in American history have Democrats enjoyed such a lopsided advantage across the Northeast.

In the Senate, Northeastern Democrats neutralized Southern Republicans. Democratic gains in Pennsylvania and Rhode Island, combined with the election of the Socialist Bernie Sanders in Vermont and the reelection of the Connecticut Independent Joseph Lieberman, both of whom caucus with the Democrats, have produced seventeen Democratic senators—the same number as Republicans in the Southern delegation. In its share of Senate seats, the Northeast has become as Democratic as the South is Republican.

Combining the House and Senate delegations, Democrats emerged from the 2006 elections with three fourths of all Northeastern seats. In no other region of the United States did a political party enjoy such a one-sided majority of elected officials. Whether Northeastern Democrats can maintain such a huge lead over the next series of elections will be critical to the national party's ability to keep majorities of seats in the House of Representatives and the Senate.

The Democrats' enormous advantages in the Northeast are based upon the party's growing lead over Republicans in the electorate as well as the popularity of its candidates among independent voters. Forty-four percent of Northeastern voters were Democrats in 2006. More Northeastern voters thought of themselves as independents or members of other parties (30 percent) than as Republicans (26 percent). In addition, a large majority of independent voters in the Northeast favored Democratic congressional candidates. Republican congressional candidates ran well only among the small and declining group of Northeastern whites who still thought of themselves as Republicans.

If the Northeast persists as a Solid Democratic region, comparable to the old Solid Democratic South, the national Democratic Party would begin each election cycle with a significant head start in assured seats for the House and Senate. The Republican Party cannot concede the entire Northeast—even a Northeast that is declining in relative size—and still remain competitive in House and Senate elections.

DEMOCRATIC CONSOLIDATION IN THE PACIFIC COAST

Democrats also dominated the 2006 elections to the House and Senate in the Pacific Coast. Gaining a single seat in the region's

House delegation, Democrats increased their regional surplus to 22 seats. Pacific Coast Democrats maintained their already large (7-to-3) advantage over Republicans in the Senate delegation. Democrats accounted for an impressive 66 percent of the region's combined House and Senate delegations after the 2006 elections.

The Democratic advantage in the Pacific Coast electorate was much smaller than in the Northeast. In the 2006 election, 38 percent of Pacific Coast voters were Democrats, 33 percent were Republicans, and the remaining 29 percent were independents or members of other parties. Just as in the Northeast, however, independent voters strongly preferred Democratic congressional candidates.

Majorities of white, New Minority, and African-American voters in the Pacific Coast voted for Democratic congressional candidates in 2006. The Democrats' success in the Pacific Coast has been greatly assisted by the growing size and unity of the New Minorities. In 2004 Latinos and other ethnic groups made up 20 percent of the electorate, and 57 percent voted for Democratic congressional candidates. Two years later, the New Minorities had increased to 26 percent of Pacific Coast voters, much larger than in any other region, and 65 percent of these voters supported Democratic candidates.

DEMOCRATIC GAINS IN THE MIDWEST

Democrats made impressive gains in 2006 in the Midwest, but it remained the only region that sent a Democratic majority to the Senate and a Republican majority to the House of Representatives. After the 2004 elections, Republicans outnumbered Democrats, 60 to 40, in the Midwestern House delegation. By campaigning aggressively throughout the region, Democrats picked up 9 House seats in 2006. A 20-seat Democratic deficit shrank to a 2-seat deficit. In short, a Republican stronghold in House elections was converted into a swing region. Cutting their losses in the Midwest helped Democrats reclaim control of the House.

Senate Democrats entered the 2006 election cycle already holding a 2-seat surplus in the Midwest. By defeating Republican incumbents in Missouri and Ohio, Democrats emerged with 13 of the region's 20 Senate seats. A swing region in Senate elections now became a new Democratic regional stronghold. Midwestern Democrats have realistic opportunities to add to their numbers in the House and Senate in future election cycles.

Democrats enjoyed a small partisan advantage in the Midwestern electorate. In the 2006 exit poll, 39 percent of the region's voters were Democrats, 37 percent were Republicans, and 24 percent were independents or members of other parties. Democratic congressional candidates drew 94 percent from their fellow partisans and 57 percent from the independents. GOP candidates were stranded with majority support only from their fellow Republicans.

DEMOCRATS CHALLENGE REPUBLICANS IN THE MOUNTAINS/PLAINS

Judging by Republican strength in the House and Senate delegations after the 2006 election, the Mountains/Plains remained a Republican stronghold. Republicans held 26 of its 42 House seats and 17 of its 26 Senate seats. The Republican share of House seats—62 percent—was the highest of any region, while the GOP share of Senate seats—65 percent—was second only to that of the South.

These favorable Republican results, however, do not tell the whole story. In many Mountains/Plains congressional districts, the Democratic Party is on the offensive. The Republicans' strength in the region's House seats peaked in 1996 and has dropped in every subsequent election. A net gain of six seats would give the Democrats a majority of the Mountains/Plains House delegation. In statewide elections, Democrats appear to be gaining ground in New Mexico, Arizona, Nevada, and Colorado. Voters in these states might replace Republicans with Democrats in future Senate elections.

According to the exit polls, Republicans continue to outnumber Democrats in the region, but by a smaller margin than in the past. In 2004, Republicans led Democrats by 16 points, 46 percent to 30 percent. Two years later, the GOP advantage in the electorate had softened to eleven points, 42 percent to 31 percent. In the 2006 House elections, Republican candidates won 52 percent of the vote, only 7 points ahead of their Democratic opponents. Two years earlier the Republican House candidates had swamped their rivals by 23 percentage points.

A smaller Republican plurality in the electorate, joined with a strong shift among independents and members of minor parties toward Democratic congressional candidates, accounts for the weakened GOP position in the Mountains/Plains between 2004 and 2006. If the Mountains/Plains cannot continue to produce sizable majority delegations of Republicans for the House and Senate, the Republican Party will be reduced to the level of an uncompetitive national party, a party whose only remaining regional base of strength would be the South.

REPUBLICANS CONTINUE TO LEAD IN THE SOUTH

The South remained a Republican stronghold in 2006. Democrats made gains in House and Senate races, but Republicans still held large majorities of the South's delegations to Washington. In the 2004 election, Republicans outnumbered Democrats, 82 to 49, in the region's House delegation. The Republican Southern surplus of 33 seats was the largest lead enjoyed by either political party in any region in 2004. In the same year, five incumbent Democratic senators vacated their seats. All of these open seats were won by Republicans to give their party an 18-to-4-seat lead in the South. The GOP's success in the South was a major reason the national party continued to control both houses of Congress after the 2004 elections.

Ethics violations and personal scandal put many Republicans on the defensive in 2006, and the party lost five House seats in the South. The Southern Republican surplus, so important to Republican control of the House of Representatives after 1994, shrank to only 23 seats and was swamped by an unprecedented 44-seat Democratic surplus in the Northeastern states. Virginia Democrat Jim Webb's upset of the incumbent Republican senator George Allen reduced the GOP's advantage to 17 to 5 in the South's Senate delegation.

A Republican advantage in the Southern electorate has now appeared in three consecutive elections (2002, 2004, and 2006). According to the 2006 exit poll, 41 percent of Southern voters identified as Republicans, 34 percent as Democrats, and 25 percent as independents or other parties. Among white voters, Republicans enjoyed a 2-to-1 advantage, 50 percent to 24 percent. Nonwhite voters in the region were heavily Democratic, 63 percent to 15 percent. In a truly bad year for the Republicans, GOP congressional candidates in the South still managed to win 53 percent of the vote, 8 points more than the share gained by Democratic candidates. Republicans remain strong in the Deep South and Texas, while Democrats are highly competitive in Florida and the Upper South states of Arkansas, North Carolina, Tennessee, and Virginia.

THE BATTLE FOR THE WHITE HOUSE

The 2008 presidential election is the Democrats' to lose. For both parties the ideal national candidate would be a widely known and highly respected politician whose favorables far exceeded his or her unfavorables among partisans and independents. Neither party has such a candidate for the 2008 general election. Nonetheless, Democrats are in much better shape than Republicans. With the sole exception of George Herbert Walker Bush's succession of Ronald Reagan in 1988, no party has won the White House three times in a row since the New Deal era. The retiring Republican president's unpopularity and public dissatisfaction with the Iraq War have produced an excellent opportunity for the Democrats to achieve a solid popular vote and an electoral college majority.

Just as unpopular wars undermined the administrations of Democratic presidents Harry Truman (Korea in 1952) and Lyndon Johnson (Vietnam in 1968), so the war in Iraq eventually destroyed much public support for the Bush administration. And just as Republicans regained the White House in 1952 (Dwight Eisenhower) and 1968 (Richard Nixon), Democrats have mounted a strong challenge to the American presence in Iraq as a centerpiece of their 2008 general election campaign. More visible and sustained success in Iraq via a new military strategy would probably be necessary for the Republicans to reclaim an advantage on issues of national security.

Since 2004 the partisan balance in the electorate has become more favorable to Democrats. The parties were tied in size in 2004. Two years later, according to the national exit polls, Democrats opened a small lead over the Republicans, and the 2008 electorate may well display an even larger Democratic advantage. If that were to happen, all that the Democratic Party would need for success is a presidential candidate who can duplicate the pattern of support that its congressional candidates achieved in the 2006 elections: sweep the partisans and win the independents.

Democrats could realistically be optimistic about their chances to regain the presidency because of the narrow Republican electoral college victory in 2004. Recall that Bush was reelected president with a national surplus of merely 16 electoral votes. Democrats were thus only one big state or several smaller states away from victory. The net effect of Bush's second term has been to strengthen Democratic prospects in the states they have already been winning while weakening the Republicans in many of the states (such as Ohio, Iowa, New Mexico, Missouri, Florida, and Virginia) they carried in 2004.

Any Democratic nominee could expect to unify most of the party's voters against any of the Republicans. By holding the Democratic strongholds of the Northeast and Pacific Coast and by improving the Democrats' record in the Midwest—trying to add such states as Ohio and Missouri—as well as targeting particular southern and Mountains/Plains states, a Democratic candidate could easily win the presidency.

Given their bleak prospects, how could Republicans hold the White House in 2008? To be truly competitive, Republicans would probably need a forceful and optimistic leader who is based outside the party's regional strongholds and who could credibly campaign as a strong commander in chief in the age of protracted global terrorism. Such a candidate would then need to draw a sharp contrast with the Democratic nominee over the most realistic ways and means to maintain and enhance the security of the United States.

Republicans especially need a presidential candidate who can compete seriously in some states ordinarily carried by Democrats. No Republican from the South or the Mountains/Plains is likely to win many electoral votes outside those regions or the lower Midwest. George Bush's double failure to achieve more than the narrowest of presidential victories underscored the Republicans' need for an articulate candidate who could appeal to voters far removed from the Republicans' regional strongholds. Republican weakness in the Northeast, Pacific Coast, and upper Midwest has been one of the most important features of presidential politics since the 1980s.

THE BATTLE FOR THE HOUSE OF REPRESENTATIVES

Led by Speaker Nancy Pelosi of San Francisco, Democrats enter the 2008 elections with a 31-seat advantage, only one seat larger than the Republican lead from the 2004 elections. What are their chances of maintaining control of the House? We think it would take a tremendous upset for Republicans to regain control of Congress in 2008. Democrats now enjoy very large surpluses of seats in their coastal strongholds. They emerged from the 2006 elections with 70 percent of the House seats in the Northeast and Pacific Coast. With current leads of 44 seats in the Northeast and 22 seats in the Pacific Coast, if Democrats can hold all those seats, they would enjoy a huge head start from their regional bases of 66 seats.

Moreover, Democrats neutralized the Republicans' Midwestern advantage in the 2006 House elections. The Republicans' share of House seats dropped from 60 percent to 51 percent, thus shifting the Midwest from a previously Republican stronghold into a swing region. Republican retirements in the region may yield additional Democratic gains in the next round of elections.

Republicans continue to hold strong majorities of the House delegations from the South and Mountains/Plains. However, the lead from their two regional strongholds now amounts to only 33 seats. If the status quo prevails in the rival parties' regional strongholds, Republicans would need a massive surplus of 34 seats in the Midwest to regain control of the House in 2008. Such an outcome—need it be said—is highly improbable.

THE BATTLE FOR THE SENATE

Democrats gained six Senate seats in 2006, enough to produce a narrow Democratic majority of 51 to 49. Harry Reid of Nevada became the new majority leader. With the retirement of Tennessee senator Bill Frist, Mitch McConnell of Kentucky became the leader of the minority Republican Party. Because of the Republicans' weakened position in the electorate, and because the Republicans must defend considerably more seats in 2008 than the Democrats will, the Democrats have excellent opportunities to increase their Senate majority.

The Republicans' advantage in the Senate prior to the 2006 elections was based largely on the size and unity of the South and Mountains/Plains. The two Republican regional strongholds contain almost half (forty-eight) of the nation's Senate seats, and Republicans held 75 percent of them in 2004. Two losses in 2006 reduced the GOP majority to 71 percent of the combined Southern and Mountains/Plains delegations. At the same time, Democrats improved their performance in the Northeast (gaining two seats) and continued to hold a large majority of seats in the Pacific Coast (no change). Although these regions account for only thirty-two Senate seats, Democrats increased their shares of these seats from 69 percent in 2004 to 75 percent in 2006.

The critical change came in the Midwest, where an increase of two seats gave Democrats 65 percent of the region's twenty Senate seats. These victories converted the only swing region in Senate elections into an additional Democratic stronghold. The three regional Democratic strongholds possess fifty-two Senate seats. Democratic senators held 71 percent of these seats after the 2006 elections, an overall rate of success that matched Republicans' performance in their two regional strongholds.

In the next round of Senate elections, Democrats will seek to enlarge their current majorities in the Northeast, Pacific Coast, and Midwest, while trying to further reduce Republican majorities in the South and Mountains/Plains. For the most part, Republicans appear to be playing defense in the 2008 elections, far more concerned about avoiding additional losses than making gains.

THE RENEWED AMERICAN POWER STRUGGLE

There are no sure things in politics, of course, and there are especially no sure things in a nation that has such deep partisan and ideological divisions as the United States. Were the Republicans able to rally from their current weaknesses, their best chance for a victory would be for the presidency. An upset here would probably require a weak performance by the Democratic nominee as well as the nomination of a far different type of Republican candidate from Bush.

Barring extraordinary developments favoring the Republicans, the Democratic Party appears poised to return to complete control of the White House, Senate, and House of Representatives. This last happened in 1992 when Bill Clinton of Arkansas and Al Gore, Jr., of Tennessee led the Democrats to victory. At that time, the Democrats' control of all three institutions lasted only two years. President Clinton's early agenda shifted to the left, surprising and alienating some of his supporters. His complex plan for health insurance became so controversial that Democratic leaders never brought it up for a vote in Congress. The failure of the Clinton health care plan disillusioned liberal Democrats but simultaneously motivated conservative voters and interest groups to replace Democrats with Republicans in the 1994 House and Senate elections.

The return of congressional control to the Democrats in the 2006 elections has not established a new majority party in the American electorate. In our view, realignments represent long-term shifts in the partisan preferences of voters that are validated over a series of elections. It is crucial for the party in power to maintain its strength—even better to increase its strength—as the party actually governs the United States.

In more than a decade after the Republican Party returned to power in Congress, for example, Republicans never approached a majority in the electorate. Republicans could do no better than draw even with Democrats among the nation's voters, and they were never able to substantially increase their share of House seats beyond their initial gains of 1994. Conservative Republican rule based upon the agenda of Southern and Mountains/Plains leaders in the early twenty-first century eventually had the effect of increasing Democrats' strength in that party's coastal strongholds and tilting the Midwest in a Democratic direction.

In 2006, twelve years after the Republicans won back control of Congress, the Democrats finally solved their "Northern problem." Democrats swept the North with 59 percent of the seats in both chambers and thereby finally overcame the Republicans' Southern advantage. In the House of Representatives, the Northern Democratic surplus increased from only 4 seats in 2004 to 54 seats in 2006. In the Senate, Northern Democrats rose from a surplus of four seats in 2004 to *fourteen* seats in 2006.

A Democratic victory in the 2008 presidential contest, accompanied by continued Democratic control of both houses of Congress, would create an opportunity for the party to pass its liberal policy agenda and possibly govern in such a way as to win the backing of a substantially larger plurality or majority. Democrats may soon have the opportunity to see if American voters want a very different foreign policy involving some form of withdrawal from Iraq and different national security policies in an era of global terrorism, as well as full-fledged national health insurance, more liberal tax policies, and legislation dealing with illegal immigration.

In America's modern power struggle the difficulty of winning presidential elections is exceeded only by the difficulty of successfully governing the nation. In pursuing their ambitious policy goals Democratic leaders would then confront the same challenges that eventually undid the Republicans—the imperatives of pleasing the most ideologically fervent of their partisans while maintaining the support of voters in the middle. Success for the Democrats is certainly possible. Over time, however, this task may prove to be as difficult for a liberal party grounded in the Northeast and Pacific Coast as it has been for a conservative party based in the South and Mountains/Plains. Whatever the outcomes of the 2008 elections, America's power struggle will continue to be ferocious. Such is the nature of American politics and government in the first decade of the twenty-first century.

APPENDIX

Appendix 1:
States and the Presidential Battleground in 2008*

Regions	Presidentially Democratic	Swing	Presidentially Republican
Northeast	New York 31	New Hampshire 4	
	Pennsylvania 21		
	New Jersey 15		
	Massachusetts 12		
	Maryland 10		
	Connecticut 7		
	Maine 4		
	Rhode Island 4		
	Delaware 3		
	District of Columbia 3		
	Vermont 3		
Pacific Coast	California 55		Alaska 3
	Washington 11		
	Oregon 7		
	Hawaii 4		
Midwest	Illinois 21	Iowa 7	Ohio 20
	Michigan 17		Indiana 11
	Minnesota 10		Missouri 11
	Wisconsin 10		Kentucky 8
			West Virginia 5

(continued)

Appendix 1:
States and the Presidential Battleground in 2008* *(continued)*

Regions	Presidentially Democratic	Swing	Presidentially Republican
Mountains/ Plains		New Mexico 5	Arizona 10
			Colorado 9
			Oklahoma 7
			Kansas 6
			Nebraska 5
			Nevada 5
			Utah 5
			Idaho 4
			Montana 3
			North Dakota 3
			South Dakota 3
			Wyoming 3
South			Texas 34
			Florida 27
			Georgia 15
			North Carolina 15
			Virginia 13
			Tennessee 11
			Alabama 9
			Louisiana 9
			South Carolina 8
			Arkansas 6
			Mississippi 6

* "Presidential" states are those won by the same party in 2000 and 2004. All other states are "swing" states. Within each region, states are ranked (highest to lowest) according to their electoral vote in 2008.

NOTES

1: Competitive America

1 Richard E. Neustadt, *Presidential Power* (New York: Wiley, 1980), p. 26.

2 Calculations by the authors from the 1976 and 2004 exit polls.

3 Alan I. Abramowitz and Kyle L. Saunders, "Is Polarization a Myth?" paper prepared for delivery at the Annual Meeting of the Southern Political Science Association, Atlanta, Georgia, January 5–7, 2006.

4 Calculations by the authors from the 2004 exit poll.

5 On divided partisan control, see David R. Mayhew, *Divided We Govern* (New Haven: Yale University Press, 1991).

6 The information charted in figure 1.1 for American voters comes from two different sources. Data for the 1952–1972 elections come from surveys conducted by the Center for Political Studies, University of Michigan, as part of the American National Elections Studies (hereafter referred to as ANES). Data for the 1976–2004 elections come from the exit polls of voters conducted for the national news organizations. The exit polls are based on much larger numbers of respondents than the ANES surveys.

7 Michael Barone, *The New Americans* (Washington, DC: Regnery, 2001); John B. Judis and Ruy Teixeira, *The Emerging Democratic Majority* (New York: Scribner's, 2002).

8 For analyses of Latino politics, see Roberto Suro, *Strangers among Us: How Latino Immigration Is Transforming America* (New York: Knopf, 1998); John A. Garcia, *Latino Politics in America: Community, Culture, and Interests* (Lanham, MD: Rowman & Littlefield, 2003); and F. Chris Garcia, ed., *Pursuing Power: Latinos and the Political System* (Notre Dame, IN: University of Notre Dame Press, 1997).

9 Michael C. Dawson, *Behind the Mule: Race and Class in African-American Politics* (Princeton, NJ: Princeton University Press, 1994); Katherine Tate, *From Protest to Politics: The New Black Voters in American Elections* (Cambridge, MA: Harvard University Press, 1993).

10 Earl Black and Merle Black, *The Rise of Southern Republicans* (Cambridge, MA: The Belknap Press of Harvard University Press, 2002), p. 206.

11 Earl Black and Merle Black, *Politics and Society in the South* (Cambridge, MA: Harvard University Press, 1987), pp. 249–256; Earl Black and Merle Black, *The Vital South: How Presidents Are Elected* (Cambridge, MA: Harvard University Press, 1992), pp. 357–360; Black and Black, *The Rise of Southern Republicans*, pp. 205–240; Edward G. Carmines and Harold W. Stanley, "Ideological Realignment in the Contemporary South," in *The Disappearing South?*, ed. Robert P. Steed, Laurence W. Moreland, and Tod A. Baker (Tuscaloosa, AL: University of Alabama Press, 1990), pp. 21–33; Alan I.

Abramowitz and Kyle L. Sanders, "Ideological Realignment in the U.S. Electorate," *Journal of Politics* 60 (August 1998): 634–652.

12 Newt Gingrich, "Reagan's Majority: What the Class of '94 Learned from the Gipper," *The Weekly Standard*, June 28, 2004, p. 12.

13 On modern American conservatism, see John Micklethwait and Adrian Wooldridge, *The Right Nation* (New York: Penguin Press, 2004).

14 Abramowitz and Saunders, "Polarization," pp. 7–8.

15 Roger Finke and Rodney Stark, *The Churching of America 1776–2005* (New Brunswick, NJ: Rutgers University Press, 2005).

16 William B. Prendergast, *The Catholic Voter in American Politics* (Washington, DC: Georgetown University Press, 1999), p. iii. See also George J. Marlin, *The American Catholic Voter* (South Bend, IN: St. Augustine's Press, 2004); Finke and Stark, *The Churching of America*, pp. 253–274.

17 Prendergast, *The Catholic Voter*, p. 178.

18 The secularization of the national Democratic Party is analyzed in Geoffrey Layman, *The Great Divide* (New York: Columbia University Press, 2001); Louis Bolce and Gerald De Maio, "Our Secularist Democratic Party," *The Public Interest* (fall 2002): 3–20.

19 For analyses of white evangelical Protestants, see John C. Green, James L. Guth, Corwin E. Smidt, and Lyman A. Kellstedt, *Religion and the Culture Wars* (Lanham, MD: Rowman & Littlefield, 1996); and Layman, *The Great Divide*.

2: America's Political Regions

1 Earl Black and Merle Black, *The Rise of Southern Republicans* (Cambridge, MA: The Belknap Press of Harvard University Press, 2002), pp. 14–19.

2 David M. Potter, *The South and the Concurrent Majority* (Baton Rouge, LA: Louisiana State University Press, 1972), p. 68; Ira Katznelson, *When Affirmative Action Was White* (New York: Norton, 2005).

3 Jordan A. Schwarz, *The New Dealers* (New York: Knopf, 1993), p. 287; Robert A. Caro, *The Path to Power* (New York: Knopf, 1982), pp. 471–472; William E. Leuchtenburg, *The White House Looks South* (Baton Rouge, LA: Louisiana State University Press, 2005), pp. 29–143.

4 See Black and Black, *The Rise of Southern Republicans*.

5 The 1952–1972 results are based on the party identification of respondents who said they had voted in the presidential-year surveys conducted by the Center for Political Studies (CPS) of the University of Michigan as part of the American National Elections Study (ANES). The 1976–2004 results are based on presidential-year exit polls of voters sponsored by national news organizations.

6 1952 ANES survey. For analyses of the one-party Democratic South, see V. O. Key Jr., *Southern Politics in State and Nation* (New York: Knopf, 1949), and Alexander Heard, *A Two-Party South?* (Chapel Hill, NC: University of North Carolina Press, 1952).

7 Robert Mann, *The Walls of Jericho* (New York: Harcourt Brace, 1996); Chandler Davidson and Bernard Grofman, eds., *Quiet Revolution in the South* (Princeton, NJ: Princeton University Press, 1994).

8 The destabilizing impact of the Great Society on the Democratic Party went far beyond white Southerners. See Thomas Byrne Edsall with Mary D. Edsall, *Chain Reaction: The Impact of Race, Rights, and Taxes on American Politics* (New York: Norton, 1992);

Kevin M. Kruse, *White Flight* (Princeton, NJ: Princeton University Press, 2005); and Matthew D. Lassiter, *The Silent Majority* (Princeton, NJ: Princeton University Press, 2006).

9 Merle Black, "The Transformation of the Southern Democratic Party," *Journal of Politics* 66 (November 2004): 1001–1017.

10 Black and Black, *The Rise of Southern Republicans,* pp. 205–240. See also Alan I. Abramowitz and H. Gibbs Knotts, "Ideological Realignment in the American Electorate: A Comparison of Northern and Southern White Voters in the Pre-Reagan, Reagan, and Post-Reagan Eras," *Politics & Policy* 34 (March 2006): 94–108.

11 Especially insightful examples of comparative regional analysis are Kevin P. Phillips, *The Emerging Republican Majority* (New Rochelle, NY: Arlington House, 1969); James L. Sundquist, *Dynamics of the Party System,* rev. ed. (Washington, DC: Brookings Institution, 1983); Charles S. Bullock III, "Regional Realignment from an Officeholding Perspective," *Journal of Politics* 50 (August 1988): 553–574; Charles S. Bullock, III, Ronald Keith Gaddie, and Donna R. Hoffman, "Regional Variations in the Realignment of American Politics, 1944–2000," paper prepared for presentation at the Southwestern Political Science Association Annual Meeting, New Orleans, Louisiana, March 27–30, 2002; and James G. Gimpel and Jason E. Schuknecht, *Patchwork Nation: Sectionalism and Political Change in American Politics* (Ann Arbor, MI: University of Michigan Press, 2003).

12 The regional figures combine two different sources of data. Because of very small numbers of voters in some of the regions in the ANES surveys, we have grouped respondents in the following time periods: 1952–1960, 1962–1970, and 1972–1982. The exit polls contain much larger numbers of respondents, and we prefer to use them when possible. Beginning with the 1984 exit poll, respondents could be recoded into one of our five regions. All regional results from 1984 to the most recent national election (2004) are based on exit polls. These data are averaged from 1984–1990, 1992–2000, and 2002–2004.

13 Phillips, *The Emerging Republican Majority,* pp. 44–186.

14 John Shelton Reed, *The Enduring South* (Lexington, MA: Lexington Books, 1972), pp. 57–81; Samuel S. Hill Jr., *Southern Churches in Crisis* (New York: Holt, Rinehart and Winston, 1966); John C. Green, Lyman A. Kellstedt, Corwin E. Smidt, and James L. Guth, "The Soul of the South: Religion and Southern Politics at the Millennium," in *The New Politics of the Old South,* 2d ed., ed. Charles S. Bullock III and Mark J. Rozell (Lanham, MD: Rowman & Littlefield, 2003), pp. 283–298.

15 For discussions of the importance of evangelicals, see James L. Guth and John C. Green, "God and the GOP: Religion among Republican Activists," in *Religion and Political Behavior in the United States,* ed. Ted G. Jelen (New York: Praeger, 1989, pp. 223–241); John C. Green, James L. Guth, Corwin E. Smidt, and Lyman A. Kellstedt, *Religion and the Culture Wars* (Lanham, MD: Rowman & Littlefield, 1996); Tod A. Baker, Robert P. Steed, and Laurence W. Moreland, eds., *Religion and Politics in the South* (New York: Praeger, 1983).

16 George J. Marlin, *The American Catholic Voter* (South Bend, IN: St. Augustine's Press, 2004).

3: The Republican Strongholds

1 U.S. Census Bureau, *Statistical Abstract of the United States: 2002* (Washington, DC: 2002), pp. 26–28. For analyses of the states in these regions, see Michael Barone, *The Al-*

manac of American Politics, 2006 (Washington, DC: National Journal, 2005), and *CQ's Politics in America 2006* (Washington, DC: CQ Press, 2005).

2 Dan Balz and Ronald Brownstein, *Storming the Gates* (Boston: Little, Brown, 1996), p. 226.

3 Earl Black and Merle Black, *The Rise of Southern Republicans* (Cambridge, MA: The Belknap Press of Harvard University Press, 2002), pp. 205–240.

4 1992–2000 ANES surveys of voters.

5 Ibid.

6 Kevin P. Phillips, *The Emerging Republican Majority* (New Rochelle, NY: Arlington House, 1969), p. 473.

7 See Dan Morgan, *Rising in the West* (New York: Knopf, 1992).

8 V. O. Key Jr., *Southern Politics in State and Nation* (New York: Knopf, 1949), p. 277. See also Alexander Heard, *A Two-Party South?* (Chapel Hill, NC: University of North Carolina Press, 1952).

9 Black and Black, *The Rise of Southern Republicans.*

10 Key, *Southern Politics in State and Nation,* is the classic analysis of the one-party South.

11 Samuel S. Hill Jr., *Southern Churches in Crisis* (New York: Holt, Rinehart and Winston, 1966).

12 See Donald R. Matthews and James W. Prothro, *Negroes and the New Southern Politics* (New York: Harcourt, Brace & World, 1966).

13 ANES surveys.

14 Robert Mann, *The Walls of Jericho* (New York: Harcourt Brace, 1996).

15 See Michael C. Dawson, *Behind the Mule: Race and Class in African-American Politics* (Princeton, NJ: Princeton University Press, 1994).

16 1992–2000 ANES surveys.

17 Ibid.

18 Merle Black, "The Transformation of the Southern Democratic Party," *Journal of Politics* 66 (November 2004): 1001–1017.

19 Jonathan O. Knuckey, "Racial Resentment and Southern Republican Voting in the 1990s," *American Review of Politics* 22 (summer 2001): 257–277.

20 David Lublin, *The Republican South* (Princeton, NJ: Princeton University Press, 2004), p. 22.

21 Black and Black, *The Rise of Southern Republicans,* pp. 205–211; and Dan T. Carter, *From George Wallace to Newt Gingrich* (Baton Rouge, LA: Louisana State University Press, 1996).

22 Earl Black and Merle Black, *The Vital South: How Presidents Are Elected* (Cambridge, MA: Harvard University Press, 1992), p. 9.

23 Earl Black and Merle Black, *Politics and Society in the South* (Cambridge, MA: Harvard University Press, 1987), pp. 138–144; Black and Black, *The Rise of Southern Republicans,* pp. 28–30; Joseph A. Aistrup, *The Southern Strategy Revisited: Top-Down Advancement in the South* (Lexington, KY: University Press of Kentucky, 1996); and J. David Woodard, *The New Southern Politics* (Boulder, CO: Lynne Rienner Publishers, 2006).

24 Black and Black, *Politics and Society in the South,* pp. 23–72; Black and Black, *The Rise of Southern Republicans,* pp. 4–5, 241–267.

25 Black and Black, *The Rise of Southern Republicans,* pp. 205–240; Black, "The Transformation of the Southern Democratic Party," 1001–1005.

26 John C. Green, Lyman A. Kellstedt, Corwin E. Smidt, and James L. Guth, "The

Soul of the South: Religion and Southern Politics at the Millennium," in *The New Politics of the Old South,* 2d ed., ed Charles S. Bullock III and Mark J. Rozell. (Lanham, MD: Rowman & Littlefield, 2003), pp. 283–298.

27 1992–2000 ANES surveys and 2004 exit poll.

28 1992–2000 ANES surveys.

29 Black, "The Transformation of the Southern Democratic Party"; and Earl Black, "The Newest Southern Politics," *Journal of Politics* 60 (August 1998): 591–612.

4: The Democratic Strongholds

1 U.S. Census Bureau, *Statistical Abstract of the United States: 2002* (Washington, DC: 2002), pp. 26–28. For analyses of the states in these regions, see Michael Barone, *The Almanac of American Politics, 2006* (Washington, DC: National Journal, 2005), and *CQ's Politics in America 2006* (Washington, DC: CQ Press, 2005).

2 See Neal R. Peirce, *The New England States* (New York: Norton, 1976), and Neal R. Peirce and Michael Barone, *The Mid-Atlantic States of America* (New York: Norton, 1977).

3 Nathan Glazer and Daniel Patrick Moynihan, *Beyond the Melting Pot* (Cambridge, MA: The MIT Press and Harvard University Press, 1963); Duane Lockard, *New England State Politics* (Princeton, NJ: Princeton University Press, 1959); and Kevin P. Phillips, *The Emerging Republican Majority* (New Rochelle, NY: Arlington House, 1969), pp. 93–105.

4 Frank Munger, "The Northeast," in Frank Munger, ed., *American State Politics: Readings for Comparative Analysis* (New York: Crowell, 1966), pp. 105–110.

5 Phillips, *The Emerging Republican Majority,* p. 44.

6 Quoted in Theodore H. White, *The Making of the President 1964* (New York: Atheneum, 1965), p. 109.

7 Phillips, *The Emerging Republican Majority,* p. 102.

8 Ibid., p. 44.

9 George J. Marlin, *The American Catholic Voter* (South Bend, IN: St. Augustine's Press, 2004), pp. 294–295.

10 Quoted in John Kenneth White, *The New Politics of Old Values,* 2d ed. (Hanover, NH: University Press of New England, 1990), p. 147. White's book has much valuable information on Reagan.

11 Marlin, *The American Catholic Voter,* p. 295. See also Samuel G. Freedman, *The Inheritance* (New York: Simon & Schuster, 1996).

12 According to the New York State Board of Elections, Kerry won 72 percent of the vote in New York City in 2004. He ran ahead of Bush by more than 1.2 million votes.

13 *The New York Times,* May 29, 2001.

14 See Neal R. Peirce, *The Pacific States of America* (New York: Norton, 1972).

15 See generally Roberto Suro, *Strangers among Us: How Latino Immigration Is Transforming America* (New York: Knopf, 1998); John B. Judis and Ruy Teixeira, *The Emerging Democratic Majority* (New York: Scribner's, 2002); Michael Barone, *The New Americans* (Washington, DC: Regnery, 2001), pp. 181–183; Victor Davis Hanson, *Mexifornia* (San Francisco: Encounter Books, 2003); Kevin Starr, *Coast of Dreams* (New York: Knopf, 2004); and Samuel P. Huntington, *Who We Are: The Challenge to America's National Identity* (New York: Simon & Schuster, 2004).

5: The Divided Midwest

1 Frank Munger, "The Midwest," in *American State Politics: Readings for Comparative Analysis*, ed. Frank Munger (New York: Crowell, 1966), p. 207. See also John H. Fenton, *Midwest Politics* (New York: Holt, Rinehart and Winston, 1966), and Neil R. Peirce and John Keefe, *The Great Lakes States of America* (New York: Norton, 1980).

2 For analyses of the region's states, see Michael Barone, *The Almanac of American Politics 2006* (Washington, DC: National Journal, 2005), and *CQ's Politics in America 2006* (Washington, DC: CQ Press, 2005).

3 U.S. Census Bureau, *Statistical Abstract of the United States: 2002* (Washington, DC: 2002), pp. 26–28.

4 Munger, *American State Politics: Readings for Comparative Analysis*, pp. 208–209.

5 Calculated by the authors from ANES surveys and exit polls.

6 Calculated by the authors from official election results posted by the Michigan secretary of state.

6: The Presidential Power Struggle

1 On American party politics from the New Deal onward, see especially James L. Sundquist, *Dynamics of the Party System*, rev. ed. (Washington, DC: Brookings Institution, 1983), pp. 198–449; Everett Carll Ladd, *American Political Parties* (New York: Norton, 1970), pp. 180–311; and Everett Carll Ladd Jr. with Charles D. Hadley, *Transformations of the American Party System* (New York: Norton, 1975).

2 Throughout this chapter, presidential election results for sections and regions have been calculated by the authors from appropriate editions of *Congressional Quarterly's Guide to U.S. Elections* (Washington, DC: CQ Press); appropriate volumes of Richard M. Scammon, ed., *America Votes* (Washington, DC: CQ Press); and appropriate issues of the *CQ Weekly*.

3 On Reagan's political career, see Lou Cannon, *Reagan* (New York: G. P. Putnam's Sons, 1982); and Lou Cannon, *President Reagan* (New York: Simon & Schuster, 1991).

4 For the South's transformation in presidential elections through 1988, see Earl Black and Merle Black, *The Vital South: How Presidents Are Elected* (Cambridge, MA: Harvard University Press, 1992).

5 The House Republicans' inexperience in governing is examined in Richard F. Fenno Jr., *Learning to Govern* (Washington, DC: Brookings Institution, 1997); and David Maraniss and Michael Weisskopf, *"Tell Newt to Shut Up!"* (New York: Simon & Schuster, 1996).

6 2004 exit poll.

7 *St. Petersburg Times*, February 1, 2004.

7: The Power Struggle in the House of Representatives

1 On contemporary House elections, see Gary C. Jacobson, *The Politics of Congressional Elections*, 5th ed. (New York: Longman, 2000).

2 D. B. Hardeman and Donald C. Bacon, *Rayburn* (Austin, TX: Texas Monthly Press, 1987), p. 346.

3 See David R. Mayhew, *Party Loyalty among Congressmen* (Cambridge, MA: Harvard University Press, 1966).

4 Increasing numbers of liberal Northern Democrats after the 1974 elections allowed House Democrats to institute many reforms that further weakened the power of conservative Democrats. See David W. Rohde, *Parties and Leaders in the Postreform House* (Chicago: University of Chicago Press, 1991).

5 On the Republicans' House breakthrough, see David Maraniss and Michael Weisskopf, *"Tell Newt to Shut Up!"* (New York: Simon & Schuster, 1996), and Richard F. Fenno Jr., *Learning to Govern* (Washington, DC: Brookings Institution, 1997).

6 Earl Black and Merle Black, *The Rise of Southern Republicans* (Cambridge, MA: The Belknap Press of Harvard University Press, 2002), pp. 391–399.

7 Throughout this chapter, House results for sections, regions, and states have been calculated by the authors from appropriate editions of *Congressional Quarterly's Guide to U.S. Elections* (Washington, DC: CQ Press) and appropriate volumes of Michael Barone's *The Almanac of American Politics* (Washington, DC: National Journal).

8 See Black and Black, *The Rise of Southern Republicans.*

9 The old one-party South is examined in V. O. Key Jr., *Southern Politics in State and Nation* (New York: Knopf, 1949). On modern Southern politics, see Earl Black and Merle Black, *Politics and Society in the South* (Cambridge, MA: Harvard University Press, 1987); Black and Black, *The Rise of Southern Republicans;* Richard F. Fenno Jr., *Congress at the Grassroots* (Chapel Hill, NC: University of North Carolina Press, 2000); and James M. Glaser, *The Hand of the Past in Contemporary Southern Politics* (New Haven, CT: Yale University Press, 2005).

10 See "Apportionment in 2010," www.polidata.org.

11 See Michael Barone, *The Almanac of American Politics, 2004* (Washington, DC: National Journal, 2003), pp. 1350–1351.

12 *The Almanac of American Politics, 2006* (Washington, DC: National Journal, 2005), p. 598.

13 Here and elsewhere in the chapter, information on the presidential vote in particular House districts is taken from various editions of *The Almanac of American Politics.*

14 *CQ Weekly,* December 11, 2004, pp. 2954–2955.

15 Ibid.

8: The Power Struggle in the Senate

1 Earl Black and Merle Black, *The Rise of Southern Republicans* (Cambridge, MA: The Belknap Press of Harvard University Press, 2002), p. 56. See also Ira Katznelson, *When Affirmative Action Was White* (Norton: New York, 2005).

2 *The Atlanta Constitution,* September 4, 1936. Here and in the following paragraphs, we have not attempted to modernize the capitalization practices of *The Atlanta Constitution* in 1936.

3 Ibid., July 24, 1936.

4 Ibid., July 16, 1936.

5 Ibid., July 5; September 1, 3, 1936.

6 Ibid., September 10, 1936.

7 See Black and Black, *The Rise of Southern Republicans,* pp. 40–57; William E. Leuchtenburg, *The White House Looks South* (Baton Rouge, LA: Louisiana State Univer-

sity Press, 2005); David M. Potter, *The South and the Concurrent Majority* (Baton Rouge, LA: Louisiana State University Press, 1972); and Katznelson, *When Affirmative Action Was White.*

8 In this chapter, Senate results for sections and regions have been calculated by the authors from appropriate editions of *Congressional Quarterly's Guide to U.S. Elections* (Washington, DC: CQ Press) and appropriate volumes of Michael Barone's *The Almanac of American Politics* (Washington, DC: National Journal).

9 Earl Black and Merle Black, *Politics and Society in the South* (Cambridge, MA: Harvard University Press, 1987); Black and Black, *The Rise of Southern Republicans;* and Robert Mann, *The Walls of Jericho* (New York: Harcourt Brace, 1996).

10 Black and Black, *The Rise of Southern Republicans.*

11 Lott's version of events appears in his autobiography, *Herding Cats* (New York: Regan Books, 2005).

12 *CQ Weekly,* December 11, 2004, p. 2956.

13 Ibid.

14 Compiled from Michael Barone, *The Almanac of American Politics, 2006* (Washington, DC: National Journal, 2005).

9: The American Power Struggle

1 Earl Black and Merle Black, *The Rise of Southern Republicans* (Cambridge, MA: The Belknap Press of Harvard University Press, 2002), p. 369.

2 Results are based on the 2004 state files.

3 Alan I. Abramowitz, Brad Alexander, and Matthew Gunning, "Incumbency, Redistricting, and the Decline of Competition in U.S. House Elections," *Journal of Politics* 68 (February 2006): 75–88; Bill Bishop, "The Schism in U.S. Politics Begins at Home," *Austin American-Statesman,* April 4, 2004.

4 Michael Barone, *The Almanac of American Politics, 2006* (Washington, DC: National Journal, 2005), p. 30.

5 Zell Miller, *A National Party No More* (Macon, GA: Stroud & Hall, 2003).

ACKNOWLEDGMENTS

I T IS A PLEASURE TO ACKNOWLEDGE THE AID AND support of the people who have made this book possible. Without the prompting and guidance of Andrew Wylie there would have been no book. At Simon & Schuster we have benefited from the counsel and advice of our editor, Alice Mayhew. Thanks also to Roger Labrie and the rest of Simon & Schuster's skilled production staff.

Among our political science colleagues, we particularly wish to recognize three individuals. Charles S. Bulloch III's work on regional realignments eventually got us interested in comparing developments in the South with those of other regions of the United States. We have also greatly benefited from the expert knowledge of Alan Abramowitz and Randy Strahan.

Matthew Gunning, Jonathan Williamson, Adam Cooper, Terry Chapman, Brad Alexander, and Scott Wolford provided able research assistance.

As they always have in the past, our families gave us steady encouragement for this book. We wish to thank Sena, Shameem, Andy, Debra, Claire, and Julia for their enthusiastic support.

Any errors of fact and interpretation are our responsibility.

INDEX

Page numbers in *italics* refer to figures and tables.

ABOUT THE AUTHORS

Earl Black is Herbert S. Autrey Professor of Political Science at Rice University. His twin brother, **Merle Black,** is Asa G. Candler Professor of Politics and Government at Emory University. They are the authors of *The Rise of Southern Republicans,* *The Vital South: How Presidents Are Elected,* and *Politics and Society in the South.*